OUR DON BRADMAN

OUR DON
BRADMAN

EDITED BY PHILIP DERRIMAN

ABC
BOOKS

Published by ABC Books for the
AUSTRALIAN BROADCASTING CORPORATION
GPO Box 9994 Sydney NSW 2001

First published 2001

National Library of Australia
Cataloguing-in-Publication entry
Our Don Bradman.
  2nd ed.
  ISBN 0 7333 0997 6.
  1. Bradman, Donald, Sir, 1908–2001. 2. Bradman, Donald,
  Sir, 1908–2001 – Anecdotes. 3. Cricket players – Australia.
  I. Derriman, Philip, 1943– . II. Australian Broadcasting
  Corporation.
796.3580994

Text designed by Jim Shepherd
Cover designed by Toni Hope Caten and Robert Taylor
Set in 11/16.5 pt Bembo by Midland Typesetters Maryborough, Victoria
Printed and bound in Australia by Australian Print Group Maryborough, Victoria

5 4 3 2 1

Contents

INTRODUCTION

IN 1987, THE YEAR THIS ANTHOLOGY first appeared, someone made a count of all the books that had been published about Don Bradman up to that time and found the total came to twenty-one. Since then, new Bradman books have kept appearing, almost year by year, and if we were to do the count again today we would probably find the total was over thirty and still rising. Clearly, interest in Bradman is as high today as it has ever been. If anything, it may be higher. People at the Bradman Museum at Bowral, who make it their business to know such things, report that for whatever reason the public's interest in Bradman appeared to intensify in the late 1990s, roughly half a century after he ceased to be a player. It's as if the further Bradman the cricketer recedes into history, the more fascinated we become with Bradman the man.

Why is this? The simple answer, surely, is that we haven't yet exhausted the subject. We haven't got to the bottom of the Bradman puzzle: we haven't had it explained to our satisfaction what kind of person he was and how, as a cricketer, he managed to do all he did. Maybe we never will, yet it is to be hoped that in the pages which follow the reader will find plenty of clues. Over the past seventy-five years any number of writers have tried to analyse the Bradman phenomenon from any number of angles, and this book, I believe, is a compilation of the best of their conclusions and insights. It is also a compilation of some of the best writing about Bradman. By excelling with the bat, Bradman always inspired those who wrote about him to excel, too. He still does.

This new edition of *Our Don Bradman* is an expanded version of the previous one. Much of the added material consists of older items which have only lately come to light. Even more of it, though, is recent material—that is, writing and quotations that have appeared since 1987.

Many of today's finest writers on sport are represented among the new contributors—Gideon Haigh, Peter Roebuck, Michael Parkinson, Peter FitzSimons, Les Carlyon, Matthew Engel, Simon Barnes, Evan Whitton, Don Watson, Neil Marks, Martin Johnson—as is the leading student of all matters relating to Bradman the batsman, Charles Davis. As before, the bulk of the contents have been arranged more or less chronologically according to the events described, although much of the recent writing is to be found towards the end of the book. Not that the order of contents really matters: this isn't a book to be read from cover to cover but one to be dipped into here and there.

One of Sir Donald's sisters is said to have remarked: 'I can't see why people make such a fuss about Don. All he was good at was cricket.' There's a touch of Bradman-like pragmatism in the comment, yet it really misses the point. The reason people make such a fuss about Bradman isn't that he was good but that he was so much better than everyone else—that he really defied, and continues to defy, comparison. This also helps to explain why, to a remarkable degree, his reputation is as fresh as it ever was. This itself is unusual, for most of us tend to be rather contemptuous of sporting champions of the past. We see them on some flickering newsreel film and think how inept they look. Bradman is different. Even in those old newsreel films he looks immensely competent. You watch him in action and you feel quite sure he could do to the world's best bowlers today what he did to the world's best in his own day.

Years ago when the Kennedy-Miller people were working on the television series *Bodyline*, a drama in which Bradman was, of course, a central character, someone raised as a talking point one day the question of why nobody had ever made a movie about him. It was accepted by those of us present that the reason was simply that there were not enough contrasts in Bradman's life—it seemed to be all light and no shade. He was a world-beater in sport at 21 and he remained a world-beater until he retired at 40. His cricket career was a virtually unbroken succession of triumphs. He was still married to the woman he wed half a century earlier and he was still living in the Adelaide house he built in 1935. Hardly the stuff, everyone agreed, that screen dramas are made of.

So in the pages that follow there may necessarily be more light than shade, yet, movie or no movie, I hope the reader will find drama, too.

Philip Derriman
Sydney

DON'S SIXER

By C. Cropin

From an account by one of Bradman's old school friends, Adelaide Mail, *1930.*

ON ATTENDING THE BOWRAL High School for the first time as a scholar I made my way during recess to where a group of boys were having a hit at a cricket ball, using a short pine stick for a bat and the time-honoured bell post for a wicket. I was soon having my dig at the wicket with Bradman bowling. Not being an expert like Don with a pine stick, I was unlucky enough to hit a ball through the school window. Bradman and myself were duly hauled before the headmaster and given a sixer each for playing in a forbidden place, and had to listen to a lecture in which we were told that the caning hurt the headmaster more than ourselves. He must have thought that we doubted his word at the time, for there was a twinkle in his eye when he told us we could go. He halted us when we got to the door and told Don to get all the practice he could—but not in the playground—as he expected him to do great things for his country one day. How true his words were!

YOUNG DON BRADMAN

By Bill O'Reilly

From 'Tiger': 60 Years of Cricket, *1985.*

I HAVE OFTEN WONDERED about the strange fact that I still have the clearest possible recollection of the very first time I heard Don Bradman's name.

The strangeness of it comes from the present knowledge that the name must have meant absolutely nothing whatever then to a young Sydney Teachers' College student, as I was, just reaching the final stages of his two years' scholarship course and preparing to take up a job as a primary school teacher with the New South Wales Department of Public Instruction, as the Education Department was then known.

A small group of us were making our way past the 'Greasers' School', as we called Sydney University's School of Engineers, on our way down to the Forest Lodge exit from the University grounds, en route to the Jubilee Oval at Glebe Point where we were due to take part in some sporting programme. To make some sort of appropriate conversation I mentioned that I would be returning to my Wingello home where I hoped to take part in some of the cricket fixtures in the Southern Tablelands Cricket Competition during the coming two months' summer vacation. Len Kelsey, who hailed from Bowral and who had spent his two years' training at the College in close association with me, informed me that it would probably pay some dividends if I were to keep a wary eye open for a young man named Don Bradman, whom he had known as a fellow-pupil at Bowral High School, and who was presently scoring lots of runs in the local competition. I passed the matter over in the same way a good chairman in a humdrum public meeting skims over the general business, setting it aside for later consideration.

But my meeting with Bradman came much sooner than I had anticipated. Boarding a passenger train leaving Sydney's Central Station for Goulburn one Saturday morning in December 1925, I travelled peacefully for 80 miles, blithely unaware of what was to happen to me before I arrived at my little home town, situated 104 miles south. As the train came to a halt at Bowral, an attractive township popular as a health resort and holiday mountain town, I was startled out of my peaceful reverie by the weird sensation of imagining that I heard my name being called. I jumped up, leaned my long frame from the carriage window and called out 'Here I am.'

It was the stationmaster from Wingello doing the bellowing. His instructions were terse and forceful. 'Grab your bag and get out.'

My reluctance to obey him must have been plain for him to see, for he added in explanation, 'We are all down here to play Bowral this afternoon and you are going to get the new ball.' I jumped out smartly. And that was a dreadful mistake, I must admit.

The stationmaster, with the same organizing ability which had induced the Railway Commissioners to promote him to his dizzy height of responsibility, put my fears to rest by informing me that he himself had been in close contact during the week with my dear mother, who had packed my cricket gear and given it to him to set me up for the afternoon. Misguidedly I silently gave three hearty cheers for the good luck which had given me such a welcome start to the Christmas holidays.

On the way to the Bowral Oval in an old 1918 T Model Ford truck I was well and truly briefed on the growing reputation of a kid named Don Bradman—there it was again—who had been showing such unusual skill that they had decided to enlist my services at short notice.

We were a motley looking crew I suppose as we began to peel off under cover of a clump of gum trees beside the ground. Young and old, all shapes and sizes. Moustaches were popular with the more mature members, but no youngster dared then to run the risk of wholesale criticism by encouraging the reluctant growth of a few goose-down hairs on the top lip to give the false impression that he had entered the state of manhood. It wasn't done then. There were no beards. It was long since the days when cricketers found it necessary to add to their ferocity, glamour, sex appeal—call it what you will—by hiding behind a thatch of fearsome whiskers.

Bowral won the toss and batted. I got the new ball.

You might well ask, 'Why did O'Reilly get the new ball? He wasn't a fast bowler who thrashed them down at headlong speed. There has never been any suggestion that he could move the new ball in the air sufficiently to claim recognition as a worthwhile new ball operator.'

Quite true.

O'Reilly got the new ball regardless. The reasons were basic. O'Reilly could bowl consistently at the stumps. He had earned himself a noticeable reputation as a wicket-taker in the Sydney Moore Park Saturday morning competition. Furthermore the Wingello captain and the entire team—including O'Reilly himself—thought that O'Reilly was a good bowler.

Play began.

In my first over I hit the stumps of one of Bowral's openers. That warmed me up for the entrance of a diminutive figure, approaching with what appeared to be the diffident gait of a stop-gap performer sent in to hold the fort long enough for the real number three in the batting order to get his pads on. What struck me most about him was the difficulty he seemed to be having in taking normal steps as he approached. His pads seemed to reach right up to his navel. His bat was small and had reached the sere and yellow stage, where the yellow was turning to dark tobacco.

Still, he shaped up as though he knew what the game was all about, and the expression on his face publicized the fact that he felt quite at home and was ready to cope with anything that I had in store for him.

The battle was joined. As the game proceeded I was quick to realize that I had come into contact with my very first 'problem child'. My training as a prospective primary school teacher was supposed to have prepared me for dealing with the occasional hard case who would turn up from time to time, but nothing could have prepared me for the confrontation with this particular youth.

As the precocious lad began to handle my quickish leg breaks, bouncing high off the coir mat which always favoured spin, I was made aware that here at last I had a real job of work on my hands, and I wondered what I should have to say to Len Kelsey the next time I saw him.

I had a bit of bad luck early in that memorable afternoon. Twice before he had reached 30 the youngster was dropped in the slips off my bowling. To elucidate, it is necessary that I give an honest pen-picture of the captain who led Wingello in that great struggle.

Selby Jeffery was a railway fettler. He had worn the Australian uniform which proudly displayed the big brass 'A' denoting the fact that he was present on the Sunday morning of 25 April 1915, when the Australian and New Zealand forces went into action at Gallipoli in their attempt to open up the Dardanelles. Selby was an Anzac, and as such held the unbounded respect of every man on the field. He sported a fairly robust black moustache. His face was rosy with blatant good health and his persistent good humour was heralded by the most pleasant smile one could wish to see.

His snow-white shirt and duck trousers were immaculate, as were his rubber boots. He wore a black waistcoat, unbuttoned, over the shirt. The idea of the waistcoat was quite original—it held his pipe, his tobacco and his matches. It was not unusual in those far off days for a country cricketer to light up and take a few draws on a pipe or cigarette. Nobody took umbrage at it. I saw it happen outback many times. Indeed I once saw it in first-class cricket on the Sydney Cricket Ground, when Freddie Mair, the gifted allrounder and Balmain captain for many years, playing for New South Wales against Victoria, let his craving for a few draws get the better of him at the fall of a Victorian wicket. And I seem to recall that he had to get a match from the man fielding at short leg, but I can't remember who that was.

Selby used to slip his big-bowled bent-stemmed Captain Peterson pipe into the top pocket of his unbuttoned waistcoat. His tobacco pouch fitted snugly into the other top pocket, with the tin box holding his Wax Vestas matches in the bottom pocket along with a penknife for cutting the plug of dark 'Conqueror' tobacco.

It would have been senseless for him to field in any position where it might have been necessary to raise an occasional canter. Had he run there would have been a scattering of smoking paraphernalia in all directions. Wisely therefore he placed himself invariably at first slip where he was splendidly covered by a magnificent 'keeper named Tommy Lynam and always supported by an active and mobile second slip.

Very early in the day I got one to lift and bite. Young Bradman edged it and the ball travelled speedily and straight in the direction of Selby's midriff. It would have been an extraordinary effort had the catch been taken. It struck him in the solar plexus just at the moment when he was, with both hands well and truly occupied, lighting his pipe.

Bradman soon gave our skipper a chance to redeem himself by snicking my quicker ball straight to him again. This second time Selby made a manful attempt with both hands to make the catch, but he had blown such a dense cloud of bluish smoke from his startled lungs that he must have lost sight of the ball well before it reached him.

'Sorry Bill,' he called, as if nothing untoward had happened. Selby's inconsistencies in the slips were part and parcel of the Wingello team's programme. I was probably the only one among us who felt that he might have been wise to deny himself just a little longer.

Who in the name of all that is holy could ever possibly hope to get away unscathed when Don Bradman had been given two lives. If I said earlier that I experienced some early worries as the boyish Bradman started his innings by methodical employment of the middle of his bat, I could certainly go much further in describing my own mental reactions as this young man tore the Wingello attack apart. Even though his size suggested that he would have been better fitted physically to have been riding winners at Randwick racecourse, he summoned up the energy required to land the ball right over the fence on half a dozen occasions. One wondered where he was hiding the battery that generated the power.

To draw a convenient veil over the desolate scene, Selby Jeffery's team finished the day a crestfallen crowd who listened more to the rattles of the old Model T Ford than to any animated flow of conversation on the thirty mile return trip by road to Wingello. Their chief bowling hope had nothing whatever to say. The boy Bradman was 234 not out.

Back at home I questioned my mother's wisdom in aiding and abetting my downfall by so carefully collecting my gear, but she seemed to think I had come to little harm, really, and that I should have considered myself lucky to have spent such a lovely day out in the fresh air playing cricket.

As the game was to be continued on our Wingello wicket the following Saturday afternoon, I could not help feeling that I was due to face up to another hammering from this pint-sized powerhouse a week later. I saw no hope ahead for me. All was gloom. I began to count my blessings in that I had other sports to choose from. As an athlete I had spent two happy years with Botany Harriers, where I had done reasonably well without ever having really tried to train assiduously for the three events—high jump, triple jump and shot putt—in which I competed. I had done well enough in tennis to promise myself some sort of a future there if I cared to concentrate. All these thoughts went through my troubled boyish mind, but it was difficult to find one alleviating premise upon which to base my deep-dyed love for cricket. Having been belted unmercifully by a schoolboy was a pill too bitter for me to swallow. My pride had been badly injured.

The next Saturday afternoon arrived. I lined myself up manfully for another serve of what the game I had loved so much might have to offer.

The first ball again was mine to bowl, and the not out Bradman was there to deal with it. I let go my accustomed leg break, aimed at the leg stump. It spun sharply past the Bradman bat and crashed into the top of the off stump. Suddenly, I thought, the grass round our Wingello ground began to look greener than ever it had done before. The birds began to sing. The sun shone becomingly. One ball changed my whole sporting outlook. Gone were the dismaying plans to give the game away forever. I was prepared to go on and take whatever it had in store for me, and I made the personal pledge that as I was taking it on the chin in future I would be unsparing in my efforts to deal out as much as I could of what I was getting.

There were lots of encounters for the two of us in the years that were to follow. There were times when I felt the full weight of Don Bradman's bat—many of them indeed—but there were many occasions too when I had ample reason to rejoice in the lesson I learned on those afternoons at Bowral and Wingello in 1925.

PERFECT TOWN, PERFECT TIME

By Rodney Cavalier

From an article in Sir Donald Bradman AC, *co-ordinated by Mike Coward, 1998*

As a result of Sir Donald Bradman's own writings and the efforts of more than a dozen biographers, we have the image of the child pursuing his destiny from the moment he hurled a golf ball against the base of the water-tank in the backyard of Shepherd Street. It is a picture of loneliness and discipline, the beginnings of the hand-eye coordination which would astonish the cricketing world.

The image serves the fable of a country childhood distant from care and the troubles of Empire, a time of competitive games, fishing, cycling, meeting young Jessie Menzies, and conquering the bowling from all comers. The image premises, as other writers have put it, a Huck Finn heaven in which World War I largely passed Bowral by. It is a beguiling portrait but not one which withstands a cursory knowledge of Australian social history.

For a start Don did not live far from his friends. No one in Bowral lived very far from anyone else: his home was less than one kilometre from the centre of town, only a few hundred metres to Glebe Park where serious cricket was on offer. If Don spent a lot of time alone, it was because he chose to. Don was approaching six when World War I broke out and ten when it ended. Australian society had changed forever. Don did not escape its impact, he could not have been unaware of it.

The surnames of the players in the Bowral cricket team are consonant with the names of recruits and the war dead. Young men who played with George Bradman, Don's father, did not return; older men who played with George and Don had sons who did not return. In September 1916 Shepherd Street learned of the death of a resident, Private J. J. G. Riley. In the streets of Bowral for all the years between the wars was the constant sight of men whose bodies had been wrecked by the war. The grieving of widows and fatherless children, Don's contemporaries, was a reality behind the need of Bowral, like Australia, to make sense of its grief and get on with living.

Cricket continued throughout: life had to go on. The *Southern Mail* carried notices from G. Bradman, hon secretary of the Berrima District Cricket Association, setting out the organisational details of a competition based on the major towns of Bowral, Moss Vale and Mittagong and the tiny settlements which were always struggling to field a team. The matches played by Bowral were hard affairs: batsmen continue until dismissed, there is no such thing as retirement, declarations are made only when the innings total is nigh-unreachable.

In addition to his duties with the district, George was assistant-secretary and treasurer of the Bowral Club and a selector. The nature of George's world brought him home for most nights of his children's childhood; his work for cricket was a part of their home life. Perhaps there is another image of the young Bradman, shared with his siblings: all the family at home most nights, a father at the dining table under the flickering light of a kerosene lamp, working on the correspondence and the minutes of the local cricket clubs. For years Don will not understand what his father is doing, then he will be absorbed by it, and in due course he will want to be a part of it.

Before he was old enough to be playing, Don was appointed scorer for the Bowral club, a position of significance in a club which took its cricket so seriously. The scorer was wholly absorbed in the progress of a match. Like the umpires, he could not relax for a single ball. Before Don famously substituted for a missing player, he was learning so much about the game by scrutinising the strengths and weaknesses of players and wickets and circumstance.

The celebrated visit to the Sydney Cricket Ground in the company of his father to see the first Test of the 1920–21 Ashes series takes its place in the Bradman legend as a life-changing moment for Don — as the first visit to the SCG remains for anyone who has ever loved sport. Yet, three months earlier, back in Bowral, Don had revealed a commitment to cricket well beyond the game on the field. Having seen how the game worked behind the scenes, Don wanted to see for himself what happened at night when the men assembled in committee to arrange the coming season. In September 1920 Don Bradman attended the annual general meeting of the Bowral Cricket Club. He had just turned 12. He found that committee politics were to his liking.

Don was to attend every subsequent annual meeting until his departure from the district. From his father at home, then in the presence of worldly men in the formality of a meeting, he learned about the precarious financial basis of local cricket, the crucial importance of sympathetic local government to provide facilities for cricket's benefit at the expense of others, the logistics of assembling a team and transporting them when required, the hard decisions involved in streaming limited personnel into grades and separate elevens, the politics of selection. To the home team fell the responsibility of hosting the visitors at dinner, a duty faithfully observed by Bowral with all its attendant costs and organisation. While most of the players took no interest in the affairs of the club, this non-player could not get enough of it.

Before he was eligible to join, the enthusiast was made an honorary member. As soon as he was eligible, he was elected to the social committee; like his father he became the assistant secretary and treasurer. The first resolution in his name defines eligibility for the bowling trophy to a player who has delivered a minimum of 20 overs. Don's attention to the organisation of the game was at least as painstaking as his mastery of batsmanship.

Some have sought to rewrite the Bradman story as a triumph against the odds, an unlikely journey from rural Australia to the lawns of Lord's and Sandringham. It is a view which blithely overlooks the organisation of Australian cricket, it was always throwing up cricketers from nowhere, uncoached and unworldly.

The Bradmans had picked the perfect town and the perfect time for a cricketer to grow up. Bowral was sufficient distance from Sydney to be a separate world yet close enough for a traveller to reach it within hours. The town deified cricket; the cricket club backed their prodigy all the way. Don's emergence coincided with radio broadcasting and the newsreel, the basis of the mass audience for sport.

It is hard to perceive what element of the Don's magnificent triumph was against the odds — he had inherited uncommon prowess in all games, his parents afforded him the discipline and character to explore that prowess to the frontiers of the possible. Don grew up in a loving home, where cricket was encouraged but kept in perspective, a view reinforced by siblings who made no fuss about their youngest. In the entire history of Australian cricket it is not possible to find another instance where the odds were stacked more decisively in anyone's favour.

FIRST TRIAL

By Jim Mathers

From a newspaper article written in 1949. Mathers, a well-known cricket writer before and after the war, gives a first-hand account of young Bradman's trial in the nets before New South Wales selectors in October 1926.

WITHOUT ATTEMPTING TO JOIN that great army of critics who periodically stake their claim to the discovery of Bradman, here is the Bradman history as I saw it right from the inside during the springtime of that wonderful career Bradman began in Sydney 22 years ago. It was the summer of 1926–27. Bradman was 18. He was playing in country cricket at Bowral. His huge scores attracted the attention of officials of the New South Wales Cricket Association. The boy was regarded as a cricket prodigy.

At the request of Mr R. L. ('Dick') Jones, now chairman of the Sydney Cricket Ground Trust, then a State selector, Bradman was invited to Sydney for trial. The Association paid his expenses.

The day arrived. Bradman walked out to the practice wickets on No. 2 SCG. He was wearing elastic braces, white duck pants, and white shirt.

Bradman donned batting pads and walked to the wicket with the nonchalance of a cocky veteran. He played all bowling with ease and confidence, albeit his stroke equipment was as graceful as the turn-out of Dad and Dave in stiff shirt and tails at Mabel's wedding party. Still, this boy from Bowral—he was born at Cootamundra on 27 August 1908—moved out audaciously to the slows, even although he nearly always hit across the flight of the ball, and he survived his baptism that day to go on to a career of glamor and wealth.

Briefly here are the facts: I was standing with Mr Dick Jones 22 years ago on the afternoon of Bradman's trial at SCG when the selector told him he showed great promise and ought to play in Sydney club cricket. Bradman replied: 'But I cannot afford to come to Sydney. I'll have to go back to Bowral and play tennis.'

After some further discussions, Bradman was found 30 shillings a week expenses to come from Bowral to Sydney at weekends and play club cricket with St George.

A RIVAL FOR ARCHIE JACKSON

A newspaper report of Bradman's 62 retired for Goulburn against the South Coast at Goulburn, 13 November 1926.

LAST EASTER IN GOULBURN with the Balmain Cricketers we had young Jackson, our youngest interstate player and the present idol of Sydney cricket, but I think Donald Bradman of Bowral, given experience in the right class of cricket, is destined to become even a greater player than Jackson. Young Bradman never had a lesson in batting in his life and has had to think out the strokes for himself, and besides possessing unique natural ability he has developed his play marvellously all round the wicket. Once or twice on Saturday at the start of his innings on a strange wicket, for he has very little practice on turf, he nearly made a faulty stroke by not getting well over the off ball, but otherwise his innings was a masterpiece. Not even Jack Hobbs in his more brilliant days used his feet better to get to a slow ball, and it was glorious to watch this Bowral youngster step out yards like a flash of lightning and play a perfect off or cover drive.

A BATSMAN OF PROMISE

A press comment on Bradman's debut for St George in Sydney grade cricket in November 1926. He made 110 against Petersham in less than two hours.

THE OUTSTANDING SUCCESS OF young Don Bradman is but an example of what may be gained through experimental channels. There are many such potential champions who are hiding their lights under country bushels, and if sufficient encouragement were offered, many a country star could be persuaded to step it out with the city masters.

Bradman is not by any means a polished batsman of all strokes, but this deficiency is more than balanced by a super abundance of confidence, a natural desire to force the game, and a very broad mind to assimilate any good advice that is offering. Bradman has made a wonderful debut as a grade cricketer, and his innings stamps him as a batsman of promise.

NICE FOOTWORK, EASY CONFIDENCE

A newspaper report of Bradman's appearance in the final Country Week fixture at the end of November 1926—for a Combined Country XI against a Combined First Grade XI. He made 98.

THE COUNTRYMEN'S BEST PERFORMER with the bat on the day was Bradman. He played a fine innings, using his feet nicely to the First Grade slow bowler Morris, and playing the other types with easy confidence. He is rather weak on the on-side, however, and has a bad habit of walking away from the wicket when playing defensive strokes. The latter fault is a common hard-wicket players' error.

Bradman has every possibility of being a State player in the near future, and, provided he overcomes these faults, will be a very classy one. His cutting and driving were his main strokes, and were made very powerfully. Everyone was sorry to see him miss by two runs the century which he so well deserved.

THE BOWRAL WONDER

A newspaper description of Bradman's 320 not out for Bowral against Moss Vale in May 1927.

AFTER GIVING A POOR exhibition the previous Saturday, Don Bradman excelled himself on this occasion, and the few spectators were given a rare treat. Getting his eye in quickly, Don commenced to pepper the bowling, and was not long in reaching his century, after which he gave a remarkable exhibition of batting activity. Never before has the Moss Vale bowling received such an unmerciful flogging; good and bad were treated alike, the balls whizzing to every part of the field, and only those who attempted to stop them know how much ginger was behind them. His experience in Sydney first-grade cricket this season has made a marked improvement in Bradman's play, and he gave one of the most exhilarating displays one could wish to see. By making the phenomenal score of 320 not out, in which there were six sixers, he broke the district high score record of 300 made by himself against Moss Vale last season. He had a few lives, but then he was after runs off every ball, and after all, how many such scores are made in any class of cricket without a few chances being given?

GOOD RIDDANCE TO BRADMAN

From an Australian newspaper, 1930.

I HAPPENED TO BE holidaying in the district whence came Bradman when that young man began to shine in Sydney grade cricket. 'Well,' I observed to a local chap, 'you've lost Bradman for good.'

'And good riddance,' rejoined the native, 'we could never get the cow out!'

LIKE A VETERAN

A review in the press of Bradman's 118 for New South Wales in his first Sheffield Shield match, against South Australia at Adelaide, in December 1927. At this early stage of his career, Bradman's ability to bat aggressively without taking risks was already evident.

THAT AUSTRALIA HAS UNEARTHED another 'topnotcher' is the opinion expressed by old interstate and international cricketers who watched Don Bradman compile a century in his first innings in Sheffield Shield cricket. Though only 19 years old he played like a veteran, devoid of nerves, cracking Grimmett twice for four at the very outset of his innings and completing his hundred by sweeping Lee to the leg boundary.

The rise of this lad reads like a romance. Though not unique, a century at a first Sheffield Shield appearance is a fine feat, especially for a colt, and roars of applause greeted the achievement.

Bradman is a natural batsman. He uses his feet well and though he hit hard and made strokes all round the wicket, not for a moment did he take the slightest risk.

BATS A BIT

By Walter Hammond

From Cricket's Secret History, *1952.*

DON BRADMAN WAS VERY nervous before going in to bat for at least the first half of his career, and I think it was always the same, but he contrived to hide the signs later. The first time I ever saw him on a cricket field, in a match on our 1928–29 tour, he was playing for New South Wales and I remember asking Pat Hendren who the slim boy was. 'Oh, he's a lad from the backblocks called Bradman—bats a bit, they say. But he looks too frightened to do much today!' was what Pat answered. We were to learn better before the game was over, for young Don scored 87 and 132 not out.

FENDER AND THE BRIDGE

An anonymous verse which appeared before Bradman made his Test debut at Brisbane in the first Test of the 1928–29 series against England, which Percy Fender covered for an English newspaper. The verse had this intro-duction: Mr Fender, passing through to Brisbane, said he had not seen Bradman. What he wanted was a close-up view of the harbour bridge.

'Oh! have you seen our Bradman.'
   And the pressman winked an eye.
He was talking to a sad-man
   Who was passing Sydney by.
'I have seen your lovely harbour,
   And I want to see your bridge;
May have converse with a barber,

And inspect a mountain ridge.
'But I haven't seen your Bradman.'
    And Friend Fender rattled on,
'Do not think I am a madman—
    It's a bridge I gaze upon.'
And his eye turned to the far wood
    While the pressmen murmured
        'Well,
Our Bradman's seen your Larwood—
    That's another tale to tell!'

PLUCK AND STUDIOUS METHODS

By Charles Macartney

A newspaper report after the third Test of 1928–29 in which Bradman scored his first Test century.

BRADMAN IS A WONDERFUL find for Australia, and although his chief asset at present is confidence and pluck, he has made a most remarkable improvement in his actual play during his very short career in first-class cricket. A couple of seasons ago, when he was compara- tively unknown, and when one would have expressed astonishment if it had been said that he would be representing Australia in two years' time, he was a raw country player, with a strong tendency to cross-bat in his strokes. Today he has almost eliminated that defect, for which matting wickets were mainly responsible, and now faces the bowler in the same manner as a player who has never been off the turf. It speaks well for his concentration and studious methods, without which he would have been years in overcoming the fault. He can defend and attack with equal skill, and when he acquires more knowledge of the fine points of the game, which do not come to young players in a moment, he is going to be one of the finest players Australia has ever produced.

ALMOST BRAZEN AGGRESSION

A newspaper report of Bradman's century in the fifth Test, 1928–29.

IT WAS BRADMAN WHO provided the fireworks by trouncing every bowler brought against him. His unfinished hand of 109 represents one of the big Test feats of the season. He jumped straight into the bowling as though he were out for a practice knock instead of having to save Australia from a collapse.

First he hit Larwood practically off his length; then to Tate he showed wonderful skill in turning and driving. To White he used his feet, often going a couple of yards down the pitch to meet him and hit him hard, either straight or through the covers. Impishly he dragged the slow bowler around to the on—a spot to which he is rarely played.

The beginning of his innings was almost brazen in its aggressiveness. He reached his first 50 in 71 minutes, and had very few dull moments until he was in the nineties, when he played steadily for his century. Once past that he was off again, and at the end was practically doing what he liked with every ball. Only by pitching their deliveries off the wicket could the bowlers steady his scoring.

To Bradman belongs the honor of having knocked White, that most difficult of bowlers, off his length. The English captain wisely changed when he saw that the New South Wales colt was able to hit him easily, even through the well placed off field. At 46 he gave his only chance, but the catch was too hot for Geary to hold.

THE PROMISE OF BIG THINGS

By M. A. Noble

From The Fight For The Ashes 1928–29. *Noble, a well-respected captain of Australia before World War I, was counted among the best judges of the game in Australia when he made this assessment of Bradman in 1929.*

BRADMAN HAS A REMARKABLE record for one so young. Two seasons ago he was an unknown country player, at Bowral, but showed good form during country cricket week in Sydney. The following season he joined one of the Sydney district clubs, the St George, was selected to go to South Australia, and made a century in his first interstate match. During the present season he has had remarkable success, having scored more runs than any other Australian ever scored in one season. For his State he made a century in each innings against Queensland, and followed that with his double of 87 and 132 not out for New South Wales against England. This performance was responsible for his inclusion in the first Test match, at Brisbane, but, owing to his non-success there, he was foolishly left out for the second Test, in Sydney. In the third, which turned out to be the deciding match for the rubber, he was again included, and in the first innings he showed remarkable patience and skill in defence, and coolness in a difficult position, but forsook his natural breezy methods, playing Scotch the whole time. He appeared to be anxious and afraid of his defence and apparently resolved to rectify any deficiency there might be. The same methods were employed during the first half of the second innings, until White drove him backward with his good-length deliveries, beat, and very nearly clean-bowled him. This was sufficient; he had learned his lesson, fortunately for Australia, without penalty. From that time onward he was a different batsman. Forsaking the

careful methods which had proved so unprofitable to himself and disas-
trous to his comrades, he opened out into a powerful offensive. Time and
again he went down the pitch, driving White with great power. Up till
then silly-point had dominated and cramped the batsmen, but now, for
the first time, he was removed to another position. Bradman never
looked back, and history tells how he eventually completed a glorious
century and had the satisfaction of knowing that he had retrieved the
fortunes of his team and put Australia into a winning position.

That was a wonderful effort for a youth who is not yet twenty.
By seizing the opportunity he gained the experience necessary to
complete his batting education. No influence I know of has such far-
reaching effects as a century in Test cricket, and this one certainly put
Bradman on the map and consolidated his position as a certainty for
England in 1930. In the field he is a worthy successor of Australia's
great outfields. He is fleet of foot, anticipates the batsmen's strokes, is
very safe with either or both hands, and has a fast, low, accurate return.
His running between the wickets, however, leaves much to be desired;
it is his pronounced weakness. He neither has confidence in himself
nor in his partner. He is too fond of stopping his *vis-à-vis* (or himself)
from getting an easy two by signalling 'stop' instead of heeding his
partner's call to 'come again.' This, however, is but an evidence of
youthful inexperience and want of knowledge that will disappear as he
develops. In Australia we look on him as one of the most promising
players of the future. For his years, and considering his short career, his
rise has been meteoric. It is somewhat of a pity that he has not a bigger
physique, yet if he had that he might not have so many other qualities.
I like his defence and aggression. I like his versatility, his stroke play, and
his general breeziness. I like his fielding, his fast running in the field, his
sure picking up and his strong, accurate return. I like his quiet modesty,
his intelligence, and his cricket temperament. I look to him for big
things, for he has the makings of a truly great cricketer. All that is now
needed to crown his success is the experience of a season in England.

THE LAST LAUGH

By Walter Hammond

From Cricketers' School, *1948.*

IN 1928, WHEN I was in Australia with Percy Chapman's English team, 'new boy' Don Bradman was included in the New South Wales side against us as a bowler-batsman. It is always the policy of a touring team to knock any promising young bowler off his length so he shall not give trouble in a subsequent Test.

Patsy Hendren and I were batting when Don was put on to bowl and we measured him up and then began hitting. Don was taken off quickly. Later he was given another go by a wise skipper who knew you must not leave a beginner with a memory of failure, if you can help it.

Patsy whipped one ball away for four, chopped the next down, slammed the next for six on top of the stand, sent the next after it in the same place, made a grinning stroke at the next—mistimed it and was caught. He made a monkey face at me as he walked away from the wicket, as much as to say, 'You'd better carry on the job'.

I got to the end for Bradman's next over, slashed 24 off it—and again Bradman was taken off. We had knocked 55 runs off him in five overs. He went to his place in the field. Two balls later I hit in his direction and started for what I thought was an easy single. By the most astonishing cat-like leap and simultaneous pick-up and return he threw my wicket down while I was still a yard out of the crease. That was the Bradman way . . . somebody had to win and it was going to be Bradman if he knew it!

He had a capacity I have never seen equalled in any other cricketer of docketing his cricket in one part of his mind and never letting any other event intrude there. That is a quality of concentration on the game that everyone must develop who is to be successful, but not many of us, I think, have the ruthless capacity of a Bradman to perfect such a power as he did.

KIND ADVICE

A remark to young Bradman in 1928–29 by Maurice Tate, as quoted by Walter Hammond. Tate was to suffer as much as other English bowlers from Bradman's bat in 1930.

WE SHALL SEE YOU in England. But keep your bat straighter, my boy. Those cross-bat shots will come to grief on our wickets.

A FIRST IMPRESSION

By Percy Fender

From The Turn Of The Wheel, *1929. In this extract from his book about the 1928–29 series, Fender repeats the criticism of Bradman's batting which he had made during the series in his newspaper columns. It is clear Bradman took note of Fender's remarks, for he later wrote that he was determined to do well when Australia played Surrey, captained by Fender, in 1930. Bradman made 252 not out against Surrey in less than a day.*

BRADMAN WAS ONE OF the most curious mixtures of good and bad batting I have ever seen. In Brisbane he made one grand shot off Tate to the square-leg boundary in the first innings and a collection of others of a most inferior brand. During the rest of the series he improved, making more shots of the truly magnificent type, but never being able to avoid either the really bad ones or the badly made ones. One would see him cram half a dozen or more shots, worthy of the greatest, into a couple or three overs, then two or three times running he would completely mis-time, mis-judge, and mis-hit the ball. One minute one would think him a grand player, and the next he would look like a schoolboy.

If practice, experience, and hard work enable him to eradicate the faults and still retain the rest of his ability, he may well become a very great player; and if he does this, he will always be in the category of the brilliant, if unsound, ones.

THE RECORD BREAKER

By Eric Barbour

A commentary in the Sydney Mail *on Bradman's 452 not out for New South Wales against Queensland in January 1930, then a world-record score in first-class cricket.*

DON BRADMAN'S RECORD-BREAKING achievement in Sydney has thrilled the whole cricket-loving world. Congratulations have poured in on him from admirers throughout the Empire, yet he remains the most unconcerned player in the game today. It is this nonchalance combined with his all-round ability and his genial boyishness that has made him so popular with the public. He is still a mere youth of 21, and is as much in love with cricket now as he was when he first got his place in the Bowral school team at the age of 12. As a boy it was recognised that he had a remarkably quick eye, was very fleet of foot, and showed sound judgment for his age. He has never lost these attributes; instead, he has developed and disciplined them until they have become the essentials of his cricket make-up. Although small of stature, he is an athlete, and keeps himself always in splendid physical condition. There is nothing stodgy about either the man or his play. His confidence is a concomitant of his boyishness, his happy disposition, his perfect health. The way he walks down the pitch to make brilliant strokes off balls which otherwise might be difficult to play is fascinating, at times daring. But he is never afraid of going out.

He loves to hit and to hit hard—to place the ball just out of reach of the fieldsman—to punish the bowler who is overawing the batsmen. In general style he somewhat resembles Clem Hill; yet he is really a law to himself. Many cricketers declare that he is too risky, too unorthodox; and from a mechanical point of view some of his strokes are certainly not perfect, but he gets the runs, and gets them so often that he has quite dumbfounded his critics.

When Victor Trumper first came into the limelight as a batsman it was his unorthodox methods that made the selectors afraid of him. Because he did things differently they concluded that he would not last. With Bradman it is the same, except that Bradman has not yet developed the versatility or stroke-making fluency of his great prototype. The youth who can make big scores consistently against the best bowlers of the day and can cap his records with the greatest individual total ever compiled in first-class cricket has a right to be unorthodox. And one of the most fascinating things about his play is that he appears to enjoy every moment of it. At the bowling crease and in the field it is just the same; he is a live wire that neither sweltering heat nor arduous work can suppress. To see him in the outfield cutting off fours or racing around to attempt impossible catches is a perfect delight. The point is that he does not accept anything as impossible.

How complete was Bradman's mastery was indicated by his scoring rate. He passed Ponsford's record in 406 minutes. The Victorian's 437 was made in 621 minutes. There was no trace of wildness in Bradman's hitting. It was an instance of sheer resolution and machine-like steadiness. Hard but safe driving, late and back cuts to the empty spaces, and powerful pulls characterised his stay of nearly seven hours. How much further he might have gone had his captain not decided to close the innings it is difficult to say. As he came off the field he showed no sign of fatigue.

A SUNNY FACE

By Claude Corbett

From a newspaper article by Corbett, a well-known sports writer of the day, after Bradman's 452 not out.

THE DATES OF JANUARY 4 and 6 in this year of grace, 1930, will ever be chronicled by the historians of the game as the days when Don Bradman created his world's record of 452 not out. Laden with confidence of the kind which is not blatant, but of that quiet, almost magnetic, character, Bradman, the lad from Bowral, was regarded as the one and only man in Australia possessing the three attributes necessary for such a mighty performance—ability, physical condition and superlative dash.

To know Bradman is to know as clean a type of young manhood imaginable. Full of the effervescent fun, natural to a trained young athlete in the full flower of a brilliant career, Bradman enjoys every moment of his cricketing life. It is a game, not a business, with him.

There are no furrowed brows when the situation is such as to demand stern measures for the salvation of his side. Bradman goes to his game with a smile on his sunny face. The 'laughing cavalier' of cricket. They may nearly get his wicket; they may almost run him out; he may crack the bowling in all directions. It is just the same to Bradman. Laughter is the companion for ever with him.

Notable critics of the game have written that Bradman is not a great batsman, that his style is too unorthodox, and that many of his shots are crude. That may be true in spots, but the proof of his ability rests in the fact that runs are always coming from his flashing bat. A man may get big scores now and again, but not all the time unless he has the gift of mastering the bowling. Bradman has done that over and over again before and after the day he forsook the matting wickets of his home town for the turf of Australia's famous cricket arenas. Didn't he, in his first club game in Sydney for St George, score a century, and didn't he in his first Sheffield Shield match against South Australia top 100 runs?

There are many years ahead of this clean-living youngster in which to add lustre to his name and the game he loves. England will be awaiting him in a few months' time, waiting to see this boy who has set the world of cricket aflame by his remarkable run-getting prowess.

BRADMAN—BATTING MACHINE

By Sim

Penned around 1930.

Robot of all-round-the-wicket,
    A ball-bearing battery of bats:
The field's perspiration is oiling rotation
    Of cogwheels all running serene
That's—
    Bradman—Batting Machine.

'Four–six–one–into–the–grandstand,'
    That is his rhythm and rhyme.

'A cut through to cover; 18 for that over.'

The bowlers turn ultramarine.

'I'm—

Bradman—Batting Machine.'

JACKSON AND BRADMAN IN THE NETS, 1930

By H. A. H. Carson

London Evening News, *28 April 1930. Despite Bradman's world record-breaking score of 452 not out three months before, some people at this early stage of the 1930 tour, before a match had been played, still considered young Archie Jackson's prospects to be as bright as Bradman's. A few days later Bradman scored 236 in the opening match against Worcester, and thereafter comparisons of the two men ceased.*

THE AUSTRALIANS WERE OUT at Lord's again today, but did not do a great amount of work. The wickets were far too soft to trouble the batsmen, and there was no difficulty in spotting what turn there was on the ball.

Archie Jackson and Don Bradman were at the nets side by side, so that one would gain some idea of the methods of the men and the way they shaped at the ball. Jackson, on the first occasion he appeared at Lord's, gave the impression that he might prove the more dangerous bat on English wickets. His methods are more on English lines, but Bradman surprised all with the variety of strokes he possesses and the power he put into his shots.

The main things which are taught in English cricket are the uplift of the bat, which should swing parallel to a line between the wickets, and the use of the right foot in guarding the wicket. Bradman lifts his bat in the direction of point, and rarely moves his right foot to guard his stumps.

We shall have no talk of pad play about Bradman; he uses his bat to play the ball as he should, and if one may judge by what was seen of him today he is likely to turn defence into attack.

One is rather inclined to discount the wonderful performances of batsmen on those glorious Australian wickets, but I think we have in Bradman a batsman who may follow in the footsteps of Trumper and Macartney.

A LESSON FOR PERCY FENDER

By Edward Wybergh Docker

From Bradman And The Bodyline Series, *1978. Covering the 1928–29 Ashes tour for an English newspaper, Fender, Surrey's captain, wrote critically of young Bradman, saying he sometimes batted like a schoolboy. It is known Bradman resented the criticism and felt he had a score to settle in the tour match against Surrey.*

FOR THE AUSTRALIANS VERSUS Surrey, Bradman had one of those special personal reasons for making a big score. 'He does not correct mistakes, nor look as if he were trying to,' the Surrey captain had written about his batting in Australia. And throughout the 1929 English season, as busy with the pen as he was on the cricket field, Fender had gone on casting doubts on the ability of so many of these young Australians, implying that Chapman's task in 1928–29 had been a relatively simple one.

It was not actually a very auspicious occasion on which to put Mr P.G.H. Fender to rights. Dark clouds, promising yet another of those cold, cheerless May days, hung low over Kennington from horizon to horizon; the gasometer in the background seemed to loom larger than ever when Woodfull and Jackson went out to open for Australia a quarter of an hour late (the wrong-sized stumps had been set). The pitch was not specially difficult, yet not specially in favour of the batsmen either, and the two of them pottered around until Jackson snicked one to the 'keeper, 1–11 after half an hour. 'At 12.45 exactly,' said the newspaper report, 'a fair-haired, uncapped boy emerged from the pavilion to hearty applause.'

Bradman was already a favourite in England. He couldn't be murdering the bowling all the time, but always he was busy, ever on the look-out for a cheeky single, and always it had a tonic effect upon Woodfull at the other end. Woodfull in 1930 was by no means as strokeless as his reputation suggested. Skilful as he was in shielding a younger batsman from Tate or Larwood in full cry, he certainly didn't hog the strike with Bradman as a partner. In this case he kept the runs coming with ones and twos and they added 116 together in almost even time. Not until Woodfull was out for 50 however did Bradman really go to town. The cut had been his favourite scoring shot earlier in the innings. Now he began to unleash that terrible weapon of destruction, the pull-shot. Fender was bowling with a packed off-side field and only a deep mid-on on the other side of the wicket. But Bradman would get right outside his off-stump and pivoting on his right foot smash the ball forward of square-leg. Twice he played this same shot. Fender pulled a man out of the covers to block it. Bradman stroked the third ball back along the pitch, leapt at the next and drove it through the vacant spot in the covers. The cross-bat may have offended against all the canons of classical batsmanship, but Fender was perhaps too occupied with field settings and bowling changes to spare the matter a critical thought.

At 5–250 Fairfax came in, 52 runs were added of which Fairfax contributed only one, and there was great interest with rain threatening to see if Bradman would reach his own personal 250 before play was stopped for the day. When he was 240 Gregory began what would obviously have to be the last over. His first five balls yielded Bradman eight runs, then to the last he was yards down the pitch off-driving it to the fence and the crowd swarmed onto the ground as the two batsmen sprinted for the pavilion. 'Nobody say anything,' called one of the team as they stood watching from the balcony, 'Not a word.' Bradman strode into the dressing-room, threw down his gloves, and remarked, 'I wonder what Fender will have to say in the morning paper this time.'

TO SEE BRADMAN 'BAHT'

An account in the press of Bradman's innings of 78 against Yorkshire early in the 1930 tour.

BRADMAN BURST INTO BLOOM in one wonderful over from Macaulay, whom he pasted all round the ground with scintillating strokes. He drove magnificently to both sides of the wicket, a treat the Yorkshire spectators have rarely, if ever, enjoyed so much.

The wily old veteran, Rhodes, was brought on to save the pickets from being broken, but he made no difference to Bradman who clouted him with rare abandon.

Bradman seemed set for another big score when he gave an easy catch to Macaulay off the latter's own bowling. It was a brilliant innings, and the crowd applauded every step he took towards the pavilion. Macaulay warmly shook Don's hands as he left the wicket.

No doubt Bradman is the most popular figure in cricket with the English crowds at the present time. In the words of one Yorkshireman: 'We do not come to see the Australians play, we *joost* come to see Bradman *baht*.'

GEORGE'S FOLLY

By Sir Leonard Hutton

From Fifty Years of Cricket.

BRAMALL LANE, NOW, ALAS, surrendered to football, was the ground for lively wit. The Sheffield spectator had no equal anywhere in the world, and it was a treat to field near the boundary and listen to the comments. One handed down in the Yorkshire dressing room involved George Macaulay, and there is a moral to it.

Don Bradman had been batting only a short time and, as usual, looked to be in ominous form. Macaulay, who had been known to quail batsmen with a glare and a mutter, asked for the ball and in a loud voice declared: 'Let me 'ave a go at this booger.' His first over produced the considered achievement of a maiden to Bradman, but in the next he was hit for five boundaries, and a further 16 runs in his third over. As silently he took his sweater, a voice with the strength of a loudhailer came from the crowd: 'Tha should have kept thy bloody mouth shut, George.'

DONBRADMANIA

By Gwen Leach

After Bradman's 254 in the second Test at Lord's, 1930.

'DONBRADMANIA.' H'M! QUEER WORD. 'Where did it originate?'

'Originate? Why it is a disease!'

'Is that so? Well, explain yourself!'

'Well, I happen to be a sufferer from this malady myself. It is, as I suppose you have already guessed, the hero-worship of Don Bradman, OUR cricketer. Although, as I have mentioned, I am a sufferer, my state is not chronic. Oh, dear no!'

Yesterday I was walking slowly down a certain street in Bondi, meditating on the weather, when, suddenly, a hefty punch on the back almost sent me sprawling. I was about to expostulate when my friend, Nellie, as I had now perceived that it was, said: 'Oh, isn't he be . . . autiful; isn't he gor . . . geous. I'm going to send to England for his autograph.'

By now I had awakened to the fact that it was OUR Don Bradman she was referring to. After a fairly polite reply, I was about fed up of this disease, I waltzed away home.

On arriving home I discovered that a heated discussion was taking place between Gwen and Dad as to whether Don Bradman would last long. To try and draw the noise of these argumentative hero-worshippers I turned on the wireless to hear the announcer say: 'I will now read you the latest cricket scores, and also an English critic's opinion of Don Bradman.'

I savagely turned the wireless off and made my way to my sanctuary—my bedroom. I selected a magazine and prepared to read; on turning the page, the first title that greeted my eye was 'Don Bradman.' I threw down the magazine in disgust, and was about to recline on my bed for forty winks, when Dad entered and said, 'Are you going to sit up with me until 3.30 a.m. to hear the cricket scores, Mick?'

BLAME BRADMAN

A newspaper story, 1930.

DON BRADMAN, THE AUSTRALIAN batting robot, does not know all for which he is to blame. He knows that he is to blame for twisting the Lion's tail, and he knows that he is to blame for several old gentlemen at Lord's having heart failure. But he does not know that he cost a Brighton lorry driver ten shillings.

Ernest Alfred Vye was driving his employers' lorry along the Marine Parade when he saw the Aquarium Test Match score board in action. Like so many other errand boys, who have exhausted all their grand-mothers for mythical funerals, he was tempted and fell. So rapt did Vye become, that he left his lorry by the wayside three full hours, and an entirely unsympathetic policeman had something to say about it.

The Brighton Magistrates have sporting instincts, but they thought that even so small a part of Bradman's innings as three hours was worth ten shillings!

How Headingley cheered!

A newspaper report of Bradman's century before lunch in the Leeds Test, 1930. He was 309 not out at the end of the day and next day took his score to 334.

Out comes Don Bradman, the record breaker, with that curiously reluctant walk of his.

Don Bradman's bat makes a warlike music. His feet are swift and decisive in their pouncing steps. But if he is the Cavalier of cricket, his captain Woodfull, is the unsmiling Roundhead. Woodfull is taking no risks. He is all stubborn patience. The bowlers' attack breaks against his unyielding defence like waves against a cliff. Eternally he pats the ball back and back, and eternally Maurice Tate wheels the ball down at him.

There are no shadows over the brilliant cricket of Don Bradman. He flickers in and out of his crease and his bat makes fierce curves in the air. To him it is all the same—the lightning of Larwood or the slow

This is a picture of Bradman, aged three, outside his home in Shepherd Street, Bowral. The Bradmans lived here until 1924.

Bowral boy

Young Bradman in the backyard of his home in Glebe Street, Bowral.

This photo of a very young Don Bradman batting for NSW shows the suppleness and freedom of movement which characterised his batting.

An early photo of Bradman, which is believed to have been taken at Menangle.

A determined young man. This photo was taken during the summer of 1928–29 at the Rockdale home of the NSW cricket official Frank Cush, where Bradman lived for a few years after moving to Sydney.

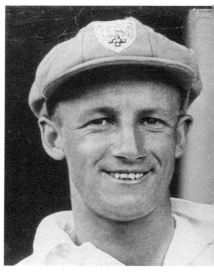

The Bradman grin. Jack Fingleton wrote: 'That grin was the cheekiest, the most challenging and the most confident thing I have seen in sport.'

This posed photo of Bradman on the SCG's old No 2 oval shows he brought his bat down dead straight even if he did pick it up towards gully.

DON. BRADMAN

t newcomers in 1928–29: Bradman, aged 20, d the spin bowler Don Blackie who made his t debut in the second Test at Sydney at the age 46 years 253 days. He is still Australia's oldest t debutant.

With his talented contemporary Archie Jackson, who made the Test side before him but died of tuberculosis at the age of 23.

Bradman awaits the umpire's decision, 1928-29. From the Ronald Cardwell Collection.

A break from the cricket, 1930. From the Ronald Cardwell Collection.

Bradman, a talented pianist, made a gramophone record at the Columbia Studios in London in 1930.

Signing bats in England, 1930. From the Ronald Cardwell Collection.

cunning of Dick Tyldesley. Round the boundary there are fieldsmen posted like sentinels and he sends the ball flashing between them almost before they can make a step.

We think of the great Macartney and the blazing century he scored before lunch on this field four years ago.

'Can Bradman do it?' we ask.

His score rushes up into the fifties, the sixties, the seventies, and though Chapman moves his men here and there and bowler follows bowler, the white figures on the scoreboard revolve dizzily. There is little beauty in this fiery art of Bradman. He cares nothing for grace; he is all efficiency.

'Let other men make exquisite gestures with the bat, my job is to get the runs,' he seems to say.

The Yorkshire crowd, massed in thousands around the field, are weary of Woodfull. This slow-motion cricket of his may be masterly strategy, but it is a great weariness to the flesh.

Don Bradman moves them to shouts of admiration—his is cricket with sunshine in it, and Headingley honours a gallant foe.

For a moment, with his score at 98, he shows that he is human after all. He actually misses the ball—and this is a thing so astounding that the field buzzes with talk. But a minute later with the lunch break still 13 minutes off, he has scored his century and has made history once more.

How Headingley cheers!

Chapman pats him on the back; his captain, Woodfull, walks across and says, 'Well done, Don!'

STONES AT GIBRALTAR

By Arthur Mailey

An account in the Sydney Sun *of Bradman's 309 not out in a day at Leeds.*

BRADMAN'S BATTING TODAY WAS almost indescribable. I was sitting with the Yorkshire cricket committee in the pavilion, listening to appreciation of Bradman's splendid innings. When Larwood bowled ineffectively at Bradman, P. F. Warner turned round to Lord Hawke and said, 'This is like throwing stones at Gibraltar!'

'Yes,' said Lord Hawke; 'the same old story—no bowlers in England.'

Bradman's innings was indescribable. The army of British overseas Pressmen were scratching their heads, trying to think of something new to say about Bradman. I can only say that Bradman's glorious innings was equal to Macartney's in 1926. Bradman's temperament is distinctly better than Macartney's. He punishes every punishable ball, but he respects those of a good length. Macartney arrogantly tried to slog good length balls.

Chapman rang the changes incessantly, but Bradman watched each move, and when occasion demanded played cautiously. In the meantime Woodfull was unperturbed by the quick scoring of his partner.

Bradman, smiling right through his innings, seemed so comfortable that he might have been playing in a village match at Bowral.

At 3 o'clock the English bowling was thoroughly collared, and Woodfull, under-rating Hammond, tried to push a ball to leg, but it broke from the off, and bowled him. Kippax was very comfortable on a perfect wicket against easy bowling. Bradman dominated the play until stumps were drawn, scoring at will throughout the day.

Returning to the pavilion, Bradman said to Woodfull, 'I am sorry I was slow today, Bill, but I've had a bit of practice, and will chase them tomorrow.'

When Bradman was hitting Tate all over the ground, Duckworth said, 'Say, Maurice, you said in Australia that you'd get Don out in England. What about trying?' Tate replied: 'You'd better try yourself, Ducky, I've had enough.'

WORLD RECORD BREAKER

By Arthur Gilligan

Gilligan, a former England captain, wrote this account of Bradman's 309 not out in one day for the News Chronicle.

AT SIX MINUTES PAST four this evening Don Bradman broke the world's record which had stood for 27 years. At that moment he ran a sharp single, making his 288 runs—a higher individual score than had ever been made in Test match history.

Australia at that time were 409 for two wickets. Tonight's play closed with Australia 458 for three, and Bradman 309 not out. His final hit was a four, a smashing drive through the cover—his 42nd four.

This is Bradman's third successive century in a Test—131 at Nottingham, 254 at Lord's, and 309 not out here today. He has scored 703 runs against England so far.

When he came in the police went out to meet him, but he made a dart for the pavilion with one policeman trying to clear the way. But it was no good. Bradman disappeared under a shower of waving arms and hands that patted him—almost as many pats it seemed as he had scored runs.

Thousands were on their feet cheering him and waving hats and handkerchiefs. If he had been an Englishman his reception could have been no greater. Even his dressing-room was not sacred. People peered into the windows, but Bradman was promptly shut off from view by sheets of brown paper.

We have spent a good deal of the day applauding this brainy boy's feats. Here are some of the things he has done that we have applauded, and that he has acknowledged by waving his cap and holding aloft his magic bat.

He came in at 11.38 when Archie Jackson was well caught by Larwood at short leg off Maurice Tate's first over; and at 11.55, having played himself well in he proceeded to score four after four.

All bowlers came alike to him.

At 12.27, with a glorious cut to the boundary, he had scored his 50. He was showing us the nectar of batsmanship. In the first hour he scored 70. At 1.16 with a hook off Larwood to square leg his century was run up.

This is a rare feat. He has thus emulated Charlie Macartney who on this same ground four years ago with the same partner, Willie Woodfull, also made his hundred before lunch.

Bradman made 102 in 98 minutes, wonderful going for the beginning of the match. At 3.15 he made an on drive off Tate which took him to 151, precisely Macartney's score on the other historic occasion. But Bradman went on and on. As the church bells chimed four the scorer put up his 200. He had now made a century before lunch, a second century before tea. Could he make a third century before dinner? He could.

At 202 he hit one over Maurice Tate's head, made on a very small chance indeed which Tate turning round and running backwards, just managed to touch with his left hand.

'Luck favours skill,' as C. B. Fry always said. The tea score was 305 for two, Bradman 220 not out. Just before tea he slowed up considerably, and for a short period afterwards he remained cautious. Twenty minutes later saw him thrashing the bowling to all parts of the field, and at 5.25 he equalled his own record score at Lord's of 254. A minute later he had broken it.

The crowd began to be on tiptoe with expectation. The question running on thousands of lips was: 'Can he break "Tip" Foster's record of 287 made in Australia in 1903?'

Australia's fourth century was reached. Larwood went on with the old ball and after a single had been scored Tom Oates, at Chapman's request, threw the new ball to him. Bradman's score then stood at 280. The new ball did not worry him at all and in seven minutes he added a further eight runs.

The world's record was smashed. The crowd cheered again and again. The game was stopped for fully a minute. Kippax, and from the English team, Chapman, Hammond and Hobbs shook hands with him. Alas, the rest of our team were too far away on the boundary to do so, but this 22-years-old cricket machine was still ticking off the runs.

At 6.10 his partnership with Kippax was ended by Chapman catching the latter in the gully off Tate, but Bradman went on with equal confidence having McCabe as his new partner.

At 6.22 a stroke past mid-off gave him his 300. More cheers. He held the fort, or rather made his sorties, to the end. His innings so far had been a galaxy of fours, and his last stroke of the day was another four—a cover drive that left the fieldsmen standing. It had the precision, finish and energy of the shots he was making at noon. When is he going to finish?

The way he is playing there seems no reason why he should not get somewhere near his own record of 452 not out made in Australia. I can assure him that all England will be delighted if he does.

A REVELATION

By 'A Man In The Crowd'

Another account of Bradman's 309 not out.

How THE SUN SHONE on Headingley Hill! The asphalt shone like the sea. Inside the ground all was shining, too; a stump lying there before beginning its day's work caught the sun and dazzled one's eyes. Faces shone all round—partly with the beginnings of an heroic thirst, but still more with joyous anticipation. ''Ow 'appy everybody looks,' as one of W. W. Jacobs's people says, after a couple of drinks. It would need the pen of Hazlitt, in the mood in which he went to the fight, to do justice to our feelings.

We arranged ourselves on those wooden seats with as little haste, with as assured a certainty of bliss, as the Blessed might on the no doubt more comfortable benches of Paradise. We, too, had eternity before us—the sun-drenched eternity of a day's cricket. We discussed many relevant matters, but most of all, and first and last, the question of the toss. Could Chapman win it again?

'Why not?' demanded a spectator of a mathematical turn of mind. He explained something of the theory of probability—at least he said it was that: he put it on almost rational grounds, when he reminded us that Chapman's coin could not know which way it fell last time. This cheered up some, but the rest of us, in spite of mathematics, felt in our bones that it was the Australian turn this time. We were right, but we didn't rub it in; it was not necessary.

Jackson came and went; we were sorry for him, of course, but not very sorry. Bradman came in; we hoped Tate would get him, too. Some thought it would be interesting to see him get a few runs before he went, just to see what he was like; others thought it would do just as well if Woodfull went. It is difficult to say when some premonition of things as they were going to be first seized us. Perhaps it was when Bradman got his first four. It was a good length ball from Tate and Bradman, with two economical dancing steps, made it a half-volley and played it (he did not drive it) straight to the screen. That single stroke was a revelation.

Tate and Larwood came off: Geary and Tyldesley came on. Very soon we began to speculate how on earth these two were going to be got out; it looked as if they would have to get themselves out. Faster and faster came the runs, but the defence of Bradman was as certain as if he was scoring 20 runs an hour, like the County batsmen we have learned to endure. To make the batsmen feel a little at home, a gentleman with a raucous voice began a little barracking of the bowlers: to judge from his vocal technique, he had studied under good masters, but he was as ineffective as the bowlers themselves.

We all had something to cheer about then, for Bradman got his century with incredible swiftness, and before lunch, too. Perhaps we had some vague idea that after scoring a hundred he would obligingly get out, and let someone else have a chance; this is generally done in English cricket, especially in Test matches. Someone ought to have drawn Bradman's attention to this social usage. Tate tried to, but his hints were ignored.

Lunch came, and our sandwiches were flavoured by the calculations of an optimist who pointed out that the Australian batting was greatly weakened by the absence of Ponsford, which some indeed were affecting to regret. He reminded us that once Woodfull, Bradman, and Kippax were out, the rest would give little trouble—and he personally didn't think a great deal of Kippax. Someone else remembered that Larwood once took five wickets in fourteen balls after lunch: if he only took three we should be in a strong position.

Out they came again. It was all too soon made clear that Larwood had not had as good a lunch as all that. Soon the position began to look serious; Bradman kept on running like a super-Felix; bowling at Woodfull was like bowling into a sandbank. We got a little sleepy; the barracker adjourned for another well earned drink; a gentleman who had been standing in the sun started a dignified, but incoherent, argument with a policeman, and his tactful obliteration was almost a welcome distraction.

Then Duckworth woke us up with an appeal; he was in quite good voice, considering how little practice he had had, and perhaps Umpire Oates hesitated a moment between patriotism and justice. Then, just when time seemed to have been standing still, Woodfull got himself out by playing across a straight ball. This reminded us that even Australians were human. We even hoped that Kippax would get out before he settled down; it took some of us a quarter of an hour to realise he had settled down. Then we began to despair, for Bradman looked as inevitable as a natural phenomenon.

It was Bradman, Bradman all the way. It is almost impossible to describe his innings, because it was all of a piece. Any one period of it was just like any other. There was no crescendo, and very certainly no diminuendo; it was as eternal and spontaneous and delightful as a Bach fugue.

Once we had put aside partisanship, with the philosophical reflection that he might as well make the runs as the others, we could give ourselves up to pure enjoyment. He showed us every stroke; where all were perfect it is difficult to particularise. There were some magnificent shots through the covers that the fieldsman hardly moved for, while the spectators did what was necessary. By way of contrast there were some most delectable shots to the on, craftily placed to beat an astutely stationed fielder, in spite of his efforts.

At one time, indeed, Bradman did become the least shade rash; possibly, with the intolerance of twenty-one, he felt himself entitled to scorn Dick Tyldesley's honest girth. He had his lesson, and gave his only shadow of a chance. After that he treated Tyldesley with great respect, and it is to be hoped that the critics will give that great-hearted worker credit for his heroic bowling for an hour after tea.

All this time Kippax was batting very picturesquely; he ran out to Tyldesley and he hit the ball as hard and as often as Bradman, but generally to the fieldsmen, by way of emphasising the difference between talent and genius. Bradman mowed down record after record; Kippax got out; the shadows lengthened. Chapman and his gallant men went on bowling and fielding as if their hearts were still high, and at last Bradman, with one last sweeping four, ran towards the pavilion to escape an ovation.

At the other end we squeezed out almost silently, a little awed at seeing history made under our eyes.

BRADMAN'S NIGHT

A newspaper description of the scene at the Australians' hotel after Bradman's 309 not out in a day.

TONIGHT IS BRADMAN NIGHT. Nobody and nothing else is talked about at the Queen's Hotel where there are more than 50 Australians, in addition to the team. It is like Cup night in Melbourne. Groups sit around toasting Bradman and discussing his epic innings of today, while Bradman is unobtrusively dining in the grillroom.

He will rest tonight hoping to add another hundred tomorrow, thereby passing the highest first-class score in England.

Even the English cricketers are toasting him. K. S. Duleepsinhji can be seen in the lounge with W. W. Bardsley, former champion left-hander, and a group of Australian friends. Arthur Gilligan, who captained the 1924–5 English team in Australia, P. G. Fender (Surrey captain and international), and dozens of other well known cricketers and former cricketers are also in the lounge.

'I must cable home,' said Bradman. 'They will want to hear about this. My feet are awfully tired, but I could have continued if stumps had not been drawn.'

Menace to England

By Chapman Jocose

From an article in the London Daily Mail *in 1930.*

So much has been written about Bradman that no superlatives are left. I said yesterday that he is a menace to English cricket. Today, I go further. I think that he will be the death of it. If he comes over more than once again we shan't be able to spare the time to get him out, and English cricket will quietly fade away.

Strange stratagems?

By Pelham Warner

From an article in the Morning Post *after Bradman's 334 in the Leeds Test, 1930. Warner's reference to the need for 'a new type of bowler' and 'strange tactics' to counter Bradman seems ominous in the light of the tactics which the Englishmen used in their next encounter with Bradman in 1932–33—bodyline.*

It is a disturbing thought that he is only a boy. England must evolve a new type of bowler and develop fresh ideas and strange tactics to curb his almost uncanny skill.

How to excel

A letter to the editor by a cricket club secretary, F. H. Molesworth, in the Sydney Morning Herald, *15 July 1930.*

In commenting on the wonderful stamina displayed by our cricket champion attention has also been drawn to his quickness of eye and the rapidity with which it telegraphs to his brain resulting in unparalleled alertness and certainty of action.

In order that young Australians may fit themselves to emulate his example and not be content with positions as barrackers may I quote Don Bradman's own words on how to excel, given in a letter to a friend:

> The man who is a total abstainer and non-smoker must necessarily have an advantage over the man who partakes of alcoholic liquor and smokes, in a contest where physical endurance and quickness of thought and movement play a part. Personally, I find a cup of tea to be the best thirst quencher and anyone is certainly better for not smoking.
>
> Your sincerely,
> (Signed) Don Bradman

Can anything be straighter from the bat of this record-breaking youth?

A CONSTELLATION

From Punch, *August 1930.*

You never saw immortal GRACE
　　Emerge from the pavilion door
On Wisden's page prepared to place
　　Another monumental score,
Although you've heard about him now and then,
My cricket-loving little lad of ten.

You knew not in his matchless prime
　　RANJI, of batsmen still the prince,
Who flourished in our alien clime,
　　Bless me! a generation since;
The thrill that stirred us as he took his stance
And gave us of his best with cut and glance.

TRUMPER to you is but a name,
　　The hero of an unknown day,
Who rather leapt than climbed to fame;
　　You never watched MACARTNEY play.
Him of the twinkling feet and jocund heart
Who left us at the summit of his art.

Yet murmur not with looks forlorn
　　That these have vanished from our view;
Rejoice that you in time were born
　　To see a constellation too;
That in his full career, to be precise,
You've seen DON BRADMAN shine, let that suffice.

PARTY TRICK

By Bill Bowes

From The Great Ones, *1967.*

W HEN DON WAS IN his early twenties I saw him give a demonstration of bouncing a golf ball with a cricket stump and he did it twenty times easily. 'When my luck's in I get towards a century,' he said. I found that other cricketers when their luck was in struggled to double figures.

BRADMAN FIRST, THE REST NOWHERE

By Geoffrey Tebbutt

From With The 1930 Australians, *1930. Tebbutt's book alleged there was estrangement between Bradman and other Australian players, caused controversy in Australia and did much to foster the notion that Bradman was a player apart. Tebbutt was an English journalist.*

F EW CRICKETERS HAVE EVER captured the public imagination like Bradman. His record-breaking feats, his astounding consistency, were alone, of course, enough to keep the mass sporting mind concentrated upon him in a season in which the rubber created such tremendous interest; but it was his youth, his romantic and meteoric rise to first-class rank, his utter imperturbability when confronting bowlers of world-wide renown, which caused him to become the most-talked-of man in England between May and August this year.

This fair-haired, smiling, cool-headed youth, who scored 236 on his first appearance in England, and whom rain deprived of another double century on his second, was quickly seen to be all that Australia had claimed for him, but few people anticipated that those deeds were but the heralds of greater triumphs to come in more trying arenas. Not even his thousand runs before the end of May—completed at Southampton in dramatic circumstances on the last day of the month, with the rain that was to descend later in bucketfuls already falling as the thousandth run was scored off an easy ball generously thrown up— quite prepared England for the shocks he was to administer, nor Australia for the games he was to save or turn into victory, in the Tests.

Nobody knew what Bradman was going to do next. The funereal progress to the wicket that became known as 'the Bradman crawl' was generally in striking contrast to the speed and aggression with which he scored, and to those amazing sprints around the boundary which have saved Australia so many runs. Nobody quite knew why he did it. To accustom his eyes to the light for as long a period as he could decently take before reaching the pitch was one explanation, but probably Bradman has not thought of it as such. If I read him aright, it is just his natural way of doing things; perhaps he has always walked to the wickets that way, for no particular reason, and the habit has become confirmed.

I suggest that possibility because of another interesting little sidelight upon him that shows his absorption in the game. Some English players had wondered why, when their batsmen reached 50 or 100, Bradman, alone of the Australians, sometimes failed to applaud. Personally, I had not noticed this alleged failing to much extent, but I asked him if there were any explanation. 'Perhaps I have occasionally forgotten to give them a clap,' he replied. 'I had not realised that I had been lax in that way, and I have certainly never intentionally refrained from joining in the usual applause.' Later, watching particularly, I noticed him quite emphatically applauding batsmen as they passed these milestones.

As this book is one for truth-telling, and as in going behind the scenes one learns more about the actors than those who, from the auditorium, applaud only what they see upon the stage, I must add that Bradman's immense popularity with the public was not echoed by his team-mates. And let me say at once that it was not a case of swollen head. Surely no sportsman has ever received public adulation to the extent that it was inflicted upon this boy from the country who, with probably twenty years of first-class cricket still left to him, became renowned everywhere the game is played. Bradman took all that with the utmost unconcern. I found him exactly the same at the end of one of the most triumphal tours anyone has ever experienced as he was at the beginning, when his greatness had yet to stand the test of strange conditions.

It would be an insult to a sharp intelligence to suggest that he did not know how good he was, or how indispensable his services were, but he kept his modesty, and he did not change his ways. And I do not want to lay undue emphasis on the occasional coldness of the relations between Bradman and the rest of the team. Any feeling that the others might have had—and I know that there was often justification for it— that they were being left out in the cold by the concentration of interest upon Bradman, was due principally to the public's demand for their idol. Except among those who realised the importance of the less spectacular parts played by the others, it was a case, in the popular mind, of Bradman first and the rest nowhere.

Of course, the generous gentleman who sent Bradman a cheque for £1,000 to commemorate his Test record of 334 at Leeds—it worked out at a little more than £3 a run—was unconsciously widening the breach between the hero and his comrades. It was a princely gift, but had Bradman's benefactor known the situation prevalent in the Australian camp, I think he would have taken different steps to recognise the merit of this amazing youngster. Let me make it plain that, among the other members of the team, there was no decrying of his cricket ability, no suggestion that he did not deserve all the success that he obtained. And I am afraid that there are few of us who would not accept £1,000 for a feat like Bradman accomplished! Hitherto unknown admirers who do things on that scale I am sure we would all like to have. Bradman deserved something out of the ordinary. He got it. Good luck to him!

The attitude of the other Australians was necessarily a little different. They were, after all, in the team; they were as necessary to Bradman as he was to them, and at least two of them performed feats of equal importance, though of slightly less magnitude. Still, they did not begrudge Bradman this handsome recognition. Their grievance was that Bradman had been rather less than human in the way he took success. Having made a score as gigantic as that at Leeds, and in the course of it having shattered so many records, surely the natural thing for the happy warrior to do would have been to bask in the sunshine of his team-mates' admiration, to have shown some human joy in achievement. And when to sporting success is added the manna of a small fortune, the inclination towards even the mildest of 'celebrations' ought to be irresistible. But not with Bradman. I believe he spent that night of triumph alone in his room, playing the phonograph! As one of the Australians said to me later: 'He is not one of us.' That did not worry Bradman. There was no open breach, he was content to lead a life aloof, and Mr. Kelly lacked the firmness to take the situation in hand before it got beyond him.

Another member of the team, who has a dry wit, also gave me a neat illustration of Bradman's position in the public eye compared with that of his comrades. It was at St Pancras station on the morning of the departure for Australia of six of the players. Some had gone the previous week, and I commented to the wit in question on the presence of twenty photographers and a great crowd, whereas only a handful of intimate friends, and only one camera-man, had taken notice of the others' farewell. Jerking a thumb in Bradman's direction, he said slyly: 'The team didn't leave until today.'

There was no malice in that remark, and, as I have indicated, the Australians philosophically accepted the situation created by the tremendous public demand for Bradman. Nor do I wish to end a study of the youth who must already be recognised as one of the greatest cricketers of all time on a note of disharmony or deprecation. I mention it out of a regard for historical truth, for I should dislike to discourage individualism. More than I have said about Bradman's supreme skill I cannot say. His has been the kind of success beyond the dreams of optimism. He has earned his laurels, and it is no disparagement that one could sometimes hope he will become, on and off the field, a little more human.

DAD AND THE DON

by Neil Marks

From Tales from the Locker Room, *1993.*

'I DON'T KNOW ABOUT you Acka, but I'm having trouble picking him up,' said Don Bradman to my father at the Gabba one summer day.

They were batting for N.S.W. against Queensland and both were having difficulty coping with the sheer pace of Queensland's Aboriginal fast bowler, Eddie Gilbert. After a couple of overs of ducking, snicking and missing, the two had come together for a mid-wicket conference.

'I'm having the same trouble, Braddles,' my father replied. 'But I'm going to take to him! Eddie doesn't like it when the batsman gets on top.' Alec Marks walked back to his crease with aggression on his mind and a prayer in his heart.

The first ball of the next over from Gilbert was well up. Marks placed his foot down the pitch and thrashed the ball between mid-off and cover for four. The next ball was a blistering bumper which my father hooked from in front of his face, over square leg for four. The third ball was a replica of the second but this time it clipped the top edge of the bat and crashed into his head, just above the left eyebrow.

The ball dropped at the batsman's feet and he nonchalantly pushed it back to the bowler. 'Well bowled Eddie', he smilingly commented. Marks did not compliment the bowler to show the world that he was a good sport; he was only obeying the time honoured maxim: 'When they hit you, never show 'em you're hurt!'

The contest continued until the end of the over and if judges had been awarding points, they would probably have declared it a draw.

Drinks came onto the field and my relieved father, with blood on his shirt, walked up to his friend, thankful for at least a couple of minutes' reprieve.

'How are you feeling, Acka?' asked Bradman.

'A bit shaky but I'm okay.'

'You know you were very lucky,' said Bradman.

'I'll say I was,' replied Dad. 'An inch lower and the ball would have hit me in the eye.'

'No, I mean you were lucky it hit you in the head, otherwise you'd have been caught behind.'

This is just one example of why 'the Don' was a better batsman than Dad—and every other batsman who ever lived, for that matter.

No Sorrows to Drown

By Bernard Hollowood

From The Punch Book of Cricket, *1985.*

BRADMAN HIT TOO MANY runs to be universally popular. He made so many runs that he was always at the wicket, often when his colleagues were in the bar. So Bradman was criticised as unsociable. After a day's play cricketers love to drown their sorrows in beer or gin, but Bradman had no sorrows to drown. Cricketers also like to remind themselves, and anyone who will listen, about their better days and better innings, but Bradman had no need for such reminiscence. Bradman was like W. G. Grace—but without the fallibility.

ENGLAND'S BRADMAN PROBLEM

By Laurence Le Quesne

From The Bodyline Controversy, *1983.*

WHEN AUSTRALIA CAME TO England in 1930, the English public contemplated the prospects with blithe confidence. Chapman's 1928 side, often regarded as one of the best sides England has ever sent to Australia, was still largely intact. Chapman himself was still available to lead it and—it was hoped—inspire it by his dazzling fielding and mercurial batting. The batting available included Sutcliffe, Hendren, Woolley, the brilliant young Indian K. S. Duleepsinhji and the prodigy Hammond. There was still Duckworth to keep wicket, and if the bowling looked thinner, it nevertheless included Maurice Tate, still close to his peak, Larwood, on the summit of his youth and ferocious pace, and two highly promising young amateur leg-spinners in R.W.V. Robins and Ian Peebles. But the outcome was shattering disappointment. Bradman dominated the series as probably no other batsman has ever dominated a Test series. At Lord's, in the second Test, he scored 254, and it became unmistakably clear that a force had made itself felt in the game that promised to tilt the whole balance of Test cricket decisively in Australia's favour for twenty years to come. This was already the highest individual score in Test cricket in England: a fortnight later he bettered it in the third Test by scoring 334, and in the decisive last Test, which Australia won to take the series 2–1, he contributed 232. Single centuries no longer seemed significant: double and triple centuries were the milestones of the new kind of cricket that Bradman introduced to the world. Well as they played, Sutcliffe and Hammond paled almost to insignificance in comparison with him, while for the English bowlers, and for Larwood above all, it was a summer of martyrdom. Slow bowlers expect to be attacked—much of their skill lies in their ability to tempt aggression into folly. But for a fast bowler of great pace to be taken by the scruff of the neck and hit all over the field—as Larwood was by Bradman that summer—is the most violent rebuff possible: an experience that might shatter a man's morale, if it could not be avenged.

SEARCH FOR A WEAKNESS

By E. H. D. Sewell

From Cricket Up-To-Date, *1931. Although after Bradman's 1930 triumphs many Englishmen pondered the question of how to contain him, Sewell was one of the few who were prepared to state publicly they knew—or thought they knew—the answer. But it does not seem any bowler was able to make his theory work in practice.*

FOR A PLAYER OF his youth, his eye, his wrists, and last but really first his head, there was really little in the bowling of England's Test elevens as chosen last season to stop Bradman reaching that 1,000 runs aggregate. Except for the one possibility, viz. that somehow or other the English captain, or one of his bowlers, should happen to discover the one flaw in Bradman's armour, I came to the conclusion, after watching every stroke in his 252 not out at the Oval, that there was nothing whatsoever in our probable Test bowling to stop a huge success by Bradman.

That there is a flaw I am satisfied so far as cricket on English wickets is concerned; just as satisfied as I am that once he discovers that he is 'found out' Bradman has the horse-sense to cut out the stroke which constitutes that flaw. This stroke is nothing more nor less than a flash at the good-length ball just outside the off-stump.

Not once in the five Tests, except here and there White at Lord's, did our fellows 'bowl for that.' If they did they hid their intention with a cleverness which deserved a better fate!

Once I thought the flaw had been spotted. That was just before Bradman was caught by Duleepsinhji off Peebles in the fourth Test at Manchester. Bradman gave a chance off the first or second ball of that over, and between them Duckworth and Hammond put it on the turf. Off the next ball but one the twin-brother of that ball was bowled—a good-length spinner outside the off-stump—and the catch was made.

In spite of that evidence the same form of attack was not served up at the Oval, with the natural result. Only, on this occasion, one of Duckworth's many dropped 'takes,' when Bradman was in the eighties, helped on that natural result.

I am not writing after the event. I wrote and published my views on this weakness in Bradman's batting before the first Test match of 1930. Later, I dropped a hint in a quarter where, had the hint been taken, the attempt would have been made in the remaining three Tests, but the hint was not taken, and after I made it Bradman scored about 450 more runs in three Test innings.

All that was required was the positioning of the off-side as follows: Two slips; a gully; deep third man as usual; cover not too square; and an extra cover on the boundary between cover and the usual third man. The remaining three fielders could stand almost where they liked while this attack was in progress, but, for choice, at long-off, long-on, and mid-on.

I do not doubt that, once bitten, this unusually wide-awake thinker might not have 'nibbled' again, but the old Adam in a man is very strong, and many a more experienced player than Bradman, with just as good a head as he possesses, has lost his wicket over and over again through the cleverness of bowlers attacking his known weakness. There is no reason why Bradman should be any different from the rest of the human race. Though at times his scoring rather gave the impression that he is!

Throughout this last rubber I never saw him in difficulties except when they pitched a decent length outside the off-stump.

He knows his limitations in that quarter right enough, even though he may not admit it.

I watched him very closely in the course of that 252 at the Oval and noted that every time Fender appeared to flight the ball on and outside the off-stump Bradman would have none of it. He refused even the start of a scoring stroke, merely putting the shutter down, declining to be 'had.' I had great hopes then that Fender had found him out and would convey the fact of his discovery to the right quarter. But if he did, nothing happened.

Depend upon it that the flaw in Bradman was, in 1930, where I have said it was.

There was no flaw in his straightforward defence, or in faulty cutting, or in lifting the ball. Bradman's bat was a bat, or a mashie. In the second Test he had made over 200 runs and in the third Test 153 before he raised a ball!

Small wonder then, when I happened to meet F. T. Mann during Gentlemen vs Players at Lord's and, thinking he was looking a bit worried, I asked him the cause, that he should reply: 'I am trying to think of a bowler who is likely to make this Bradman lift the ball off the turf.' Aye! selectors have their worries, and these are not lessened by the butting-in of unsought advisers. So I remained silent on the point.

Bradman's strong points, ignoring his eye and obviously natural aptitude for, I guess, any ball game, are his timing, his refusal to be bound by any such silly fetish as not hitting a half-volley because it happens to be early in his innings, and his ability to play forward powerfully.

In this latter respect he was a model to all English youngsters who were lucky enough to see him, and was at the same time a very visible warning to our numerous coaches who lay far too much stress upon back-play, and who are thereby so largely responsible for much of the ugliness now rampant throughout English batting.

I do not admire Bradman's back-play. It is quite unworthy of such a player. I guess, since I have no other way of getting at the truth, that, roughly speaking, Bradman never plays right back on Australian wickets. He is an expert, if ugly, half-cock player. But he comes very prominently to the front in my class of Forward-Offensive player, the class that lasts, and lives in the memory long after the other kind has been consigned to the limbo. I guess that last season he played back in the rather ungainly, crouching, all-pads-and-bat-in-a-bunch style in which he so definitely stopped an occasional good one, because somebody had dinned into him the slogan that you 'can't succeed on English wickets unless you play back a lot.' Shades of Victor Trumper, the Forward-Offensive Attacker, and the wet season of 1902! How easily the great deeds in cricket such as his performances of that year are forgotten, and with what facile destructive glibness such shibboleths as the 'Play Back on English wickets' slogan are remembered!

In conclusion, as regards this very interesting young player, ought we not all to be thoroughly impressed by the outstanding fact that a batsman who proved himself capable of scoring nearly 1,000 runs in seven Test match innings on English wickets at the age of 22 is an absolutely uncoached player, in the sense in which coaching is under-stood?

HIS NAMESAKE

By Bradman Weerakoon

From a letter to Richard Cashman in 1985, explaining how he came to be called Bradman. Mr Weerakoon had been a senior Sri Lankan Government official, serving as permanent secretary to three Prime Ministers.

I WAS BORN ON 20 October 1930, and this according to what my parents told me was the date of Don Bradman's stopover in Colombo when the ship he was travelling on docked in on the return of the Australian cricketers from England after their tour in 1930. This was I believe Bradman's best year of cricket and the year in which he scored his record 334 runs. There must have been quite a deal of excitement in Ceylon (now Sri Lanka) at the news of the arrival of the Australian cricketers. What in fact seems to have happened is that my father, who was then in charge of the Colombo Port Police, went on board the ship in which Bradman had arrived, met him and obtained his autograph. My father had then gone on to a nursing home in Colombo (Ratnam's Nursing Home) where my mother had been expecting a baby. To my father's delight he had found a baby boy had been born during the time that he had been away getting Bradman's autograph. His decision to call his son Bradman was instantaneous.

One of the things that invariably happens when people see my name on paper is to link it with cricket and to imagine that it is a kind of nickname given for apparent prowess in the game. It becomes a useful opening gambit in conversation. It has certainly helped at interviews when someone on the panel begins to ask about the origin of the name. I am sure it has helped me in starting off with an amusing anecdote and getting into a relaxed mood. It has also meant that since the name was a 'given' one, and not a nickname, I had to start playing cricket from my childhood. I didn't want people calling me Bradman and using it in a manner that indicated that they considered me the opposite of Bradman; so I feel that it did give me the motivation to try to play cricket well.

A HERO'S RETURN

A newspaper story, November 1930.

THE ARRIVAL TODAY OF Don Bradman, a day ahead of the rest of the Australian Eleven, drew a crowd of 10,000 to Essendon Aerodrome. Bradman was expected to arrive from Adelaide by plane at 3.30 this afternoon, but it was not until 5.30 that the plane reached Essendon. The crowd by this time had considerably diminished, but the welcome by hundreds of people who rushed the plane almost before it had stopped was none the less hearty. It was noticeable that not one cricketer of note or a cricket official could be seen in the crowd. It was the reception of a popular sporting hero by a crowd of sightseers, in which curiosity and hero-worship were the principal features.

When Bradman landed he was immediately lost in the crowd, and only the forcible attentions of a strong body of police enabled him to reach a lorry draped with the Australian flag that was to serve as a platform.

The captain of the 1921 Australian Eleven, Mr W. W. Armstrong, welcomed Bradman. He said that it was a welcome to the first of the team which had won the ashes. The credit of victory belonged to all the members of the team, but Bradman was the first to reach Melbourne, and was thus first to be welcomed.

Bradman, who was smiling as usual, said he was overwhelmed at the reception, and that, although there had been many welcomes, this was the best of them all. He apologised for having been late, and said that the plane was late leaving Adelaide, and was then delayed by head winds.

A LINDRUM OF CRICKET?

By Walter Lindrum

I FIND MAKING A break of a thousand in billiards comparatively easy. One of these days when Bradman is in the mood he will find it just as easy to score a thousand runs in one innings.

TRIUMPHAL MARCH REVIEWED

By Pelham Warner

This well-known essay first appeared as an introduction to Don Bradman's Book, *written by Bradman after the 1930 tour.*

As FOR MR BRADMAN'S own performances in England, they were unique in the annals of cricket. In all matches he scored 3,170 runs, with an average of 99.06. He made eleven three-figure innings— six of these over 200—and in the Test Matches his scores were 8, 131, 254, 334 (a world's record), 14, and 232—974 runs, with an average of 139.14! These great innings followed on two seasons' unbroken success in Australia, and it is no exaggeration to say that not even W. G.—at Mr Bradman's age—had attained so world-wide a reputation.

What were the secrets of his triumphal march through England? First—immense natural skill. Secondly—an idealism which urged him to learn everything he possibly could, and to profit by the lessons learnt. Thirdly—tremendous concentration of mind; and fourthly, like C. B. Fry before him, great physical strength. Fifthly—extreme fitness; and, lastly, a cool, calm temperament. As to the actual technique of his play, he was blessed with a wonderful eye, steel-like wrists, and small and beautifully neat feet, which a Genée or a Pavlova might have envied, and which made him quite exceptionally quick in moving back or forward to the ball, every stroke fully developed, except, possibly, the straight drive, and, above all, an amazingly strong defence—which, as he says in his chapter on batting, is the keynote of all successful bats-manship in first-class cricket. His hooking of anything the least short was masterful to a degree; he missed nothing on his pads; and he off-drove brilliantly; but, above all, the cut, both late and square, was his chief glory. I have seldom seen finer or *safer* cutting—for he was always right on top of the ball.

Again, he watched the ball very closely, and played all his strokes with his nose exactly over the ball—the 'smell her, sir, smell her', of the renowned Yorkshireman, Tom Emmett—and his extreme quickness of foot enabled him almost to dictate the length to the bowler—at least, so it appeared in the Test Matches at Lord's and at Headingley. Another noticeable feature of his batting was his placing of the ball, and the absolute certainty with which he hit a full pitch for four. He seldom played forward, though he was often yards down the pitch to a slow bowler, and he scarcely ever lifted a ball off the ground. His drives clung to the turf, and how clean and powerful they were, and I cannot agree that his eschewing the high drive was a weakness in his play, though so highly do I rate Mr Bradman's cricket that I am sure he could play any stroke on which he cared to concentrate.

So much for his batting—but he was also a long field of the very highest class, quick to start, a fast runner, and the possessor of a return as swift as an arrow from a bow, and full pitch into the wicket-keeper's hands. Australia have had many fine deep fields, but never a finer— judging him on his form here—and those who were at the Test Match at Headingley will never forget the manner in which he threw down Hobbs's wicket, at Oldfield's end, from deep mid-off. Never have I seen anyone move forward faster to a ball, pick it up more quickly, or throw it in harder.

What is his future? Is he destined to break his own records? Will he one day play an innings of 600 or 700, and put the aggregates of Grace and Hobbs, and their number of centuries, in the shade? Remember, he is only twenty-two, and given good health, he should have, at least, twenty more years of cricket before him. He seems certain to 'plague' and, at the same time, delight England's bowlers for many future seasons—indeed, boys yet unborn are destined to suffer at his hands. Personally, I believe him to be possessed not only of the skill, but of the ambition, the physique, and the temperament, to accomplish these feats. A batsman, as a general rule, does not attain to his best until he is thirty-four or thirty-five, and by the time Mr Bradman reaches that age he will have had immense experience to build on to his natural skill. Have I praised him too highly? I don't think so, if one remembers his youth, and the fact that it was his first visit to England, and our varying wickets.

Do people realize his astonishing figures? Take the Test Matches. In these Australians scored 2,743 runs from the bat, of which Bradman contributed no less than 974. Again, he invariably made a huge proportion of the runs scored while he was in—namely, 131 out of 255 at Trent Bridge; 254 out of 423 at Lord's; 334 out of 506 at Headingley; and 232 out of 411 at the Oval. One may also add that *v.* Worcestershire, at Worcester, he scored 236 out of 413; *v.* Surrey, at the Oval, 252 out of 363; and *v.* Kent, at Canterbury, 205 out of 302.

Mr Bradman looked every inch a cricketer. He was scrupulously neat and smart in his turn-out, and he played the game with rare zest and enjoyment. Short in height, though long in the leg, and with very broad shoulders, he is, from a cricket point of view, finely and compactly built, and one was particularly struck by the fit of his cricket boots on his small feet; and I think that he should present his boots to the Australian nation, to be placed in the pavilion at Sydney, there to be kept in a glass-case for future generations to gaze on, and to inspire them to something like his own nimbleness of foot!

Above all, Mr Bradman possesses both character and brains, and I feel sure that so well-balanced a personality will remember to 'keep a straight bat and a modest wind'. Certainly he showed no signs in England that that fair and well-shaped head of his was in danger of requiring a larger-sized cricket cap. On the contrary, he took his long succession of triumphs with a becoming modesty which is reflected in this interesting book of his.

CRICKET AND CORKSCREW

A London newspaper report.

OF ALL SUBJECTS THAT lend themselves to fatuous controversy experience must award the palm to total abstinence. The debate in the House of Commons on the Licensing (Permitted Hours) Bill produced a passage between Mr Isaac Foot and Mr Raikes which should rank as a classic of its kind. Some reference having been made to an application, once upon a time, for an extension of licence on the Sheffield cricket ground during the visit of an Australian team, Mr Foot interposed that D. G. Bradman is a total abstainer. Mr Raikes countered this deadly thrust with a battering-ram: 'Dr Grace was never known to refuse a little alcoholic refreshment.' Mr Foot picked himself up and flung at Mr Raikes the name of J. B. Hobbs. But Mr Raikes also had a secondary armament. 'It may be,' he said, 'that a number of players who have failed when faced with leg-theory would have found that the drinking of ale would have helped them.'

And so the foemen parted, with inanities easy. Neither can be said to have done his side good service. For what do their arguments prove? One knows and respects the opinions of Messrs Hobbs and Bradman that teetotalism has been the making, or the saving, of their cricket; but they can properly speak for themselves alone. Others have excelled at the popping crease without forswearing the popping cork. It cannot be proved that a Hobbs or a Bradman would have been skittled out by a glass of beer, or that a Grace who declined to be treated would have been twice as redoubtable. As well contend that Grace would have been a greater man without his beard as without his beer. Mr Raikes suggests that if Bradman had lifted his elbow occasionally it would have given more power to his elbow against Larwood. Who knows? Test Matches, happily, were not instituted to test the merits or defects of total abstinence. By a curious oversight no Nazarite has yet contended that excellence in cricket depends upon at least a partial adherence to the Nazarite creed. Grace was true to one part of it, Hobbs and Bradman to another. But perhaps it is possible to be a great player and yet remain in practice with both razor and corkscrew.

AN OLD WOMAN'S ADVICE

A letter sent to Bradman by an unnamed Victorian woman in 1931, apparently to urge him to accept an offer to play Lancashire League cricket in England.

Dear little boy,

Take the advice of an old woman. Hit while the iron is hot. Australia soon forgets, England never. You were not too well treated on your return with the greatest record in cricket. Go and marry an heiress. With your face and record you can. Good luck.

A BOY'S ASPIRATION

By T. W. Nathan of Kings Cross Road, Darlinghurst, Sydney—quoted in the press, 1931.

I WOULD LIKE TO be our idol, our star of hope Don Bradman! I would hit up wonderful scores for our team, and imagine, even while away on English ground, I could hear the encouraging cheers of Australia. And I would smile when sweet young things hunted after me, requesting an autograph!

BRADMAN'S FABULOUS CENTURY

By John Boyd

An excerpt from a privately published account of Bradman's century in three consecutive eight-ball overs at Blackheath in November 1931. Bradman and New South Wales team-mate O. Wendell Bill played as guests for Blackheath against Lithgow. Of the 102 runs scored between them in the three overs, Bradman made 100 and Wendell Bill 2. Boyd played for Blackheath.

AT THE TIME OF the match, Blackheath was a municipality and the cricket club officials and the council probably cooperated to have a new pitch laid down, composed of bitumen and malthoid, which was a new idea and was called M. A. Noble wicket, after the great cricketer of that name. The ground at that time was longer than necessary, so ropes were lined in a semi-circle at the bottom or northern end to mark the boundary and it was well grassed except for a small corner on the southern end. The western end had huge pine trees along the fence and on the other side a lane with trees and, beyond that, the park which is still there.

The work on the pitch was apparently executed early in the season, 1931, and a decision was made by the club to invite Don Bradman, who lived in Sydney then, to take part in a match to celebrate the opening of the new wicket. There was some doubt in my mind as to whether the match was on a Saturday or a Sunday, but I have found out that it must have been a Saturday, from the fact that George McCall, according to Mrs McCall, had to ask his employer, a grocer, for the afternoon off, as the shops were open all day on Saturday in those days. Another proof comes from Doug Christie, who was driving a meat cart and stopped for a while to watch the match.

Anyway, on the morning of the match, most of the players were assembled at the ground to put in boundary ropes, sweep the pitch etc, and of course discuss the coming game. I think Bradman was travelling by train, but whether he did or not, an argument developed among the players as to who was to meet him.

Wally Snelling was captain of our team and apparently had not been officially asked to be in the welcoming party. The result of this was that he dropped out of the team altogether. The remaining players had a hurried meeting on the field and decided to ask Bradman to captain the team. It was a beautiful day, clear and crisp, with warm sunshine.

There was a fair gathering of people, mostly locals at the ground when Mr Sutton assisted Bradman to cut a ribbon to open the wicket. The Don had agreed to captain the team. To open the game, Mr Sutton bowled a ball to Bradman and he hit it over Mr Sutton's head into the tennis courts for what would be a six in a match. Straight off, without even a sighter. Mr Sutton had cut the ribbon and the scene was set. I said to my young brother, Dick on the day before, something like this: 'You ought to come down tomorrow, and watch the game. You mightn't ever see anything like it again all your life.' How right I was. Dick didn't come down, but, in my opinion, nobody in the world had ever seen such an exhibition of controlled hitting and probably never will in the future.

When Bradman faced the first ball, there was no fieldsman at square leg and he played it through the gap and scored a single. The next ball he received, he did the same thing, so Dick Thorn, the Lithgow captain, placed a man there. The Don picked another gap, but after a while he was hitting the ball so hard that he created his own gaps and was also hitting some sixes. Wendell Bill was also scoring but not nearly as fast.

It was toward the finish of Bradman's innings that he scored the hundred runs in 18 minutes, which some people consider a world record. It probably is, but can never be proved, as it is not known now who timed it and other responsible persons would have had to have signed as witnesses, I presume. It would have been something less even, if time was deducted for the ball being retrieved from across the road, front yards and the pine trees, although there were plenty of small boys scrambling for the honour of returning it.

The fact of Don scoring 100 in three overs is undoubtedly true because Bill Black copied it out of the Lithgow Pottery Club scorebook; but he may have done that years ago and kept the copy for his own records. But likely as not the scorebook no longer exists.

'I THINK I'LL HAVE A GO'

An unpublished account written in 1986 of Bradman's innings at Black-heath by the batsman at the other end, O. Wendell Bill. Of the 22 balls he faced in the three overs, Bradman scored 10 sixes, nine fours, one two and two singles.

LITHGOW KNOCKED UP A very good score of about 240. We went into bat. Don Bradman said, 'We'll let the locals go in first, open up, and we'll go in four and five'. It was one wicket down for none, two for about 10. He went in to bat, someone else got out and we were 3 for 15. Then I went in and joined Don. An hour and a quarter later he was 150 and I was 77. The score was up to their score. Don came down the wicket and said, 'Wendell, we've passed their score—I think I'll have a go.' Remember, he'd already scored 150 in about 70 minutes. He had a go, all right. His shots were in front of the wicket mainly, from cover right round to square leg. There were people outside the boundary there, boys, throwing the ball back all the time from beyond the trees. The fieldsmen just stood in awe at the hitting. I don't think anyone was aware at the time that a hundred runs were being scored in three overs. It just happened that way. The hitting just went on and on. While Don scored the one hundred in the three overs I scored two singles. They were meant to give him the strike. One was a push to the off-side, I think, and the other a push to the on-side. So in three overs Don went from 150 to 250 and I went from 77 to 79. The funny thing is that of all the runs I scored in my career, all the centuries, those two singles are the ones people remember best today.

A SCORE SETTLED

An extract from an article in the Sydney Sun *in 1969 by Tom Downes, quoting one of Lithgow's players at Blackheath, Bill Black. Several weeks before this match Black had bowled Bradman in an exhibition match at Lithgow. This extract varies from Wendell Bill's account in small details only.*

W E BATTED FIRST, HITTING up 228 runs and we thought we were in a very strong position. Two local players opened the innings for them and one of them was out quickly and Bradman came in. Soon the other opener was out and Wendell Bill came in and he and Bradman really got going.

When Bradman was about 50, George Thorn, who was captain, threw the ball to me and said, 'Here you are. Try your luck again.'

I stood at the bowler's end and while I placed my field Bradman was talking to the wicketkeeper, Leo Waters. Later Leo told me this conversation took place.

Bradman: What sort of bowler is this fellow?

Waters: Don't you remember this bloke? He bowled you in the exhibition match at Lithgow a few weeks ago and has been boasting about it ever since at your expense.

Well, my first over to Bradman provided him with 33 runs. The next bowler was the late Horrie Baker—later Lithgow Town Clerk—and he had no less than 40 runs hit off his over. There were 29 runs hit off my second over, 27 of them by Bradman, to give him an almost unbelievable century in just three overs. I pleaded with George Thorn to take me off and he did.

A MASTER TRADESMAN

By Eric Barbour

An article in the Sydney Mail, *December 1931. Barbour, a former New South Wales player, was at this time one of the best informed observers of the game in Australia.*

DON BRADMAN HAS COLLECTED another record—the highest score made by an Australian in a Test against South Africa. Bradman is an amazing cricketer. The immensity of his performances can only properly be appreciated by those who have had personal experience of the conditions under which they have been recorded. Only recently a rash critic in the Old Country has made the assertion that Bradman cannot be classed with the greatest players of the past.

Again, we are told that he has no strokes. This persistent 'whistling in the dark' is presumably intended to raise the morale of the next English side to visit Australia, but it is no wonder that the standard of *Punch* is kept up while English journalism is provided with critics of this nature.

If a batsman who in three Test innings has compiled 820 runs, and in less than two seasons of Test cricket has broken practically every record that there is to break; and has withal played for his side first and last, and produced his best when most needed—if such a batsman is not great, will someone tell us what constitutes greatness? And if a batsman who sends the ball whizzing to the pickets at every point of the compass, from fine slip to fine leg, has no strokes, will someone let us know what is a stroke and how it is made? Perhaps what the critic intended to convey was that Bradman has not the artistry in stroke production of some of the masters of the past. With this claim I think most of us would be in accord. Don Bradman is not an artist, as were Victor Trumper, Ranjitsinhji and Macartney, or even as are Archie Jackson and Alan Kippax, of the present generation; Bradman is a tradesman, and a master tradesman. Hobbs started his first-class career as an artist, and finished as a tradesman; but Hobbs at the zenith of his powers never approached the performances that Don has already established; and who knows what is to come? He is still in the very early twenties, and should have another twenty years of first-class cricket.

No; the trouble with our friend the critic is that he does not realise what constitutes greatness in a batsman. It is not grace of style, nor is it perfection of eyesight, nor any other physical attribute. It is the mentality of the player that distinguishes the great from the merely artistic. Bradman has a cricket mentality that is at his age nothing short of colossal. In a few years' experience of first-class cricket he would seem to have acquired the knowledge, experience, and judgment of a veteran. I have never known a keener or shrewder student of the game. Every batsman and every bowler he has seen has been read, marked, and inwardly digested. Even now, with his amazing record of achievement, he regards himself as still in the stage of development, and honestly believes that in a few years' time he will be a better player than he is today.

I have watched his development from the stage of initial crudity when he first came down from Bowral to the present time, when he has tumbled all existing standards and records into the scrapheap. Step by step he has eliminated weaknesses, and added the most effective shots of great players he has met to a repertoire of his own, of which some are unorthodox, but yet so well under control and made with such confidence and certainty that one would tremble to class them as incorrect. When required, he has extraordinary patience; he certainly has remarkable stamina, but in addition possesses an unusual knowledge of his physical powers.

In many of his long innings I have noted periods in which he seems to deliberately quieten down, and even avoid the strike, to allow his muscles the opportunity of recovering from the fatigue which by the laws of physiology is inevitably associated with effort. Here, probably, is the secret of the extraordinary number of scores of 200 and upwards which he has recorded in first-class cricket. The average batsman gets out from exhaustion or carelessness soon after reaching a century, but Don regards a century as merely a stepping stone to a fair score. But perhaps the most outstanding feature of his amazing psychology is his relentlessness. He may relax physically, but never mentally, and he certainly has no mercy.

BALL SENSE

By Bill Bowes

From an article in Cricket: The Great Ones.

WHEN DON WAS IN his early twenties I saw him give a demonstration of bouncing a golf ball with a cricket stump and he did it twenty times easily. 'When my luck's in I get towards a century,' he said. I found that other cricketers when their luck was in struggled to double figures.

A SOMEBODY

By A. B. 'Banjo' Paterson

From a radio talk reproduced in Song Of The Pen: Collected Works 1901–41.

A COUPLE OF YEARS ago I was in a sports depot in Sydney and a wiry sunburnt young bush chap came in, and started looking over the goods. I've had so much to do with athletes I can generally pick a man fairly well, and I said to the salesman, 'That's a hard-looking young fellow and he's very light on his feet. I should say he had done some boxing or was accustomed to riding rough horses. They have to be pretty active for that game.'

So the salesman laughed and said, 'No, you're a bit out. But he's a somebody all the same.' I said, 'Who is he?'

'Oh,' he said, 'that's Don Bradman, this new boy wonder cricketer they have just discovered.'

You see he was only Don Bradman, the Bowral boy then, and hadn't been to England. He's Mr Bradman now, and many congratulations to him.

So the salesman brought the boy over—he seemed only a boy to me—and after we had exchanged a few remarks, Bradman went out. So then I asked the inevitable question: I said, 'How good is this fellow? Is he going to be as good as Trumper?'

Now, the salesman had been a first-class cricketer himself and he gave me what I consider a very clear summing up of the two men.

'Well,' he said, 'when Trumper got onto good wickets he developed a beautiful free style, like a golfer that plays a full swing with a good follow-through. He trusted the ball to come true off the wicket, and if it bumped, or shot, or kicked, he might be apt to get out. But this Bradman takes nothing on trust. Even after he has got onto good wickets, he won't trust the ball a foot, and he watches every ball till the last moment before he hits it. His eye is so good and his movements are so quick that he can hit a ball to the fence without any swing at all. That makes him look a bit rough in style compared with Trumper, and he hits across his wicket a lot. They say that's a fatal thing to do, but I never saw him miss one of them.'

So I said, 'You wouldn't remember W. G. Grace, can you remember Ranjitsinhji?'

'Yes,' he said, 'Ranji had a beautiful style, but he was a bit fond of playing to the gallery. If he'd liked to stonewall, they'd never have got him out, but he used to do exhibition shots—late cuts, and tricky little leg glances—and out he'd go. There's no exhibition shots about this Bradman.'

I said, 'How will he get on in England? Will he handle the English wickets?'

'Yes,' he said, 'don't you worry about him on English wickets. He'd play on a treacle wicket or on a corrugated iron wicket. He's used to kerosene tin wickets up there at Bowral. He'll never be the world's most artistic cricketer, but he'll be the world's hardest wicket to get.'

Well, it's not often that a prediction works out as well as that, is it?

A TINY FELLOW IN A NEAT, GREY SUIT

By A. J. Bell

Bell, a fast bowler, was one of the South African team which Bradman scored so heavily against in 1930–31, averaging 201.50 in the Tests.

YOU NEVER HEAR THE name Bradman in Australia. He is simply, Our Don.

There were thousands of cricketing enthusiasts at the quayside, all of whom greeted us with the usual formula: 'Wait till Our Don gets you.' In Sydney we were received by the New South Wales Cricket Association and there we met many old friends of South African cricketers, including Jack Gregory, Sam Ryder, Bert Oldfield, Charlie Macartney, and dozens of others. Of course we were most anxious to get a glimpse of Don Bradman.

Imagine our surprise on seeing a tiny fellow in a neat grey suit, and then finding him to be the redoubtable Don Bradman.

Enough has been written about him to fill a book. But off the field he has a remarkable personality, more especially when one considers that four years ago he was a nonentity in the small township of Bowral and now is easily the most magnetic figure in the world of cricket. He is a good conversationalist, obviously out to learn all that he can, and he gives one the impression of being an astute businessman. You feel when you talk to him that he is probing you. His eyes are never still. You feel that he will not be satisfied until he knows all about your bowling and your batting. You can see that he makes a close study of cricket and has unusual powers of concentration.

He does not talk about himself to any marked degree. He takes all his amazing performances as a matter of course. He tells you quite candidly that he is determined to better his previous records.

Our first encounter with Don was on the Sydney Oval when we played New South Wales for the first time. Neville Quinn had been left out of this game in order to be a surprise packet for the first Test. Morkel and I had a few overs at Don, and he did not impress us as anything out of the ordinary. Quentin McMillan and Cyril Vincent then took over the bowling. For about 80 minutes Don put up a very scratchy display, finally ending his innings at 30 caught and bowled by McMillan.

Naturally we were all somewhat elated and felt that we more or less had the measure of him. On the last day of the match we declared, leaving New South Wales 450 to get to win. We disposed of Wendell Bill, and Bradman came in. McMillan promptly was given the ball. But this was not the same Bradman. McMillan's first ball was a good length, fast spinner. Don ran about five yards up the pitch and cracked it like a bullet past mid-on to the pickets (the boundary). After this we were entertained to one of the most magnificent exhibitions of footwork any of us had ever seen.

Don never allowed McMillan to pitch the ball anywhere near a decent length, but hit it on the full-toss all the time. This rather changed our views about the little wizard. However, we put our faith in Neville Quinn. He bowled over the wickets in Australia, making the ball do a little either way.

Arriving at Brisbane we soon realised that Don had shown them the way of dealing with McMillan. The story of the first Test match is simply this—Bradman was dropped twice before he had scored 20, and on both occasions off Neville Quinn. In Brisbane Don broke Trumper's record against the 1910 Springboks, giving a magnificent display of forceful hitting.

Most people in South Africa seem to be under the impression that Bradman is a great forward player. This is quite erroneous. He is the finest forcing back player any of us have ever seen. To slow bowling he uses his feet marvellously, placing the ball when and where he likes. Against fast and medium bowling he does not score at quite the same phenomenal rate, but employs entirely different tactics.

One pitches a good length on his leg stump and the ball gathers another coat of paint off the pickets of the fine leg boundary, and one's bowling average increases by another four. If you bowl the ball just short of a length on the off pin he takes great pains over his shot and is content to push it down the gully for a single, or just out of reach of the unfortunate fielder.

We tried for four and a half months to get him caught in the slips by bowling just short outside the off stump. His wonderful placing and command over the ball made life absolutely untenable for gully and point.

When batting Bradman always seems, to the weary bowler at any rate, to assume a sort of cynical grin, which rather reminds one of the Sphinx. We tried to shift that grin; but I think Neville Quinn was the only one of us successful, and that was in the third Test at Melbourne when Cameron caught him for two.

His command of shots is nothing short of marvellous. He seems to know just what kind of ball you are going to bowl and where you are going to bowl it. He makes up his mind in a flash and does not hit the ball to the fielder as a great many do, but places it just out of reach and grins cheerfully.

To bowl to him is heart-breaking. He takes risks but never seems to pay the cost which his temerity deserves. His hook shot is incredible. He steps right back on to the wicket (one does not see much wicket when he is batting) and cracks the ball plumb in the middle of the bat about 99 times our of 100. When he does mistime the ball, and that is very infrequently, the ball does not shoot up in the air and fall into the avaricious wicketkeeper's hands, but drops harmlessly on the ground. This is due to the fact that with every shot he plays he intends the ball to hit the ground just a couple of yards from his feet. In all his shots he seems to turn the wrist over so that on the completion of the stroke the face of his bat is towards the ground.

The remarkable thing about the little wizard is that while fast and medium bowling is fresh he contents himself by never attempting to score in front of the wicket but glides the ball down the leg side or hits it like a bullet between point and third man. This last shot of his is, I think, his favourite.

If I ever play against Don Bradman again I think the best thing to do will be to bowl the fast full toss straight for the top of the off-stump. That seems to be the only ball he is content to pat back to the bowler. On second thoughts, however, he probably would work out a counter-offensive and land it up against the pickets in his usual manner!

Bradman's running between wickets was an eye-opener. I have seen him make nearly 200 runs in one day and at the end of the day seem to the weary bowlers to run faster than when he began at 12 o'clock. He runs for everything. He hits the ball just short of cover-point and runs a quick single. Cover-point comes in and he then places it just out of reach of his left hand. He does this to every fielder in the team.

Consequently, when Don comes in nobody knows where to stand, and they pray fervently either that he'll go out, or that six o'clock will hurry up.

Another remarkable thing about Bradman is that he never seems to perspire. Our bowlers used to get through three or four shirts a day, but Don comes out in an immaculate silk shirt at noon and at six o'clock it is still an immaculate silk shirt.

At Adelaide the temperature was 108 in the shade. Don was in the course of making 299. We were all just about exhausted, but Don—he was as fresh as a new pin. The only sign of his 180 runs was a tiny little damp spot in the middle of his back.

Apart from Don's actual play in the field he is looked upon as a national hero in Australia. He is easily he greatest drawing-card in the cricket world of today; probably the greatest of all time. We had an instance of this in the third Test at Melbourne. Don was 97 not out on the previous night. We started the next day at noon. Old players and officials of the Melbourne cricket ground told us that they had never seen such a queue at the members' gate. At the commencement of play there were 32,000 people.

Needless to say Don dispatched the first ball for three, making his 100. If I remember he got 160 odd and lost his wicket just prior to the luncheon adjournment. On the re-opening of play at 1.45 the crowd numbered about 20,000, which goes to prove that 12,000 at least only came to the ground to see Don get his century.

As regards his fielding I saw both Andrews and Pellew in the Australian side that played in South Africa in 1919 and they were considered to be among the world's best. I think it only fair to say that Bradman outshines any outfield in the world.

His running is phenomenal. If he sees a ball travelling towards the boundary he suddenly starts off after what seems to be a certain four, and to everybody's amazement he stops it with his foot just on the boundary.

He then throws it back in much the same way as 'Tupps' Owen-Smith. One of Don's idiosyncrasies is that no matter whether the batsmen are still running or are stationary in their crease he still pelts the ball straight at the wicket. If throwing square to the wicket he hits it from the boundary once in three times.

Our running between the wickets was very bad and to some degree I think Don Bradman was responsible. One never knew how quickly he was capable of disarranging the wickets from a boundary throw.

His ground fielding was exceptionally good: but the Australians who toured England in 1930 aver that he is not a very safe catch. Whether this is so we never really had a chance of observing. As in his batting his judgment of the pace of the ball in the field is wonderful.

He is the perfect example for the budding cricketer. He neither smokes nor drinks. He keeps reasonably early hours and looks after himself very carefully. He does a course of physical training, and combines it with wrestling. As regards the bogy of golf he seems rather to explode that theory. He is very fond of the game, plays off about eight and wins various competitions. So much for golf affecting the strokes of a batsman!

He plays the piano remarkably well, and plays most tunes he is asked either from ear or music. His only downfall against the South Africans was at a charity meeting when Eric Dalton beat him in a ping-pong match.

To sum up Don is rather a difficult job. He has done enough to make 20 average men swollen-headed. And yet that is the last thing one could accuse him of. He has a queer way of talking about himself. To all appearances he is batting well, and yet he will tell you quite candidly that he never bats well on the day following a big score. We could never detect a flaw in his batting.

He is one of the most magnetic personalities I have ever met in the course of my cricket career. He speaks with a strong Australian accent. Quite definitely he is an Australian. He is proud of it and Australia is proud of him. Whether he has reached the zenith of his powers cannot be said. But I think Alan Kippax hit the nail on the head when he said to me: 'If Don played for the West Indies they would be the leading cricketing country. If he played for New Zealand they would be the leading cricketing country. If he played for England they would be the leading cricketing country. If he played for South Africa they would be the leading cricketing country.'

And at that I leave it.

BROKEN WINDOWS, ANGRY WOMAN

A story in the Sydney Morning Herald, *January 1932.*

PLAYING IN A PICNIC match at Callan Park yesterday, Don Bradman broke two windows of a neighbouring house by a mighty stroke. The indignant householder confiscated the ball and refused to return it.

The match was between teams captained by T. H. Bosward and B. J. Folkard. It provided a day of merry cricket, nearly 600 runs being scored. Bradman made 143—giving a characteristic display that was greatly appreciated. One stroke sent the ball over a high wall, and it crashed through the window of a house in Darling Road. The ball then rebounded through another window. A fieldsman called at the house and asked for the ball. 'It will be returned,' he was informed by a startled, but determined, woman, 'when the damage is paid for.' No amount of persuasion could make her hand over the ball, and a new ball was brought into play.

Bradman was particularly severe on A. A. Mailey, and it was off his bowling that the window-smashing stroke was made.

'THANKU, MASSA BRADMAN'

By Arthur Mailey

From an article in the Sydney Sunday Telegraph, *December 1948.*

BRADMAN WAS A MEMBER of a team I took to Canada and USA in 1932, and there were moments on that tour when the most phlegmatic humorist might have been rattled. Money was very scarce at times, and had to be doled out in small amounts.

Once, at Chicago, I gave him five dollars which he left on the dressing table while he had a bath. Later he was wondering where the money had gone when the dusky maid came into the room and said, 'Thanku very much, Massa Bradman, for the tip. Glory be to you for being so kind.'

DON MEETS BABE

By 'Daniel'

A New York World Telegram *report of Bradman's meeting in New York with the American baseball champion Babe Ruth in 1932. Bradman was touring North America with an unofficial Australian team led by Arthur Mailey.*

BABE RUTH TODAY WAS bound to a promise. When the Australian cricket team visits this part of the country again next May the Bam will try his hand at the old English game and bat against the visitors from Down Under. He made that arrangement with Don Bradman, the Ruth of the cricketeers and star of the Aussies, at the Stadium yesterday.

Bradman and his teammates, sitting with the crippled Babe in mezzanine boxes, watched the Yankees beat the White Sox again, 7 to 2, sweeping the series of five games.

'I'll try this cricket business,' chuckled Ruth. 'Maybe it's my game. Now, why don't you put on a Yankee uniform and see what you can do against our kind of pitching?' he suggested to Bradman. 'Maybe baseball is your game.' But Bradman begged off. He had to be on his way to Detroit.

The Babe was surprised by Bradman's lack of size and weight. The greatest batsman cricket yet has boasted is no bigger than Joey Sewell.

Don weighs 145 pounds, is 24 years of age, and, according to the cricket experts, is a Willie Keeler rather than a Ruth—a scientist rather than a powerhouse. Bradman hits them 'where they ain't,' and has been known to score more than 1,600 runs in a little more than fourteen days of cricket.

'From what they were telling me I thought you were a husky guy,' remarked Ruth. 'But us little fellows can hit 'em harder than the big ones!' roared the Bam, and at once the proper spirit of camaraderie was established.

They watched the game closely, Johnny Allen pitching for the Yankees, Pete Daglia for the White Sox. In the second inning, with one out, Arndt Jorgens grounded to Red Kress.

'Now watch this closely,' suggested Guide Ruth, who was intent on teaching all the finer points to Bradman.

'Jove a double play!' ejaculated Don. 'Hey, what's this?' snorted the Babe. 'I was told to point out the tricks of the game and you holler "double play". You don't need any teaching. Seen much of this game?'

Little Bradman smiled. 'Oh, yes; we have lots of baseball in Australia and I have taken a keen interest in it. I'd like to play baseball myself.'

'Well, what strikes you most forcibly? What's the big difference between baseball and cricket?' Ruth asked. 'The catches of the outfielders? The work of the infielders? Those things always impress the English.'

Little Mr Bradman smiled again. 'No there is nothing extraordinary about the catches or the inner-fielding. You professionals do nothing else. You work up to the leagues and then you must be exceptional or they chuck you out.' Mr Ruth chuckled. 'I'll say!' he snorted.

'In addition, baseball players are equipped with heavy gloves,' Don continued. 'It isn't the actual playing of the game that impresses me. It's the quick decision, the businesslike way in which the test is conducted.

'In two hours or so the match is finished. Each batter comes up four or five times. Each afternoon's play stands on its own.'

A demonstration of the late cut, a favourite stroke.

Don and Jessie in November 1932. They were married at Burwood in Sydney five months earlier.

The Bradmans spent their 'honeymoon' touring North America with a team organised by
Arthur Mailey. Those pictured here in the front row were all prominent in cricket:
(from left) Stan McCabe, Bradman, Mailey, Vic Richardson, Alan Kippax and Hanson Carter.
Another future Test player, Chuck Fleetwood-Smith, is in the back row, third from right.

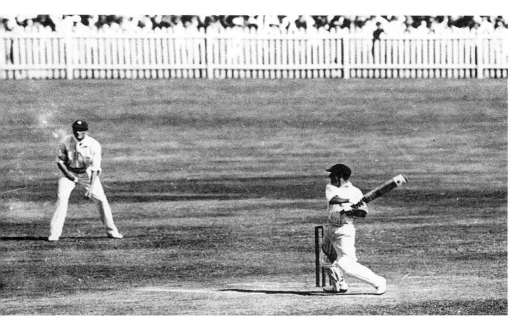

adman's daring strategy to counter bodyline: stepping back to square-cut from outside the leg stump in the third Test at Adelaide. Douglas Jardine is the fieldsman at backward point.

One of the finest of all Bradman action photos. He has skipped down the pitch to drive the England spinner Hedley Verity in the fifth Test of the bodyline series, 1932–33. Gubby Allen is at short square-leg and Leslie Ames behind the stumps.

With Jack Hobbs, who covered the 1932–33 tour for a London newspaper, and Admiral Dalglish at a Navy v Press match at Rushcutters Bay. This match, played immediately after the third Test, provided the rare spectacle of Bradman and Hobbs batting together.

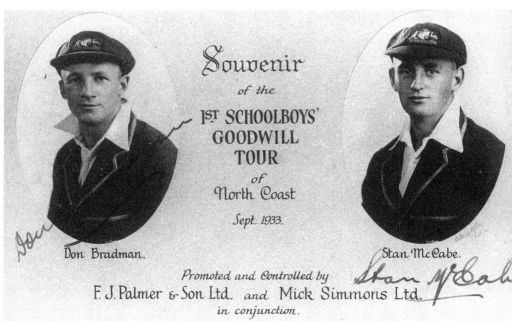

Bradman in his Australian cap. This photo was used in the souvenir of a schoolboys' tour of northern NSW, which he and Stan McCabe accompanied in September 1933.

Power

. . . in Bradman's batting and in Plume's performance

. . . The flash of a willow blade . . . then, "KLUP!" . . . (Ha! that satisfying sound of well-smitten leather!) all the well-timed power of Bradman behind it . . . the pickets rattle . . . the crowd applauds . . . the Umpire waves . . . "A BOUNDARY!"

A century maker is he who has *power* to drive and keep on driving . . . to speed the flying ball with flashing cuts and glances . . . and stand up to express deliveries the hot summer's day through. Plume too has the *power,* the *driving power,* that will enable you to take the hills in top, the *power* that means maximum mileage. Plume's *power,* proved in every motoring test, stamps it the champion among motor spirits.

PLUME
for all-round performance

Starting
Acceleration
Speed
Power
Mileage

VACUUM OIL COMPANY PTY. LTD.

Although in later life Bradman made little attempt to capitalise on his fame, as a young man he did appear in a number of advertisements, such as this 1932 ad for motor spirit.

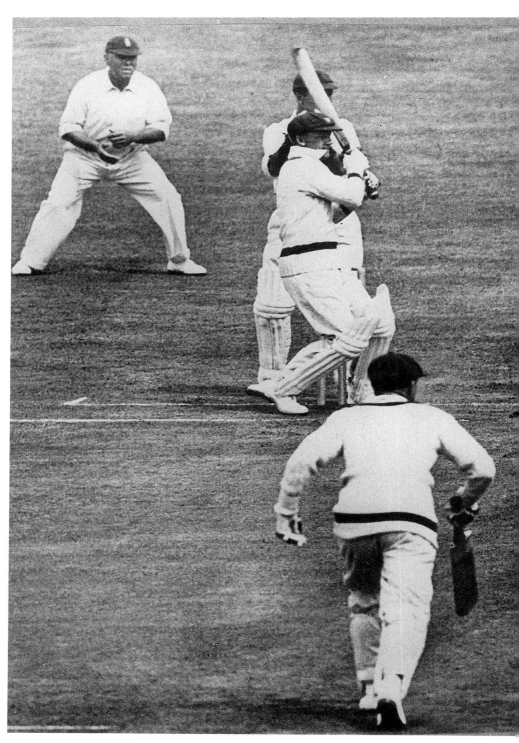

Bradman pulls to the fence during his innings of 304 in the Leeds Test, 1934.
Patsy Hendren is at slip and Leslie Ames behind the stumps.

Bradman and young Bill Brown on tour in England. They toured England together three times, in 1934, 1938 and 1948.

Bradman tosses as Australian captain for the first time in the first Test of the 1936–37 series at the Gabba. England's captain was his friend Gubby Allen.

With Gubby Allen in front of the old players' pavilion at the Gabba, 1936–37.

'Yes, cricket could learn a lot from baseball,' Bradman went on. 'Our matches are prolonged for days and days. Only four or five batsmen may come up in an afternoon's play. There is more snap and dash to baseball.'

There was little conversation through the game. The Babe sat resplendent in brown sports coat, shoes and a white cap—the true nabob.

In the fifth inning the Australians were aroused. Frankie Crosetti drove a home run, with two on bases, to left centre. As Bob Seeds and Elias Funk chased after the ball Crosetti went scampering around the bags. On he came, and there was a play at the plate. The Aussies were on their feet. But not Bradman.

'A beauty in the right spot,' was Don's comment. 'That was off a googlie ball,' remarked Fleetwood-Smith, star bowler of the visitors, who is quite a googlie-ball thrower himself. A googlie, m'lads, is a pitch with twist and spin to it—in short, a curve.

The game ultimately got a laugh out of Bradman. In the seventh inning the boys got up to stretch. 'What's all this about?' asked Don.

'Just an old American custom that takes the place of tea!' roared the Babe—and then 'Arry Stevens, of Derbyshire, sent up his boys with tiffin—ginger ale y'know.

VANISHED CROWD

By Clifford Winning

From Cricket Balmania.

IN 1932–33 DON BRADMAN accepted an invitation to play in a charity match at Gladesville Mental Hospital in the cricket grounds that were in those days adjacent to Victoria Road.

I had the very great honour, as a current Balmain first grader, of being invited to play for the hospital eleven by the manager Mr Bill McCoy, himself an ex-Balmain first grader. Naturally I was thrilled to the back teeth at the prospects of sharing a partnership with the great master and also at the thought of having a serious knock against my own club mate Arthur Mailey who was captaining the opposition on this occasion and was being assisted by another rep. player named 'Ginty' Lush.

The crowd was so dense that traffic problems never experienced before in the area were created in Victoria Road, so serious that for a time it appeared more than a possibility that the match would have to be abandoned. However when the authorities allowed the spectators to encroach upon the perimeter of the playing area in order to fit them in, the match was able to proceed.

I opened the batting for the hospital invitation team and lost my partner very early in the innings. This paved the way to provide me with my greatest cricketing thrill—waiting nervously out there in the middle amid tumultuous applause as the legendary Bradman moved out to join me. Arthur Mailey came on to bowl much earlier than was his usual custom and to my utter disbelief and the vast disappointment of the huge crowd he had Bradman caught in slips for only a couple of runs.

This was the only occasion in my long career that I ever felt like changing positions with a dismissed colleague so that he could bat on in my place. But this was against the rules so the match had to continue, and I could do nothing but watch the most prolific run-getter of all time slowly wend his way back to the tiny pavilion.

No crowd has ever dispersed as quickly as the concourse that surrounded the ground on this occasion. As a matter of fact, play was held up for nearly thirty minutes until the spectators disappeared through the many exit gates.

There I was, left out in the middle, willing and able to entertain the fans but I was less than immortal and so they were not the slightest bit interested. Indeed I went on to get the best 80 runs I ever scored in my life against a first-class attack, but I performed in what was virtually an empty arena apart from the players, the umpires, a few officials and a number of the best behaved of the mental patients who were generally allowed to watch the social games under a strong guard of warders.

THE COUNTERPLOT

By A. G. Moyes

From Bradman, *1948. Moyes, cricket journalist and former cricketer, had taken a fatherly interest in Bradman since he first moved to Sydney from Bowral. He describes here how Bradman, after illness had forced him out of the first Test of the bodyline series, tried to work out a counter to the Englishmen's tactics.*

BRADMAN IN THE MEANWHILE had gone to the country for a rest to recover in peace and quietness. Apart from his health, there was much to consider; he had to work out a plan to counter this new theory which had been devised, as *Wisden* put it, 'to curb the scoring propensities of Bradman.'

At a little beach cottage, owned by Tom Langridge, whom English cricketers know so well, he worked out his counterplot like a general who seeks to halt the enemy's attack and then advance to the assault.

When Bradman returned to Sydney he looked better, not completely well, perhaps, but ready for action. The next day he called at my office and expounded his plan. My task was to think out all possible objections and to raise them, like Aunt Sallies, for him to knock over. The plan was simple and direct as he stated it, though one could see immediately that putting it into effect would be neither simple nor straightforward.

The first fact in his appreciation of the situation was that he had to make runs. He was so quick on his feet that he could get out of the way of anything that Larwood might hurl down the wicket. He could dodge all danger—provided he was content to do that. But—and it was 'But' with a capital letter—the public would not be content with that. They would grow weary of an exhibition of gymnastics and would demand that he make runs. The 'Hill' would wax both facetious and querulous. The old law of supply and demand would operate. The public would make the demand. How was he to arrange supplies?

He would walk away from his wicket and try to hit the ball through the off-side field. If he succeeded it would put the bowler off his balance and would force him to weaken the leg field and strengthen the off field. Then he could revert to normal batsmanship. His plan was, in effect, to meet unorthodoxy with unorthodoxy—he must make runs.

I tried to counter it. If one ball came through quicker and lower, he would be left straddle-legged with a cross bat, looking as though his style was as fully impregnated with the scent of gumleaves as some of his detractors still affirmed. To this he replied that, first of all, a ball pitched short would bound over the wicket. If it was even close to a good length he would not move away. Further, if its direction was towards him, it would pass outside the leg stump whether it rose high or kept low.

The hook shot was no good, he thought. I pointed out that he played two hook shots, one (past mid-on) like the drive off a high-bounding ball at tennis, and the second a normal one. He had considered all that. In the first case, he played the stroke with the ball coming towards the right shoulder. That was easy enough against a normal bowler, but Larwood came 'in' to the body and a 'miss' would mean a broken head and hospital, which would help neither Australia nor Bradman. As far as the normal hook was concerned, he pointed out that he was not tall, that the ball was flying as high as, or higher than, his head and that he could not possibly get on top of it and keep it down.

He disposed of every argument. He had considered them all and rejected them. The crowd would not be content for him to dodge and let the ball pass, hoping that the bowler's condition would wear out before the batsman's patience. Therefore, his plan was the only one which might work.

MARVELLOUS BUT RISKY

By R. W. E. Wilmot

From Defending The Ashes 1932–33, *1933.*

BRADMAN DUCKED AND RAN. With more imagination than the others, he decided to stand well back from his wicket. Instead of the 'centre and leg' guard he had previously adopted he took block on the leg stump. He endeavoured by hitting the ball on the off side to force Larwood to weaken his leg field, and it was marvellous to watch some of his strokes. They were his own invention. They brought him many runs, but they also cost him his wicket. The fight between him and Larwood went on match after match, and in the third Test in Adelaide he was again the master, only to lose his wicket to the slow bowler, Verity, as the result of over-confidence. He felt in himself that he must take the gifts the Gods offered while he had the chance, and as he expressed it, 'I thought I had better hit Verity before Larwood hit me.'

LIKE A CAT

By Bill Voce

From an interview with Murray Hedgcock in Wisden Cricket Monthly, *November 1981.*

HOBBS—HE WAS IDEAL to watch. Hammond—ah, he had those great shoulders, and when he opened them you had to watch out. Bradman was like a cat, he was so quick-footed. He would have to be No. 1 in an all-time World XI. But he wasn't the spectacular sort like McCabe. . .

We didn't bowl short to hit Bradman, you know—it was to try to unsettle him. In those days on those Bulli-soil wickets in Australia we'd bowl our little hearts out, and after two overs the shine had gone. The pitch would be dotted with red paint from the ball. He had a bit of a weakness right at the start, trying to turn the ball away to leg, so you'd try to get him off balance there. But after that first two or three overs with the new ball, you'd had it: you'd try variations of pace or anything like that, but it wasn't so easy on Australian wickets and in that atmosphere.

Bradman didn't like bodyline, but he didn't show it the way some of them did. Kippax was scared stiff, and he let you see it. But Bradman had the right idea: he always knew the best defence was attack. He was very quick on his feet, and he could get out of trouble so fast. He wanted a lot of reckoning out.

BRADMAN'S MOST FAMOUS DUCK

By Bill Bowes

From an article in Cricket: The Great Ones. *This was Bradman's first encounter with bodyline in a Test, and his first-ball dismissal caused a sensation. He turned the tables in the second innings, scoring 103 not out.*

BECAUSE OF ILLNESS BRADMAN did not play in the first Test of this particular series which, in spite of the 187 not out by McCabe, finished with England gaining a ten wickets win.

He played in the second Test at Melbourne and, of course, there was a confident feeling among the home spectators that everything would now be in order. There was a crowd of nearly 70,000 packed into the huge Melbourne stadium to watch Bradman. Other players were merely pawns in the game. Even the potency of Larwood had not yet been realised and the word 'bodyline' had not been coined.

I happened to be bowling when O'Brien was run out and Bradman, batting at No. 4, came to the crease. Coming from the shadow of the pavilion into the bright sunshine he made a huge semicircular approach to the wicket to give his eyes a chance to get accustomed to the light. The crowd cheered his every step. No gladiator in Roman times had a more vociferous welcome. They cheered right through the ceremony of taking guard and afterwards. There was nothing to do but wait until they quietened. Eventually they did so. Bradman moved into position to take strike. I began the first steps of my run up to bowl.

The cheering started again. By the time I had taken two more steps it was almost deafening. Bradman moved away from the stumps, I stopped, and again came this period of waiting.

For the sake of something to do, rather than any bright idea on my part, I asked my mid-on fieldsman to go up to short leg for the first ball or two. After such a reception, I thought, Bradman would be very determined not to disappoint the crowd and would hardly begin by driving to mid-on.

The crowd quietened again, and once more I began my run up. But before I was half way to the bowling crease the cheering had started again. Bradman turned away. I stopped. And this time I motioned to my deep fine leg fieldsman to come more square.

I saw Bradman look at my short-leg fieldsman and then at the man moving into position almost behind the square leg umpire and I knew, as certainly as if I had been told by Bradman himself, that the batsman expected me to bowl a bouncer.

If only I can make him certain, I thought. I glared at him when the crowd again quietened and I began my run up to bowl. This time there were no cheers. As I went into the delivery stride I pulled a face as if there was to be tremendous effort. I bowled it short but did not 'dig' it into the ground, as you must to bowl a bouncer.

Almost as the ball left my hand, Bradman set himself for the pull stroke. I do believe if the ball had bounced as high as he expected, it would have been going yet!

All set for the ball at shoulder height, he suddenly realised it was coming to him at the height of the bails or less. He altered his shot and swung down at the ball, got the faintest of edges to it without altering its direction, and the ball crashed into his stumps.

I could hardly believe my eyes. For the first and only time in his career, Bradman was out first ball in a Test match.

The crowd in the vast Melbourne stadium could not believe it either. A stunned and complete silence came on the crowd as Bradman surveyed his stumps, turned, and walked slowly to the pavilion.

Jardine, fielding at short leg, seemed to be the only man abreast with things. He put his arms above his head and danced round and round in happiness like an Indian doing a war dance.

The silence held until Bradman approached the gate to the pavilion and then a woman began to clap. In the stillness of the stadium, all eyes went to the moving hands. The spell of stunned disbelief was broken, and immediately, such a hubbub broke out that the effect was startling.

An impression of Australian crowds, 1932–33

By S. P. Foenander

CRICKET SEEMS TO BE a passion with most Australians and the female sex is no exception. In fact, they struck me as being even keener on the game than most of the men. The way in which they 'let themselves go,' by cheering any good hit, bowling performance or worthy display of fielding is amusing more often than not. As for shrill shrieks the Australian girls are second to none in the world.

They queue up very early in the morning of a big match outside the Adelaide Oval, every one of them carrying her luncheon basket, stuffed with sufficient food for at least two persons for a day, a cushion perhaps and a copy of a souvenir, that is usually on sale, giving all particulars about the two teams. At least for two hours before play begins these spectators sit patiently in the stands, chatting, watching others come and go, eagerly awaiting the arrival of the players on the ground. No cricketer was ever the object of greater hero-worship than Don Bradman. At Adelaide, Melbourne, Sydney, and Brisbane, he was the idol of the crowd—particularly of the female section of it.

'There's Don' would be shouted out as Bradman's dapper little figure appeared in view. And all eyes would be focussed on the great cricketer from Bowral. And when Bradman began to punish the bowling, the crowd would grow delirious with delight and shriek and screech till they almost grew hoarse.

A TRIUMPH OF TEMPERAMENT

By R. W. E. Wilmot

From Defending The Ashes 1932–33, *1933.*

THE BEST ILLUSTRATION OF temperament I know is the case of Don Bradman. In him it is developed to the nth degree. It possesses him, radiates from him, raises him above his fellows in the most remarkable way. If Bradman's batting be examined carefully, studied in the light of the accepted standards, much can be found that is not usually associated with a first-class batsman. He does not always play with a straight bat; some of his strokes are almost crude; but he rises superior to these defects; he confounds his critics and exasperates bowlers. For four years he scored centuries with a regularity which had almost become a habit, as he passed on to his second, his third, and even his fourth century, in a manner which was altogether amazing.

I recall a wonderful innings in the Test match in Melbourne against South Africa. N. A. Quinn, the left-hander, had worried him in the first innings and had done so previously. The ordinary player would have gone in to face his rival with the memory of his previous failure, and with perhaps a shade of caution. When Bradman went in Quinn was bowling magnificently, and as Bradman walked to the wicket many wondered if, at last, he had met a bowler who was his master. There was little in his demeanour to indicate what was to follow; a slight increase in the pace of his walk, a perceptible tenseness of his lightly-knit frame, perhaps; an absence, may be, in some measure of that smile which usually radiates his face; but nothing more. The moment he took his stance, however, it was evident that the fight was on, and from the very first ball it was evident that, whatever had happened before, it was Bradman who was the master then, not Quinn. There was no hesitation, no tightening of the defence, no waiting; but an immediate and compelling aggression. Grandly as Quinn bowled, so much the more did Bradman flail him. Off drives which rattled on the iron pickets, cover drives which sent Viljoen and McMillan racing round the boundary, brought four after four to that flashing blade, and old cricketers went into rhapsodies at this classic innings. By nightfall the match was won; but Bradman was still unconquered, and Melbourne spent its weekend waiting for Monday. Long before play was due to recommence crowds streamed through the parks to see this wonderful boy. It was the first working day of the year; but that did not prevent 20,000 people breaking all their good intentions and deserting their businesses. Just before lunch he was out, and they went back to work satisfied. Temperament had triumphed.

A failure to Bradman is not defeat, it merely affords an opportunity for increased activity. Long before the English team led by D. R. Jardine arrived in Australia, Bradman knew that he was the one Australian cricketer the Englishmen feared. He also knew that there was a set plan to bring about his downfall. In England he had been the dominating factor of the Tests, and all England realized that, unless he could be conquered, there was little hope of the Ashes being regained. Wise men, good judges had discovered—though on what they based their judgment on English results it is not easy to imagine—that he could not withstand fast bowling, especially when it was directed at his body. They chose their team with this as their objective, and they put it into practice at once. Larwood was the spearhead of the attack, and Bradman at once realized that he was to be the target. From the moment that he first met this new attack he adopted his own methods. He did not tighten his defence; he increased his aggression. His confidence in his own powers did not wane. His frail body may have wilted under the virulent attack but he did not quail. It was not fear that made him adopt new methods. It was, to the contrary, a firm belief that he could overcome the devastating attack. He attempted strokes of which no other man had dreamed, and, what is more, he so frequently executed them that veterans, who could not understand his lack of the orthodox, gasped as they saw him making the most extraordinary shots, taking the most amazing risks. Though he failed to make the mammoth scores which had previously marked his career, though he seemed, at times, to throw his wicket away, the final test match saw him still unconquered, still the most dreaded of Australian batsmen, with the highest aggregate and the highest average of all his fellows. That they had subdued him to some extent was a triumph for the Englishmen; but he still maintained his confidence, his complete sense of the importance of victory and his ability to hide from an opponent any idea that he felt that he might not be able to do what he had previously done.

Temperament is the only word to describe just everything that surrounds Bradman and his cricket. In momentary failure, in success, he still remains, after a most eventful season, the laughing boy, the run-maker, the inventor of new strokes, the best batsman in the world. Though worried by contracts, by conflict with the Board of Control, by criticism, by the excitement of new and varied experiences, he is still the same modest, smiling lad, who came from the quiet of a country town into the maelstrom of international contests, and in all that he does there is never a word of self-adulation, never a hint that he has been doing aught but play a game, though to him such game is his business.

A TASTE OF HIS OWN MEDICINE

By Harry 'Bull' Alexander

From an article by Philip Derriman in the Good Weekend, *1993, in which the former fast bowler spoke of his teammates' reaction when he struck England's captain, Douglas Jardine, a painful blow with a short-pitched delivery in the last bodyline Test.*

Vic Richardson was certainly pleased. Braddles was probably pleased in his own way, but he wasn't the type to say anything. Braddles was fielding in front of the Hill. I was told that after I hit Jardine he turned his back on the play and faced the big crowd on the Hill with a grin on his face.

DESPERATE MEASURES

By the Coaching Editor

From the Australian Cricketer, *May 1933. The article from which this passage is taken was titled 'How To Play Bodyline Bowling'.*

With the moral effect of their frightfulness as a background, Larwood with one or two headers was able to bring the batsmen's minds back to the Australian Eleven match at Melbourne, when the batsmen paced up and down the dressing room nearly frantic trying to think out a way of successfully dealing with a full attack of headers on the bodyline and leg-side, bowled to a leg field. Only Bradman and Lee (who had no reputation as a batsman to worry about) were game enough to chance their arms at the head-high balls that whizzed down all day.

For the high ball over the wicket or on the off, Bradman has played a species of tennis smash, obviously not an orthodox cricket stroke. . . Bradman's method of stepping away from the fast medium-height leg ball and forcing it to the off, which stroke he may have copied from Grimmett and O'Reilly, is a dangerous stroke except for a genius. It usually necessitates hitting against the flight of the ball, and across it, and there is very little margin of error. Bradman has lost his wicket in this way several times, though he may eventually master the stroke. Previously, good batsmen used this stroke only to medium-pace or slow bowlers.

SOME PRAISE AFTER ALL

A remark attributed to Douglas Jardine

From Bodyline, *1983, by Philip Derriman. This remark about Bradman was quoted by John Arlott in an account of a conversation he had with Jardine, England captain in 1932–33, about England's controversial victory in the bodyline series.*

YOU KNOW, WE NEARLY didn't do it. The little man was bloody good.

SUPREME IN HIS OWN CONFIDENCE

By Jack Fingleton

From Cricket Crisis, *1946.*

THE WORLD HAS NOT seen his equal, nor anybody approaching his equal, in the consistency and degree of his big scores. I particularly stress the word consistency. Some of aesthetic tastes might have preferred the cultured charm of a Kippax or a Jackson to Bradman's flaying piece; I saw Macartney and knew his genius to be of a different mould from that of Bradman. Repute also has Trumper to be of a different mould; but, in the sheer consistency and robust profligacy of their respective arts, Bradman far outshone all others, the English eras of Grace, MacLaren, Hayward and Hobbs not excluded.

Other individuals might have been noted for fast footwork, unerring judgment or brilliant eyesight. Bradman possessed all these; but, if there was one faculty which made him superior to others, it was in being able to judge, almost as soon as the ball left the bowler's hand, the length, spin and merit of that particular delivery. Therein lay much of his greatness—a quicker brain, a quicker judgment than any other batsman I have seen.

But a batsman does not place himself on a pinnacle such as Bradman occupied by virtue of any one, two or three outstanding gifts. Bradman was richly endowed in all that went towards making the champion, and in none more so than in his twinkling, magical feet. I have tried to dissect their movements from the distance of the pavilion and from the closeness of the opposite batting end; but Bradman's feet were almost too quick for me, especially against slow bowlers.

A friend of mine once had an interesting conversation with

Ponsford about Bradman's batting. When asked why it was that Bradman made batting look so easy, Ponsford, with his usual modesty, replied: 'The reason is very simple. Don sees the ball about two yards sooner than any of the rest of us.'

Ponsford meant by that exactly what I have written—that Bradman was able to judge the merits of the ball two yards or so sooner than any other batsman. This, in turn, gave him what I consider the greatest advantage he possessed over all contemporary batsmen. He played forward more, he played up the wicket more than any other first-class batsman I knew, and no bowler likes to see a batsman coming forward with confidence and attacking good length balls. Unusual height with its long reach enabled Woolley to cover by forward play ordinarily good length balls; Bradman, a smallish man, got to where he wanted by quick footwork. J. M. Taylor hit Tate hard off his back foot; Bradman hit him hard off his front, delighting in the fact that Tate's excessive pace off the pitch gave him additional speed off the bat. Where most batsmen instinctively swayed on to the back foot to cope with this Tate pace off the pitch, Bradman went forward gleefully to make the most of it.

His batting stance was unique. His bat touched the ground between his feet, not behind them, like every other batsman and photograph I have seen. He stood perfectly still as the bowler approached; the end of his bat did not act as an escape conductor for energy with that nervous tap, tap, tap on the pitch so common to most batsmen as the bowler ran to deliver the ball.

Bradman at the wickets was completely at ease and at rest until the ball began its apologetic advance towards him. His lithe, compact body was a power-house of latent electricity until the switch of a ball released was turned, and then his brightness flashed in all directions. His feet took him into immediate position to offset swerve, swing or break bowling; his running feet took him three and even four yards up the pitch to slow bowling to kill the break and take advantage of the gap in the field which his eye had detected. He was at his best in making the placement of a field look foolish. He was at his greatest against slow bowling (he took 30 off a six-ball Freeman over at Folkestone in 1934), for he moved far out to the ball on the full or drew back to destroy its length and pull in that unorthodox manner which grew with him on the concrete wickets of his country youth.

I remember Bradman in his first appearance at the Sydney nets. There was a breeze of the bush and bygone years in the braces he wore, but there his rusticity ended. He was the cynosure of all eyes, and well-intentioned critics, as they always do, converged on him at the finish of his net and talked to him of his stance, his unorthodoxy on the leg-side. They would have had him change this or do that, but Bradman gave them a polite ear and then promptly dismissed them from his thoughts, internationals and ex-internationals though they were. Even at that age Bradman possessed pronounced qualities. Confidence in his own ability and interpretation of the game was one of them.

The story is told of him in those years when he was first chosen, a mere slip of a country youth, in the New South Wales touring team. An admirer had presented him with a touring cricket bag and he had gone to choose it.

'I want something big to carry plenty of equipment and I also want something that will last a long time. It is going to have a lot of work to do,' airily said Bradman to the storekeeper, and that story quickly went the rounds.

His selection, like that of others at the time, was purely in the nature of an experiment, a commendable New South Wales experiment of the period which paid and repaid handsome dividends. Mere lads were chosen in first-class games. Some fell by the wayside, others bore rich fruit (Jackson and McCabe were two), but Bradman did not consider that there was anything problematical in the scattering of his seed and its ultimate harvest. Youths walked blushingly and full of awe into the precincts of Macartney, Taylor, Andrews, Kippax, and others, but Bradman came supreme in his own confidence, determined to go his own way. And he did!

In a few short years he had the Australian sporting firmament at his feet. No Prime Minister, no inventor, no medical genius of the calibre of McCormick and Hunter, no South Polar explorer like Wilkins or world-acclaimed airman like Kingsford-Smith, Ross and Keith Smith, Hinkler or Ulm knew the publicity from the Australian Press that Bradman received.

He rose to the heights in a period of world uneasiness, the depression years and the early rumblings which were later to develop into the avalanche of European troubles. Hitler had just commenced his rise to power; economic conferences were being held in London; gold standards were crashing; Wall and Throgmorton Streets were dizzy with speculation, and one of the representatives of world finance, Sir Otto Niemeyer, had just delivered to Australians a depressing lecture on how to run their country—a lecture dictating financial belt tightening in a land of primary abundance.

As the Irish poet and author, Eimar O'Duffy, had it:

The banker in his counting-house counting out his money;
The land was overflowing with bread and milk and honey;
The shops were full of good things, the factories likewise;
The banker shut his books and said we must economise.

Bradman's colossal feats with a piece of willow gave editors a chance to depart from their usual mournful run of depression news. His deeds were so remarkable that they spilled over from the sporting pages and gave the window-dressers of the Press an infrequent opportunity in those days to instil a little brightness, some light relief, into their usually gloomy leader columns.

He became the most discussed person in Australia, conceding the limelight for a short period only to the then New South Wales

Premier, John T. Lang, when that turbulent politician became embroiled in a Government Bank crash, a constitutional tilt with Governor Sir Philip Game and a ribbon-cutting episode at the opening of the Sydney Harbour Bridge.

Bradman became the continent's number one idol, not merely because of his prodigious batting feats, but, in a sense, because they happened at a time when Australian national life was sick and apprehensive. Business men on the verge of bankruptcy said, 'To hell with business' (it invariably finished there, anyhow, in those days!), closed up their doors and went out to forget their woes and themselves with Bradman. It was usual to see thousands leave the ground when Bradman was dismissed. The atmosphere and most of the interest in the game walked back with Bradman to the pavilion, a bitter pill for previous headliners to swallow and none too happy a prospect for those who had the interests of the game at heart; but circumstances and his own genius surrounded Bradman with an atmosphere and a publicity value no other player could approach.

People who had never been to a cricket match before, who did not know a bat from a ball, flocked to see Bradman. A carnival spirit hung over every ground on which he played, and the first sight of him as he emerged from the pavilion was sufficient to send the whole ground into ecstacies of delight. No other batsman in my time, which corresponded with Bradman, could approach his terrific skill with the bat or his unlimited popularity with the crowd. He was the planet, solely inhabited; the others revolved around him, shining intermittently in the early 1930s in his reflected glory.

His colleagues frequently felt that they were mere lay figures or items of scenery to be arranged to provide a background for the principal actor, but, from a public point of view, Bradman was responsible for a very great percentage of the enormous public interest in cricket between the two wars.

He seemed to bring out through the gate with him a breath of power and a confidence which made everybody feel that the whole fortunes of the game would be changed by him—as they invariably were. He walked slowly to the wickets with a slight rolling gait, the slowness so that he could accustom his eyes from the dark of the pavilion to the light of the ground (a gentleman named Lyon took him to task for this slow walk, in England, in 1930, but as Lyon had also played the game he should have known better).

Where 99 batsmen out of a hundred make their last few yards to the wicket with a grim, haunted look on their faces, determination alternating with nervous hopefulness, Bradman's mien when at last he reached the creases was one of supreme and disarming happiness. A few seconds' business with the umpire and then he looked about him with a huge grin. That grin was the cheekiest, the most challenging, and the most confident thing I have seen in sport. It was such as to rip the innards out of any bowler, sending him hurtling down to spreadeagle the stumps of this cocky young man, but always the tale was the same. Bradman opened his score with the cheekiest and most confident of shots, and there he was at the other end or walking back down the pitch from a boundary shot, grinning, grinning, grinning!

The crowd loved and adored him for his tradesmanlike activities at the wickets. His worth was apparent and intrinsically honest. He gave them even more than they asked for their admission money.

He was at once the despair of the bowler, the captain and his fieldsmen, the batting worthy struggling at the other end and his comrades in the pavilion. He made it all look so easy, so simple, so prearranged. He always made the onlooker feel that a loose ball would be lifted for four to the very place on the boundary to which batting science required that that ball should be sent.

He was the genius absolute. To bat with him was an education and revelation, not given by any other batsman of the period. Great artists like Trumper and Macartney varied the direction of the shot for sheer artistic satisfaction, but Bradman was implacable. He was more interested in runs than art, and in the days when he was playing for Australia you would have searched a long time before you found an onlooker who seriously disagreed with him. He was the undisputed hero of the new-found public, the broadcasting public. He was the darling of the spectator's heart—and justifiably so, because no batsman in history had been so prolific and none of the moderns could approach the standard he set for consistency and sheer honesty of batting purpose.

Sydney citizens asked the visitor whether he had seen our Harbour, our Bridge and our Don. It was embarrassing to walk down the street with Bradman, to ride in a street car or dine with him. He was instantly recognised and acclaimed, even staid professors permitting themselves a childlike chuckle as they obtruded a pen and a piece of paper on Bradman for an autograph. The life of the champion seemed to be one long succession of autographs. The post disgorged hundreds of them at him daily, and almost the only peace he knew from them was while he was at the wickets—which was probably a reason why he stayed there so long.

In all this adulation, in all this hero worshipping, which came at its flood when he had just passed his 21st birthday, Bradman never lost his balance. He never allowed his head to expand in the vapourings of flattery. The ground was always in contact with his feet, though once established he did not temporise with any challenges against his domain.

Once in a game in Sydney against Victoria there had been the bold claim in a newspaper that Ironmonger, who had taken his wicket in the first innings, had the measure of the champion. It was dangerous for Ironmonger that such stuff should have been written. Bradman made a close study of what the critics wrote. His most spectacular innings in Australia was played in Sydney (Fleetwood-Smith being the chief operating medium) the day after a leading critic had written that he did not possess the spectacular flair of a Trumper or a Macartney.

As he opened his huge mail this other Sydney morning he casually asked several of us if we had seen the particular article about Ironmonger and himself.

'Yes,' somebody answered, 'we did.'

'It will be quite interesting,' said Bradman, with a smile, 'to see what happens today.'

The tone in Bradman's voice suggested that he himself was in no doubt. Ironmonger was to be put through the Bradman hoops, but Bradman was not boasting. In his 'it will be interesting to see what happens today,' he was letting us know that he had accepted the Iron-monger challenge, and he wished us to note how he accepted it.

Until he reached the sobriety or comparative sobriety of his late twenties, Bradman was always impish in his batting. It amounted almost to a point of honour with him, as I have written, to take at least a single from the first ball bowled to him, but in this innings against Ironmon-ger, the innings which was to prove whether a mere bowling mortal could hold a cricket god in chancery, Bradman's audacity took on the flavour of contempt.

It was not sufficient for Ironmonger first to be subdued and then flayed. A Jackson or a Kippax might do that. Ironmonger, or rather the critic, had to be put in his Bradman place.

From the very first ball Bradman took the most daring risks. He cut Ironmonger fine off his middle stump, he flicked him off his stumps to the fine leg fence, he on and off drove him, hit him high to the outfield (always difficult with Ironmonger), and then, in a final flourish of contempt for the critics, Bradman hit Ironmonger over the fence. No batsman could have done more against a bowler, and in all this it was difficult not to believe that Bradman was laughing hugely, not at Iron-monger so much, but at those critics who suggested Ironmonger held an option over him.

Bradman returned radiant to the pavilion. 'What was in that article again?' he asked.

That was Bradman's nature. He liked nothing better than slaughter-ing bowlers and critics alike.

There was another occasion, on the eve of a charity game in which

Mailey and Bradman were opposed, when a statistician found that Mailey, then a cricket veteran, had taken Bradman's wicket several times. The newspapers displayed the fact. It was an interesting news item, but for Mailey it could mean only one thing, even though the game was a charity one. It meant for Mailey his offering on the sacrificial altar of Bradman's greatness, for the little chap never missed a cricket item in the newspapers.

I lunched with Mailey that day and he was obviously ill at ease.

'They shouldn't write stuff like that,' he said, referring to the newspaper item.

Mailey knew his Bradman. He knew, as a consequence of that item, that there would be a hot Bradman reception awaiting him.

Thousands thronged the small ground, and there was a buzz of excited expectancy as Bradman made his customary slow walk to the wickets. The test was to be immediate. Mailey was bowling. As Mailey apprehensively twiddled the ball from hand to hand at the other end, Bradman meticulously took his guard and looked about the field as if to say: 'So Mailey, one of the Old School, has my measure. Well, well! Let us see if there is anything in this rumour. I'm ready when you are, Arthur.'

Mailey began his ambling run, his arm came up and over—and Bradman was running yards down the wicket with his bat poised aloft. There was a succulent swish of Bradman's bat and away in the distance, as if fearing what was to come, the ball lost itself in the crowd.

Then followed cold and deliberate cricket murder. Mailey's deliveries speeded to the fence and over the fence, and from one of the latter soaring hits came the tinkle of falling window-glass, the orchestral accompaniment to a stage plot of murder that had thousands calling for blood, blood, still more Mailey blood. Bradman put Mailey in the stocks that day for all to see. Then he hanged, drew and quartered him. Mailey was butchered to make another Bradman holiday.

That was another glimpse of Bradman. He was the dominant cricket

figure of his age, and if fate delivered to him one of an older generation, then his treatment would be such as to suggest that Bradman was
the dominant cricket figure of all the ages. Mailey had then retired
from the first-class stage and was far past his best, but had he been in
his prime I venture to say the story would have been much the same.
Bradman paid respect to no bowling save bodyline.

All bowlers, with the possible exception of O'Reilly, whom he first
met in a country game, came alike to Bradman. At one time or another
he took up Tate, Larwood (before bodyline), Geary, Voce, Freeman,
Verity, Constantine, Francis, Griffiths, Grimmett, Fleetwood-Smith,
Ebeling, Blackie, Ironmonger, Oxenham, Quinn, Bell, Morkel,
McMillan and the rest of the world's best. He was wary and respectful
always with O'Reilly, but the others he closely analysed and then slashed
them apart before he left them bewildered, abashed and out of breath.

MORE THAN ONE SECRET

By J. R. M. 'Sunny Jim' Mackay

From an interview in the Referee *with Mackay, who had come to
Sydney to see Bradman in action for the first time—and had seen him
score 128 in 96 minutes for New South Wales against Victoria, in
January 1934. Nearly 30 years before, Mackay, from Uralla, had scored
runs in Bradman-like profusion for New South Wales until an eye injury
brought his career to a tragically early end.*

HE IS A WONDER, and the greatest run-maker I have ever seen.
They say that he uses a cross-bat. Well, what is wrong with it? His
footwork is so perfect that he is always in the right position to make
any of the strokes he employs. Those two terrific fours he hit off Ironmonger, past the bowler, were made with a cross-bat. But did you

notice that he had got into the correct position to make the strokes. He left nothing to chance.

The secrets of his success?

There's more than one secret. First of all, he has a wonderful eye. Second, he has a wonderful brain for cricket. Third, he has wonderful power in those forearms and wrists. How he does make the ball travel! His placing is grand, but did you notice that the pace he gets into the ball greatly helps the placing. He hits it so hard that the fieldsman who would intercept an ordinary stroke cannot reach most of his. Then on top of it all, his footwork is wonderful. The difference between an ordinarily good batsman and a great one is often to be found in the use they make or do not make of their feet in getting into position to execute the stroke.

Bradman will do me. Those big hits were the result of perfect timing of the ball. He is only a little chap. But those sixes! He has mastered the art of timing the ball.

'GIVE HIM 300 AND ASK HIM TO GO OUT'

By Trevor Wignall

From an account in the Daily Express *of Bradman's 206 against Worcestershire in the opening match of the 1934 tour.*

ONE HOUR AFTER THE start of the second day's play in the Australians' opening match with Worcestershire, Cyril Walters, the home county's captain, could almost be heard saying despairingly, 'What on earth are we to do for a bowler now?'

Walters was standing in the middle of the field, surrounded by some of his men, and Brook, the nearly-forty-year-old bowler, had just been taken off after only two overs. Don Bradman had treated the veteran in the most unmerciful fashion. His slamming of the ball was easier than shelling peas, and Walters wore a perplexed, anxious expression. The best he could do was again to 'ring the changes.' The sole consequence of this was that Bradman went on his relentless way without let or hindrance until he completed his double century.

The end of his innings was typical of the man and his sense of showmanship. It was palpable that he was weary of the fashion in which runs were being presented to him. He had started his knock soberly and slowly enough, but that was chiefly because the wicket had been softened by the overnight rain. Once his eye was in, however, he did everything except make his bat recite.

But this—much more significant—was the end of his innings. In the final over he skied one ball, which was fumbled for a catch by a fielder. The next he missed by half a yard: the third he sent to the boundary; and the fourth he deliberately missed, knowing it was straight and would hit his wicket.

He had had enough. His decision to conclude his own particular proceedings was wise. Spectators all round me were announcing that they were wearied of the constant boundaries, and of the sad effect the Australian had produced in the Worcestershire team. One man near me loudly shouted: 'Give him 300 and ask him to go out!'

SECRETS OF SUCCESS

By Pelham Warner

An article in the London Daily Telegraph, *1934.*

WHAT ARE THE SECRETS of the amazing success of Don Bradman, who, with his fellow-Australians, makes his first appearance of the season in a match in London at Lord's today? Bradman has immense natural skill. An idealism which urges him to learn everything he possibly can and to profit by lessons learnt. Tremendous concentration of mind. And, too, he is in perfect physical condition, while he has a cool, calm temperament.

As to the actual technique of his play, he is blessed with a wonderful eye, steel-like wrists, and small and beautifully neat feet, which make him exceptionally quick in moving back or forward to the ball. Every stroke is fully developed, and, above all, he has an amazingly strong defence, which is the keynote of all successful batsmanship in first-class cricket. Bradman's hooking of anything the least short is masterful. He misses nothing on his pads; he off-drives brilliantly; but, above all, the cut, both late and square, is his glory. I have never seen finer or safer cutting, for he is always on top of the ball. Again, he watches the ball very closely, and his extreme quickness of foot enables him almost to dictate the length of the bowler. Bradman's eye is quick and his balance perfect. He has very small hands, but his forearm is all power, and the muscle between his right thumb and first finger is abnormal. It sticks out like a hard cushion.

What is Bradman's future? Is he destined to break his own records? Will he one day play an innings of 600 or 700? Remember he is only 25, and, given good health, he should have at least fifteen more years of cricket before him. Bradman looks every inch a cricketer. He is scrupulously neat and smart in his turnout, and he plays the game with rare zest and enjoyment. Above all, he possesses both character and brains. Bradman, indeed, bats like no one else. He is a genius—a law unto himself.

'To an Australian cricketer'

By Jane T. Stoddart

A poem from 1934.

Any Schoolboy
Sign your name, sign your name, here in my book, Don;
Ten cricket heroes' for yours any day.
Now for a close-up and don't you escape us;
Dozens of us are barring your way.

A Newspaper Critic
What was the mystery, what were you hiding,
All these first games when the scoring was low?
Dazzling, deceiving us, waking our pity;
Many a trick the wild wood doth know.

A London Scot
I watched you away from the Langham that morning,
And saw the two flags hung out on your car.
War tune of Donald, the pipes with the banner,
Were they not sounding to me from afar?

Any Citizen
We wish you calm seas, and a joyful returning;
Fresh triumphs, my wizard, as life draws to noon;
Friendships and health where the home-stars are burning,
You've given us our summer, Don; come again soon.

INSPIRATION FOR A GROUNDSTAFF BOY

By Denis Compton

From Compton On Cricketers Past And Present, *1980.*

FUTURE GENERATIONS MAY, I fear, become slightly sceptical about the legend and achievements of Donald George Bradman, and dismiss such scribblings as mine as exaggerated hero-worship, or a judgment warped and coloured by time. No single player, I can imagine it being said, could have been so impossibly gifted, or endowed with a temperament to match his extravagant ability. Or, it may be thought, the bowling of his age must have been ordinary—spanning twenty-one years?—and the field-placings naive.

The late Sir Pelham Warner was once asked by a group of players if W. G. Grace was as good as history made him out to be. His answer was: 'Only those who played with and against him could have appreciated his true greatness and his impact on the game.'

As with Grace, so with Bradman, who played havoc with all types of bowling, created records never likely to be surpassed, and fascinated all with the psychology of his make-up. He was unique, a batsman appearing not just once in a lifetime but once in the life of a game. His like will not be seen again, and I count it as my privilege that I was able to study his technique and methods from the closeness of slip and gully. I also came to know him as a man and in my experience the Don was far from 'a solitary man with a solitary aim', as an eminent critic claimed.

If any should doubt the crushing power of his strokes please, I beg you, take the word of one who fielded on the boundary to him and watched a round red bullet repeatedly pass at unstoppable speed, and placed with such precision that I had no earthly chance of getting within reach.

When I first played against the Don I was a precocious twenty-year-old. My mind was flooded with mixed sensations of awe, respect and plain curiosity—one could imagine a recruit to Winston Churchill's war-time Cabinet undergoing the same emotions. The mere presence of the greatest cricketer the world had known on the same field as myself was unnerving, and after encountering Bradman in two home series and one in Australia, I never lost the sense of being in contact with history.

Far from breeding contempt, familiarity nourished my wonder at everything Bradman did. He was a living miracle, defying comparison with any other player before, during or since his time, and an early description of him has stood the test of time. Jack Ryder, a former captain of Australia, was asked how Bradman played. He replied, 'He just belts the hell out of anything within reach.' He did just that, and, unlike Jack Hobbs and Victor Trumper, never threw his wicket away when he thought he had had enough.

I suppose my attitude to Bradman had its roots in my sporting background and my immersion in the game. My father and I once took a No. 13 bus from our home at Hendon to Lord's in 1930 to watch the phenomenon everyone talked about, but I am ashamed to admit that my memory of the occasion is blurred and I remember nothing of the Don. At least I didn't suffer the disappointment I had on a Bank Holiday at the Oval when Hobbs, my idol, was bowled for a modest 22, though there was a wondrous exhibition of cutting from his partner, Andy Sandham, the memory of which excites me to this day.

In 1934 Bradman was back in England, and I had been a ground-staff boy at Lord's for two years. Sometimes the leading players of Middlesex might stroll to the Nursery to cast critical eyes on young hopefuls like me, and the conversation inevitably turned to Bradman, who seemed to score at will and at a fantastic pace. Bradman was the constant subject. His very name was magic, and the inimitable 'Patsy' Hendren, who had played in the Don's first Test at Brisbane in 1928, fed me with every scrap of detail. 'Patsy' scored 169, England won by 675 runs, and the way Australia were ground in the dust was said to sour and fashion Bradman's attitude to the way a Test had to be played.

Unfortunately contact with the foremost players was seldom possible for groundstaff boys—the lowest form of cricketing life!—and I was able to see Bradman in action only briefly as I sold scorecards during the famous second Test, when the late Hedley Verity took 14 wickets in a day and 15 all told. Frank Chester, the umpire, told me an overnight storm left a patch at one end no bigger than the circumference of a frying-pan. It was enough for Verity.

Bradman had been out when the game was resumed for a small but brilliant 36, but, oddly, he served as an inspiration to me even in failure. Australia followed on, and I was at once fascinated and impressed at the way Bradman met aggressive bowling with a counter-attack. Though he gave a skied catch to Les Ames at the wicket I could not forget his positive approach in what was really a hopeless situation, and there can be no doubt that a firm Compton philosophy which was to serve me well throughout my career was conceived on that occasion. He made me realize that in the final analysis attack is the best form of defence, and it is better to take the fight to the enemy than be dominated by him. I have never changed my opinion that the successes gained by intelligent assault far outnumber the failures.

It was invariably held against Bradman that, in contrast to Hobbs, he was not a master in all conditions and was vulnerable to the turning ball, particularly with his unconventional grip if it was leaving the bat. Aren't we all? Verity did not share the conventional view, and I am inclined to agree with his opinion that the Don's attitude on sticky pitches was a form of protest.

He was never one to hold a weak belief on any subject, and he was very much against uncovered pitches. The argument was that Lindrum and Davis would never be expected to perform on a lumpy billiards table, and it was wrong to play cricket on a pitch open to the vagaries of the weather besides being grossly unfair to one side. As a batsman I agreed, and for my part I find it inconceivable that the Don, who batted with ultimate perfection and saw the ball on the bat as late as it was possible, could not have devised a technique for wet conditions if he had put his mind to the problem.

It seemed a matter of principle to him not to overcome a bad wicket, and he shrugged his shoulders like a renowned actor enduring bad acoustics at a one-night stand. Nor did I pay much attention to the criticism that he would hold himself back and expose his less fortunate and less talented team-mates to the torments of a drying surface. To me that would be simple logic, and totally in the interest of his side.

To the Don there was no mountain high enough. His cricket was planned to the last detail, and I confess that on the occasions I bowled to him I was in near-despair. Every basic requirement of batting was there in abundance—the lightning reflexes of brain and eye, footwork which would not have come amiss in the Bolshoi ballet, a delicate balance and the self-confidence springing from a belief in his own dazzling ability.

He had a marvellous gift of getting into position quicker than any batsman I have ever seen, played the ball very late, and was never off balance, or stretching out of control. With his judgement of length he would make his quick decision and play either back or forward without hesitation. Brain and body were in perfect harmony. I could understand the temptation to regard him as simply a run-machine with such built-in powers of concentration and personal drive as to be incapable of human error. Certainly he lacked the charm at the crease of an Alan Kippax or a Tom Graveney. He was not in that sense a stylist. But he was fallible to the occasional error for the simple reason that he made his runs at a fantastic rate and never refused a challenge. Often I would look at the scoreboard and be surprised to find he had twice as many runs as I figured he had scored. He was forever finding the gaps and taking the singles and the twos.

Modern bowling and field placings might have crabbed and confined him to a degree, but would not have finally defeated him. It might have taken him longer to make his scores, but he would not have been utterly shackled or have allowed the bowlers to dictate their terms. Instead of being 300 at the end of that remarkable day at Headingley he would possibly have been 220 or 240 not out. In any case with the slow over rates he would not have received anything like the number of deliveries.

With his uncanny ball sense Bradman could master any ball game. He flirted with lawn tennis for a time and doubtless would have become a champion. Within weeks of starting billiards he made century breaks, and he had the same success with golf and squash.

His cricket was uniquely Bradman. No coaching manual was intended for him, and despite what is said to the contrary I am sure that had he been born English no coach would have dared to interfere with him. His grip would have doubtless caused some consternation. Both hands were turned over the handle with the fingers of the left hidden from the bowler. The swift answer to those who said it was wrong was in his murderous hooking and cutting. The only doubt raised by his unorthodox grip was his cover drive and his defence against the ball leaving the bat.

But I cannot honestly recall him as an ineffective cover driver, and his record scarcely suggests that he was ever technically handicapped! If he once reached 30 or so the fielding side were thankful if he was satisfied with a single century.

He gathered runs at such a speed that it was impossible to set a field for him, and it occurred to me at times that he had a private game with a slow-moving fielder or with the opposing captain. His placements were so exact that he could have a fielder moving backwards and forwards from one position to another. There was, in fact, no precise field setting for the Don because he was able to improvise brilliantly as I found to my cost at Sydney in the 1946–7 series.

Bradman's hook was pure magic. There has not been a batsman I have seen able to match his special skill with a shot that gets so many able batsmen in difficulties. Today's batsmen, plagued with the obsessive use of the bumper and the short-pitched delivery, ought to study every action picture and film they can get of Bradman playing the hook. Never once did I see him hook in the air, and, unlike even the best who aim for deep square or fine of square, Bradman whacked the ball in the direction of mid-on. Bradman was different because he was fractionally quicker in picking up the ball, and was in position faster. His secret was to pick up the flight path and pitch of the ball so soon that he actually seemed to be in position and waiting for it from the moment it left the bowler's hand. He was unsurpassed in his timing and execution, and I am certain bowlers would have been disinclined to use the bouncer too often against him.

Bradman was the unwitting cause of the so-called bodyline form of attack. If ever there was a back-handed compliment to genius it was the invention and employment of bodyline. Douglas Jardine and his ally Harold Larwood roughly halved Bradman's output and average to 396 runs at an average of 56.57. By Bradman's standards a failure, but even with seven fielders on the leg side and the ball screaming at his head at a speed of ninety miles an hour or so Bradman improvised with shots placed on the off side. He also had a tennis-style smash back over the bowler's head.

The cut was one of the Don's favourite shots. As with his hook, the ball was kept on the ground. Anything fractionally short of a length or over-pitched was murderously assaulted, and his moral ascendancy over the bowlers was enough to give him an advantage before a ball was bowled. Understandably Bradman's reputation was enough to send a chill down the spine, and bowlers knew they had to pitch an immaculate line and length or they were set for merciless punishment. I suffered a definite sense of inferiority on the occasions I bowled to him. I admit I was an unpredictable slow-left-arm spinner with an inclination to experiment. But precisely because I felt I must not bowl a bad ball to Bradman, I invariably ended up doing so. And he never failed to hit a bad ball.

'I LIKE THE LITTLE DEMON'

By C. B. Fry

A newspaper column, 1934.

UNTIL YESTERDAY I'D NEVER seen Bradman play. Of course, I was immensely interested in him, and asked the experts to explain him to me. I got nothing but the usual adjectives—and these cloud any subject. My madame told me: 'He's a little man with fairy feet, who watches the ball.' That did convey something.

This Don Bradman, we all know, is a marvel. Merely on figures. But the interesting point is why and how. I will tell you. He's beautifully built for physical fine art: by conformation an athlete of the light-weight type. Many great batsmen have not been athletic. Arthur Shrewsbury wasn't: he was a podgy plodder. Tom Hayward wasn't: he was a comfortable sergeant-major. And others.

Bradman has a gem of a body for batsmanship, conformation perfect: hence perfect poise. A bundle, beautifully shaped, of what the Greeks called harmony. He is light-armed, free and ever so quick with his bat. He need not begin his stroke till the last fraction of a second. Hence, never compromised before he sees, *actually* sees, the ball right up to its full development.

It is a simple point: moderate giants play at the ball as they figure it will come. This little master plays at the ball as it is. The difference between mastery and mediocrity—with a bat.

He has lovely wrists—that grace in batting. He moves on his feet ever so neatly and ever so easily in good time. He is poised on the ball of the feet not the flat. Like a good dancer. More, he does trust his eye utterly. Not afraid really to wait and see.

Remains, the psychic side. And this is a big plus for your Don. This young man owes half his perfection to an outright power of concentration. Native or acquired, it's the *sine qua non* of mastery. You can see it in his face. Firm little mouth. Winner's chin. He has the quality as a settled habit and no doubt subconscious. His sheet anchor.

He has humour, too. A great asset. If only the Australian Board of Control would let him, he'd amuse us with words as well as shock us with runs.

I like the little demon. I've never spoken to him. Perhaps never shall. You should see the dour Australian discipline! No expansion, boys! Keep your tongues tied and think of cricket.

It is not raining at Worcester. I want to see Don bat all day. I want to learn. I wish I could have used my bat like Don. He's a gem of a batsman. I just love his finished technique and inevitable surety. How he must enjoy getting his runs. After all, cricket worth while is physical fine art. Isn't it?

Bradman is still not out—he is flicking, persuading and forcing the ball all over the field, pretty well as he chooses. I note an interesting point. All these Australians, including our Don, drive off the back foot. Half the beauty of Lionel Palairet's off drive and Stanley Jackson's and Billy Gunn's was the fluent force due to moving the weight smoothly onto the left foot—the forward foot. But Ranji drove like these Australians—a method that gives less margin of error and needs acuter timing. This is a matter for pavilion critics. I'm not sure which way is the better. But I'd rather myself drive and teach my pupils (you, for instance) to follow the Palairet practice.

I wish Don Bradman would bite some of our batsmen, I've just seen him deliver a full-fledged straight drive clean and high over the bowler's head. He chasséd out on his nimble toes and just let drive—gave me quite a thrill. And I simply hate the Australians—with a playing-at-hate.

I want 'em beaten. Don't you?

THE BRADMAN FACE

By Neville Cardus

From a 'Famous Faces' series in the press, 1934.

It is a jauntily confident face, isn't it? Eyes and mouth surely never conveyed a plainer message of abundant self-reliance. It is there to see in the shrewd half-pucker of the eyes, with their air of watching your next move in the secure knowledge that you won't make anything of it at this individual's expense anyway.

The little creases at the eyes lead directly somehow to the cocksure smile that reinforces the eyes' expression. Quite a pronounced smile it is, though the lips never forsake their curiously tight line. Under these eyes it seems to be the smile not so much of spontaneous amusement or of the real deeps of humour as of a superiority that knows it can be discomfiting to the people who measure themselves against it. It belongs to a man who knows not only exactly what he can do but also how few other people can do anything like it.

Jauntiness of this sort somehow suggests sport. There is an intelligent forehead to this face, but the features convey the idea of mental sharpness rather than of, say, a permanently constructive power of thought. It ought to be the face of an alert and successful business man, but even business success would hardly bring this degree of 'gallery conscious-ness' into a face. Bradman the cricketer is, of course, the idol of a vast public. And he knows it. It may perhaps be just a question whether he loves the game as much for the chance it gives him to measure his skill and cunning against the bowlers as for its opportunity to let him fill the public eye with the picture of a master of cricketing art.

A CRICKET CALAMITY

Anon.

On Bradman's duck against Cambridge, 1934.

There's a great ado
Among the bats,
The old, the cracked, the new;
The country bats,
The city bats,
The home-made sloggers, too.

There is a stir
Amongst the balls
Of leather, rosy red,
The leg-break balls,
The off-break balls,
The one that swerves instead;
The kicking balls,
The one that crawls,
The wretch that hangs
Before it falls,
And all the other
Wicked balls
That strike a batsman dead.

The very pads,
The gloves and bails,
The cricket-pitch,
The light that fails,
The tool-bag and
The scoring-book
Are wearing an
Astonished look.

And should you ask
The reason why,
The downcast kid
Will make reply:
The cricket world
Is up to Putt;
The King doth emulate
The mutt.
Australia's down
And out—of luck—
Don Bradman's made—a duck!

LE DON INSPIRED

By William Pollock

A newspaper report on Bradman's 160 in just over two hours against Middlesex in 1934, reckoned to be one of his most brilliant innings.

AN INNINGS THAT THOUSANDS of us who love cricket are going to enshrine in our memories was played as the sun went down over Lord's on Saturday.

For more than forty years I have watched great batsmen—W. G., Ranji, Trumper, Frank Woolley, Macartney, Jessop, Hammond, Hobbs—and am grateful for many precious hours from them, but never have I seen a masterpiece of batting more glorious than Don Bradman's 100. It was a supreme. It was epic.

Le Don came in when the Middlesex J. Smith (ex Wiltshire) had got both Woodfull and Ponsford out for noughts with his village black-smithy fast stuff, and for a ball or two he was not quite sure of himself. But the bit of luck that all batsmen need at the start was with him, and within five minutes the bowling was his toy. His timing was marvel-lous, the power he got into his strokes extraordinary. Through the covers, straight past the bowlers, round to leg, down through the slips, the ball raced from his almost magic bat. All the shots were his, the whole field his kingdom.

Smith's quickies, Walter Robins's slows, Ian Peebles' length ones, including an occasional googly, were just so much meat and drink to him.

The ball no question made of ayes or noes
But right or left, as struck the player, went

Le Don seemed to be inspired; he danced down the pitch and hit, he flung out his left leg and drove, he lay back and pulled.

I do not believe that any bowling in the world could have stopped the torrent of his run-making during this wonderful hour and a quarter. It was an honour to bowl and field during such an innings. It is no more than the frame of the picture to say that he put the ball to the boundary nineteen times, and that he got the one run he wanted for his hundred off the last ball of the evening.

Le Don has played the great innings of the season. If there is anything better to come from him or any one else, may I be there to see and share. The really great things of cricket are treasure.

Music for Men

By C. B. Fry

A newspaper column after Bradman scored 160 against Middlesex.

Don Bradman is a monopoly. Drama is afield the moment this jaunty dignity and purposeful poise emerge from the pavilion.

This terrific little batsman was never spoon-fed in a nursery or flattered into early folly. He ploughed his way to the top through stiff club cricket in Australia. Here is a master. He paid the price of struggle and has achieved success extraordinary.

His innings has been simply smashing. Fancy 100 out of 135 with Darling, a fast scorer, at the other end!

Like every transcendent player Don bags inadvertently 75 per cent of the bowling. Ranji was the same, and Gilbert Jessop. One might be 80 not out when they arrived, and would be perhaps 120 when they reached 100. It's a funny feeling.

Adjectives do not quite describe him. He just does it. Slogs the bowling—as we have seen him in this match. Batting is relative to bowling. Frankly, I do not know what class the bowling has been, because Don has just gutted its quality. I have seen Ranji and Macartney and Trumper perform in similar fashion. Ranji was more sinuous and electric, Macartney more impudent and risky, Trumper more stylish and graceful. None of them put across such unremitting and undiluted dash and devil.

It is interesting that technically Don has faults. He dips when he cuts—he punches on the off from his hind leg. He hits across the break. But his exquisite timing and his faculty of holding back the delivery of his stroke to so late that he knows each ball by heart before he hits it— these supreme excellencies cover every error and to spare. Personality does count in cricket.

Such humour in his batting! He smashes with a sort of sardonic smile in his strokes. When the runs are up he hazards a bit of a lark. He really does. All in, he's a lovable little enemy. I hate to see him hit out!

What are we to do about him? But I tell you this. Many runs as he would have made he could not have treated the big bowlers of 20 years ago—our Lockwood, Richardson, Jack Hearne and Peel—as he deals with the county bowlers of today. The difference sticks out a fathom to anyone who has seen both eras. The perfect length, powerful pace and dominance of skill is absent nowadays.

The end has come—dramatically. Punch after punch, and finally a high, hard drive—for fun almost—finely held by Hulme. A grab, a tumble and a recovery. Just by the pavilion middle gate. Well, we've seen an historic innings. We'll talk about it for years.

Never was [there a] batsman who did so many wrong things right. The crack of his bat against the ball is proper music for men.

HUMAN, AFTER ALL

By Philip Lindsay

From Don Bradman, *1951. Lindsay, the Australian-born novelist, was a son of the artist Norman Lindsay.*

WHEN NEXT I SAW Don Bradman it was during the 1934 tour of England and I had tickets for every match in which he was to play in London. Those years between had been hard years, yet I cannot call them miserable because there cannot be misery while there is faith. Hunger, bailiffs and cold can be exasperating tribulations but little more to youth when it remains certain that it carries its fortune in a typewriter. Of that literary pilgrimage I have written elsewhere, and in 1934, when the Australians again visited England, it lay in the past and

I had my tickets like any millionaire, my seats safe, my passport paid for into paradise.

As a man in love must parade his beloved in his pride, I had bought three tickets for each match to be played in London—against the MCC, the Gentlemen of England, Middlesex, Surrey and the second and fifth Tests—that I might take friends with me to share my happiness in good company. Many were those friends—countless they became when the news spread that I could show them Bradman on the field—and some joined in my worship, while others were patriotically stung by their country's defeat, looking on Bradman as a personal affront, but even in their atrabilious sneers there was pleasure for me in knowing that they, poor wretches, were merely jealous. Others, however, became embarrassing with their adoration.

Particularly do I recall that day at Lord's against Middlesex—Bradman's 160 made in 120 minutes—when an Australian stuntman for the films I had met by chance that morning in the Strand and who could not be shaken off when he discovered what I had in my pocket, made even me and my hard-bitten cousin, Peter Lindsay, want to crawl under our collars with his irrepressible barracking. Only by enticing him now and then into the bar could we choke him into silence, but once back in his seat, his bawling thundered round the sacred ground. That day we had a member of the Hill with us and, hotly though he made me sweat, I could not blame him for his excitement, for he expressed only what I was feeling.

Few of my memories can equal that warm day at Lord's when, unconquerable, Don Bradman stood with the impish glee of a boy doing what he liked with the ball. Both Woodfull and Ponsford were out for a duck; Woodfull the dour, Ponsford the patient, two of our greatest, safest batsmen, back in the pavilion, and our hearts sank down to our bellies until Don Bradman came to laugh for us. His pointed collar up, his cap drawn green over his eyes, he ambled to the wicket in that high-shouldered way of his and, seeing him after those years of stubborn poverty, I felt as happy as a man who meets again his loved one after long parting, with that joy edged with tears, bringing a grin to the lips and no words.

That was a day forever red–lettered in my calendar.

What mattered that in the early Tests he failed? That at Lord's I saw him trapped by Verity, most foxy of bowlers? The defiant hit of his in the second innings of that match which sent him back to the pavilion when he was needed so terribly was the kind of knock at fate for which I loved him. Hammond in his *Cricket My Destiny* tells us that afterwards as Bradman 'passed Woodfull at the other end, his skipper gave him a look so compounded of anger and disappointment and woe that I have never forgotten it. Verity, standing at the wicket, showed not the slightest expression on his face, though he knew, as we all did, that that ball had won the match'.

With woe and disappointment certainly, but not with Woodfull's natural anger, I saw him turn on that long road back, because, as I have said, almost I loved him for that cheeky stroke. Certainly, it was not a Test match stroke. It was practically a swipe, if one dare use such a schoolboy word about anything attempted by Don Bradman, but it had in it the heroism of Ajax defying the lightning, for that day Hedley Verity was lightning, although lightning is definitely not the word to describe his artful bowling. It was snakish, it was cunning, it was crooked, it was venomous bowling. Rarely have I seen a mere ball perform such extraordinary dodges as Verity made it do that day. The turf was to his liking, and in conspiracy with the ball, as though witches had crooned there all night to make a hellbroth of it, it spat the ball from directions it should not, by any act of reason, have possibly come. Only Woodfull with his dogged patience was able to remain at the wicket, content to block and not to hit; and then, on that bedevilled pitch, Bradman had to act with the fury of a lunatic instead of imitating his captain's noble caution. Verity tempted him. With cruel cunning, he left the long field open.

Those who insist that Bradman is a batting-machine and little else should have been at Lord's that day. Verity plainly did not believe such nonsense. He knew that this so-called machine was human and that, being human, it had its weaknesses. Almost he taunted Bradman with that open field; and a man of flesh and blood, child of Eve, can tolerate such insolence only for a time. It must have been a continual ache to Bradman to have to stand and block when he knew that sixes and fours were being offered by the serpent and he dared not accept the challenge. St Anthony with all the whores of Satan in their voluptuous nudity could not have known such agony as Bradman must have known while the minutes ticked past and, as he tapped the balls dead, he knew that he had only to make one real hard hit. . .

He made it. This 'machine' was human, after all. There must come the moment when restraint grows beyond bearing and the singing heart can be stifled no longer. In a burst of heroic rage, Bradman lost his head and his wicket. The insult had been too much and could no longer be tolerated, so he did what Verity had been begging him to do. With a frenzied bat he swung at the ball and, instead of flying fast to the outfield to zip over the rails as it should have done, that wizard's ball, crooned to by Verity, spun up for Ames with gluttonous gloves to hold easily, gracefully; and the young god was out.

Certainly, at the opening of that season Bradman had often behaved like a schoolboy; and for those insect-minds which feed on statistics, it was a record of humiliation, but in his autobiography he has explained that he was not well before the tour, and an enforced rest after the fourth Test in which he tore a muscle on his right thigh gave him the needed breathing-space that he might restore his strength for that glorious feast at the Oval in August.

No doubt he was suffering from the penalties of genius. Others might make a small score and nobody would complain, but let Bradman make one mistake and that meant headlines. To live at such pressure must be soul-destroying and the impulse to give a wild hit, as he did that day at Lord's, must have been strong in him every time he walked to the wicket and heard the mob clapping, demanding further records for every occasion. The heart must rebel against such incessant strain. That devil which lives in all of us, that imp of perversity, had Bradman during that tour. It was as though he were determined on blasphemy, like a god weary of sacrifices who would steal off to romp on Earth, or like a king sighing for the anonymity of his subjects who have no fear of cameras, so that he struck out with his bat, metaphorically poking out his exasperated tongue, with the desire to be left alone and no longer badgered for centuries.

The enforced rest, however, calmed rebellion and after it he was ready for what proved to be, on the whole, that tedious final Test at the Oval. I call it tedious because that last hot day returns to me with a feeling of sickness and of dust up my nostrils. The vast crowd pushing on to the grass, letting newspapers deliberately flutter into the wind to distract the batsmen, the eruption of brawls to release the angers of an embittered mob, with England in a hopeless position, Ames having been stabbed in the back with lumbago when he seemed the only batsman capable of bringing delight back into the game, and then the pitiful sight of the great Woolley helpless behind the sticks: no, that is not a game I like to remember, except for Bradman's batting.

The great Cardus, again in *Good Days*, has recorded that lovely innings and it would be impertinence for me to do other than to follow his pen, save for one reservation.

'Beautiful strokes,' he wrote, 'delighted the eye continually . . . Eighty runs an hour in first-class cricket can be achieved only by brilliant batsmanship . . . Bradman was flawless; he gave no sign that in his extensive machine there was any seat of error. His first stroke was a mishit along the ground through the slips off the middle of his bat; this was his only miscalculation. When he was 77 he chopped a ball from Hammond and put his arm over his eyes in self-criticism; at 97 he achieved another chop—quite safe, of course. (And a stroke not perfect was indeed an

achievement for Bradman today.) He began with a calmness and quietness that were sinister. Tamed was the imp of mischief that pricked him
to wayward and lovely and dangerous hazards in June. At the right
moment in the cricket match of the year Bradman called back the
Bradman of 1930, only here we had a Bradman richer by four years in
experience. He did nothing all day that was not fine.'

Only must I quarrel again about the use of that word 'machine', and
it is surprising to find it from the pen of so subtle a critic as Cardus:
one who is a lover of music, too! To call that innings at the Oval
mechanical both astonishes and angers me. Here was perfection, and
man, unable to account for perfection except as something miraculous,
must denigrade it to machinery, as though should a goddess walk on
Earth, her beauty, being beyond the beauty of women, must be
compared to a doll's or a painting's, as being inhuman. But machines
are not the only inhuman things: gods are inhuman, great artists are
inhuman, rare beauty is inhuman, because they are above the norm
which is you and me. Must such miracles then be put lower instead of
higher than us? Far from mechanical, Bradman's batting that day was
inhuman only because it was chanceless. Nor was it just the dogged
chancelessness of a bore who will take no risks; he took what to any
ordinary mortal would have been risks enough to stop one's heart, only
one's heart missed no beat because here was Bradman at work, Apollo
on Earth, and one knew that he could not fail. Machine, indeed! Show
me a machine that can drive and cut and glance so merrily, with that
brisk footwork, that saucy contempt for any devilishness the bowler
might think to put with burning fingers in the ball.

Probably his speed was enhanced by Ponsford's ponderousness, for
he came on to the field hugely padded against possible bodyline, and,
a stocky man, he at times looked like Mrs Gamp in flannels, nor did he
seem at ease against the bumpers of Clark. One began almost to fall
into rhythm with the crowd—and it was no pleasant crowd, being fired
with resentment because Woodfull had threatened to abandon the

recent game against Notts should Voce continue bowling: I like to believe that tale a myth but unfortunately the evidence is against me— when it jeered at his persistent use of the pads, his shrugging away from every ball that even faintly rose. Although he reached 266, he never seemed really safe and his behaviour towards legitimate bumpers, the haughty scowling down the pitch as though he were a basilisk, made one a trifle ashamed, but this majestic dourness added spice to Bradman's gaiety at the other end. While Ponsford, with the supreme gesture of contempt, turned his back on the bowlers, Bradman hit out at them. This was no swashbuckling innings, but neither was it a dull one: very far from it, indeed, for it had all the grace of poetry in every rhythmical stroke. To my thinking, it was one of the most perfect innings I have ever seen and remains the flourish on which I like most to dwell as Bradman's farewell for many years to England.

YORKSHIRE SMITTEN

By Neville Cardus

An account of Bradman's innings of 140 against Yorkshire in 1934, scored between lunch and tea. This remarkable performance marked Bradman's return to form after a run of low scores.

BRADMAN FOLLOWED, WEARING A sweater in the hot sunshine; he fumbled with two balls from Smailes, one not too far from his leg-stump, and then he broke his duck with a shot to leg. He tried a cover-drive off Bowes and mistimed it; he tried to cut and nearly played on; he tried to drive off Bowes again, and the ball turned in from the off-side, hit the inside edge, and narrowly missed the leg-stump. He lashed Bowes off his face to the leg-boundary and glanced him to fine-leg; then got into a tangle with a ball swinging from leg and gave a

Bradman pulls a short delivery from Gubby Allen in the first Test of the 1936-37 Ashes series at Brisbane and starts off for a run. Courtesy of Film World.

Bowled by Verity for 82 in the second Test at Sydney, 1936–37.

Down the pitch again. Bradman cover-drives Morris Leyland on the first day of the fifth Test at Melbourne, 1936–37. He made 169.

radman faces the newsreel cameras after docking at Southampton at the start of the 1938 Ashes tour. From the Ronald Cardwell Collection.

Australia's best-known couple.

Squash player. He won the South Australian title in 1939.

Cricketers in uniform: Lieutenant Bradman and Sergeant-Major Fleetwood-Smith at Frankston, 194

Bradman and Arthur Morris, wearing his NSW cap, on their way to the middle in an Australian XI-MCC match in Melbourne in November 1946. Both made centuries. Courtesy of the Herald & Weekly Times Ltd.

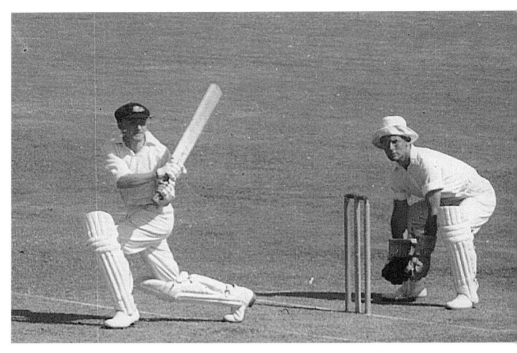

Bradman swings to leg during his innings of 187 in the first Test at Brisbane, 1946–47.

\Opposing captains in the 1946–47 Ashes series, Bradman and Wally Hammond.
Relations between them were sometimes strained.

Courtesy of the Herald & Weekly Times Ltd.

An autograph hunter, Brisbane, 1946–47.
Courtesy of News Ltd.

Bradman with Sid Barnes, second Test 1946–47, at Sydney. Both scored 234.

chance to Leyland's left-hand at 8. He smashed Bowes past cover. Woodfull stood watching him gravely, and then walking up and down in his tense way even more than usual he could say with all sincerity: 'It hurts me, Bradman, more than you.' For Woodfull would not mind if his side went down for 120 if Bradman could only make 100 of them in the 1930 way.

Bradman began to find himself. Back strokes flowed to the boundary; a man was moved from slip; he cut the next ball past the space. As sometimes in a symphonic movement group after group of instruments enters, so came new stroke after new stroke, until at 50 in seventy minutes the whole orchestra was on. He ran out to Macaulay and drove him for a mighty six over mid-off's head, not a hit but a drive, left shoulder forward and the bat swinging true down the line of the ball. Macaulay retreated, and two fours to cover came in the same over: Yorkshire blocked the cover-point boundary, and he hit the off-side ball over mid-on. When they blocked there he swept it in front of square leg, and then went back to the off-side boundary over mid-off's head. Verity, getting nothing from the wicket, set an off-side field, with Wood, the wicket-keeper, standing a foot outside the off-side stump and slip twenty-five yards away. No ball dropped on the wicket, and Bradman accepted the challenge, swinging his body over and driving without fear; twice he got through, once square and the second time through cover. The second 50 came in thirty minutes, and the last 40 in fifteen, a perfect kaleidoscope of stroke-making, balls pulled from a yard outside the off-stump and then, with four men out, a late cut.

Leyland, the heaviest sufferer, bowled him in the end. As he went in the Sheffield crowd rose at him; few, if any, had ever seen an innings like this, and, apart from the runs, it is an innings charged with significance. The Australians from the balcony of their dressing-room applauded him heartily. Was it a return to form? No living batsman and few dead ones could surpass the ease, the variety, and the power of the 22 fours and two sixes which were the boundary strokes of this marvellous display;

but there was that nasty quarter of an hour at the beginning; one cannot ignore it. It is not bowling, nor wicket, nor anything; the trouble origi- nates from Bradman, and it is Bradman who will solve it, and on whether he does so or not this season hangs the whole issue of the Tests.

ADMIRABLE IN WHATEVER GUISE

By Lord Tennyson

Tennyson, the former England captain, wrote this in a newspaper column after Bradman's 304 in the Leeds Test in 1934.

BEFORE I OFFER (with all humility) my team for the Oval, I would pay tribute to Don Bradman. You may search the records of international cricket as you will, and you will not find a greater feat than he performed at Leeds.

His effort may not be valued by his colossal score; it was the iron discipline of the man, the sacrifice of his real self for his country, his unsuspected patience, the scorn with which he answered his critics, that was the wonder, the delight, the masterfulness of his innings; his defiance, his magnetism—that was the mightiness of his conquest. At heart Bradman is, I am sure, all for gaiety and high adventure; he has to a greater degree, perhaps, than any other batsman, the faculty to make a success of any role he chooses to affect.

There have been occasions when sticklers for what we are pleased to call style have professed to see flaws in his batsmanship. I make bold to say that Bradman has all the strokes, and then some. He is compe- tent to play any game—the game that, in its dash and gusto, is typically Bradmanesque, or one that tells of the complete scholar. And in what- ever guise he compels admiration. He is no run-getting machine; Bradman is a genius.

STILLNESS, THEN LIGHTNING MOVEMENT

By Pelham Warner

From a commentary in the London Daily Telegraph *on Bradman's 304 in the Leeds Test, 1934.*

A PURIST MIGHT ARGUE that Bradman's bat was occasionally not straight, but ordinary rules do not govern a player who, perhaps, is the greatest batting genius the game has produced. Bradman showed in the last half hour that he could, if he wished, be one of the greatest of drivers pure and simple.

It is strikingly apparent how absolutely still Bradman stands until the ball is half way down the pitch. Then follows a lightning movement of his feet and the bat, and the ball crashes into the crowd. His stamina is remarkable. He never seemed the least bit tired, and was running as quickly at the end of the day as if he were just beginning.

SCORING MACHINE

By Wilfred Rhodes

From a newspaper report of Bradman's innings in the Leeds Test, 1934. Bradman was 271 not out at stumps.

THE SCORING MACHINE—THAT is Bradman—got to work again today and our bowlers had to pay tribute, as we all knew they would have to do, as soon as Bradman decided that the time had come for him to move seriously along the run-getting road.

He never hurried—never dashed, as cricketers say—yet at the end of a day on which he was at the wicket for five minutes less than six and a half hours he had 271 runs to his name. He scored over a hundred runs in the last hundred minutes, and just as there was no indication of quick-scoring in his general outlook, so, when he left the field, there was no suggestion that he was tired after the strain of standing at the wicket for so long.

Frankly, I do not know which is the most remarkable feature about this very remarkable young man, who is, all the way round, the best scoring batsman I have seen. He has all the shots; he can apparently use them at will: he has wonderful strength in his wrists and forearms, and his timing is so perfect that one knows the quickest of eyesight is allied with lightning footwork and an astonishing judgment of the length of a ball; and, with all this, he has the confidence he has a right to have in his power, and a determination that enables him to do almost as he pleases.

I have heard a story that when he was playing his record Australia vs England Test innings at Headingley on the last tour—a record that he may easily beat on Monday morning—he was asked at lunch-time how he felt. His reply was characteristic: 'Good for the day.'

And I am prepared to believe that when he got up this morning he (knowing the beautiful condition of the Headingley wicket) said to himself: 'Well, I think that, seeing we are at Headingley again, I'll get a few runs for Australia, and, incidentally, have a go at topping the 334 innings I played here four years ago.'

All today he batted like a man determined to fulfil a promise to himself, and he has served Australia as well as a batsman can serve his country. Do not overlook the fact that when Bradman and Ponsford went to the wicket this morning there was the threat of Bowes, the man who took three wickets in 10 balls last night, hanging over their heads. What happened? Bowes had two balls left in the over in which he took the wickets of Oldfield and Woodfull, and Bradman had to face

Bowes. Now Bowes had to loosen himself, and each of the balls was understandably a trifle short. Bradman played two beautiful back shots to get two 4's, and ever afterwards he was the commanding figure of the day.

It may be that his innings was not an innings for the spectators. They probably looked, after all they have heard of the other Bradman of whom we have seen so much this season, for some fast and furious hitting of the type we saw at Sheffield on Monday. They got the furious hitting, but it was served to them in doses.

Whenever a loose ball was sent along Bradman was there to hit it safely with a wickedly vicious bat—I don't think I have seen a man so vicious with a loose ball as Bradman can be—and all the time he missed very few scoring chances, without ever noticeably seeking to rush the score along. The Bradman we saw today was a sound Bradman taking, in the correct way, the right toll of steady bowling on a wicket good enough to delight the heart of any batsman.

He was, so far as I could see, only beaten once, and then, when his score was 56, he played over what appeared to be a half-volley from Mitchell. It was a difficult stumping chance, for Ames would be blinded by the batsman and he would have to guess a little in going for the ball, but nevertheless it was just a chance. For the remainder of the day, if one excepts the first period in which Bowes desperately tried to bounce the ball, Bradman's bat simply met the ball and dealt with it on its merits. As I saw Bradman's score mount steadily with Ponsford's and Australia's, I had a feeling of sympathy for our bowlers, for I have always said, since I first saw this young man from Australia, that he is the hardest man to keep quiet I have ever bowled to.

He has so many shots—every one of them—he is so sharp at judging the length of a ball, and, what is more, he can place the ball with such astonishing accuracy. When you watch Bradman seriously at work you see hitting as crisp as anything you ever will see, you see forcing back shots played with a dead straight bat, and you see leg hits that are leg hits, made with timing that is the acme of perfection. Watch Bradman's leg-glide. Not only does he glide the ball to place it, but he jabs hard to help that ball along, and there the steel that's in his wrists and forearms makes itself felt. It was Bradman all the way today.

DON BRADMAN

By 'Cornstalk'

A poem from 1934.

Do you know Don Bradman?
Our Bowral boy Don Bradman.
Whose 19–30 history
Has oft been sung before?
Well, then you know that Bradman.
The marvellous Don Bradman.
Became a man of mystery
In 19–34.

For you recall how Bradman.
When critics wrote: *'Don Bradman*
Has reached a stage that's tragic.
His golden days are o'er.'
At Leeds with bright blade flashing.
Irresistible and dashing.
Enthralled us with his magic
And the splendour of his score.

'Twas there the peerless Bradman.
The one and only Bradman.

Carved out for Young Australia
A lesson and a law:
Not his to knuckle under.
He tore Fate's web asunder.
HE CONQUERED SELF—we'll thunder
That lesson evermore.

PERFECT ARTISTRY

By Reverend R. Birch Hoyle

A press comment on Bradman's 244 in the fifth Test, 1934.

IF EVER THERE WERE a wizard with a cricket bat, it is Don Bradman. From a quarter to twelve till a quarter past six those of us who were lucky to be at Kennington Oval last Saturday saw record after record go by the board, and saw in the centre of the emerald patch the slight figure of a youth withstanding what one newspaper called 'England's treble battery of fast bowlers.' Coming in when the score board read 21 for one wicket, though the bowlers tried all kinds of wiles, not till the score had reached 472 did Bradman leave the centre of the Oval, and amid an upstanding, uproarious crowd pass into the pavilion to doff his pads. Even then he need not have got out, for the fatal stroke was a two-handed slam at a 'bumper' which he could safely have left to wing its flight high in the air. He had given no chance while over 450 runs were scored, 244 of then coming from his own bat, while Ponsford, his partner, amassed 205 runs.

To see perfection in any art is a joy to the soul. We saw the perfect artistry of the world's greatest batsman. Even as a study in psychology the innings was a gem. Four crashing strokes to the boundary signalled his arrival at the wickets. *Joie de vivre* was at the back of each stroke.

One wondered if the wild, untamed lust to smite would get the upper hand, as so often in his earlier innings this year. Then the subdual of the champing steed was seen. For nearly forty minutes his score stood at 25. Every ball was watched with an eye as keen as a hawk's. At the other end, Ponsford was steadily putting on fours and singles, what time Don had played himself in. Then his cannonade began. No fewer than fifteen fours were in his first hundred. All eyes were riveted on that slender figure. He stood perfectly still until the ball had crossed more than half the distance of the cricket pitch, then swiftly the brain measured the length, the bat was poised for the stroke, and, like a flash, the ball was away among the spectators seated on the grass behind the ropes.

The agile motion of Bradman's feet were worthy of a Pavlova. One shot, among many, lingers in the memory most bewitchingly. The ball looked like hitting his boot—a 'Yorker'—from the Yorkshire Son of Anak, Bowes; then, *hey presto*! the feet twinkled, stepped a pace back; bat and ball were in perfectly timed contact, and lo! the ball was in the crowd in the twinkling of an eye! All kinds of bowling came alike to the silvery willow he wielded. Now it was pulled hard to the 'on'; next moment a flashing blade had sent the ball between the stately Woolley and the kingly Hammond in the slips. What power there is in Bradman's forearms! Again and again balls pitched close up were forced away to the boundary, where first-class batsmen would have been satisfied to have simply defended their wicket. And so hour after hour went by and one wondered if ever that lissom figure could get out.

Two Australians, 1934

By J. M. Kilburn

From In Search Of Cricket, *1937.*

D. G. Bradman and W. H. Ponsford, batsmen of Australia, have at least one characteristic in common; they amass huge scores. Fifty to them is merely indicative of the playing-in period safely passed, the century but 'a milestone along the road to progress, the end of the journey lying ever beyond'. Time and again these batsmen have made scores of over 200, not infrequently they have passed the 300 mark, and innings of 400 and more are not unknown to them.

Batsmen cannot make such big scores with such consistency without having something in common in their method, and in the case of Bradman and Ponsford the common factor is their determination. Determination to succeed in their self-appointed task makes them forego the delights of ordinary batsmen, makes them ignore or quell the craving for one wild glorious moment leading inevitably to destruction, and keeps them along the same road all the time. For them there is no wandering in the fragrant bypaths of big sixes and improbably unorthodox shots. They have their limitations, of which they are fully aware, and they never venture beyond the boundary fence of their own proved ability to dabble in the prohibited lands of uncertainty. Thus, and thus only, are great scores made with regularity.

But with this much in common, Bradman and Ponsford then diverge widely in matters of detail. Test match spectators have had rare opportunity to study the difference between these two men, for this year they have been together in two stands which developed into affairs in which the only records left to be broken were their own.

Bradman is unquestionably the greater batsman of the two. Ponsford is always a little hesitant in starting; there is always a certain straining of his eyes and tentative pushing of the bat at the start of his innings, and there is always a period when the bowler can delude himself into believing that he might easily get Ponsford out. With Bradman there is no such hesitation. If he is to play a big innings, the signs are there from the first; without any delay or preamble he is hitting the ball in the middle of the bat and scoring runs with contemptuous ease. Nobody who saw those two back shots in the first over on that memorable Saturday at Leeds could help but read the writing on the wall or fail to appreciate its significance.

Bradman deals safely and profitably with balls that Ponsford makes no attempt to master. It is very doubtful if there is any batsman in the world who hits so hard as does Bradman the ball, of whatever pace, pitched only just short of a length on or outside the leg stick. Not for Bradman the swift covering up movement and the bat loosely held lest the ball spring off into the waiting leg trap. He stays where he is in line with the ball and, timing his shot to the last fraction of a second, hooks with all the incredible power in his wrists. Were he to miss the ball he would himself be hit, but that accident occurs very rarely indeed.

For this particular ball, Ponsford has no counter. He could, no doubt, play the usual defensive back shot and risk a simple catch to short leg, but he invariably prefers to turn his back and allow the ball to hit him in a manner which has more than once drawn derisive and scornful laughter from the spectators. Ponsford apparently admits his inability to deal with this particular ball, and rather than risk losing his wicket in attempting to master it, he prefers to suffer what must amount to considerable physical pain. In view of these methods one can readily appreciate that leg-theory as bowled by Larwood, and as bowled by anyone else, is a distinctly variable quantity.

Not that Ponsford is without many good shots; he cuts delightfully and as safely as anyone can cut, but he has this stroke under control and reserves it for the appropriate ball; never will he cut at anything not simply asking to be cut.

Bradman does not cut as late as does Ponsford. He requires less time to see the ball and prefers to play it more towards (and invariably past) point, the ball leaving the bat with the speed of a bullet from a gun. Generally speaking, all Bradman's shots are played harder than Ponsford's, because Bradman's timing is so immeasurably superior. Ponsford gives the impression of playing forward more than Bradman; Ponsford plays forward as a defensive measure without any intention of making a scoring shot. To such balls Bradman finds an extra instant in which to play a forcing shot off his right foot, the ball generally going towards mid-on.

Bradman goes forward to drive, and drives with a full swing of the bat, hitting the ball with tremendous force through the covers, but rarely straight. Ponsford is more sparing in his use of the drive, waiting patiently for the half-volley, without ever going to look for one on his own. Bradman, of course, is far and away the more beautiful bat. Where Ponsford crouches at the wicket, Bradman stands upright, creating no impression of tenseness and strain, simple as a monarch surveying his all. Ponsford can become boring to watch, but Bradman, because of the miraculous power and perfection of timing, holds the interest to the end.

It may seem that Ponsford does not come out too well from the comparison. Let it be remembered that it is only a comparison, and however superior in technique and attraction Bradman may be, Ponsford must have proved to his own and the satisfaction of everyone else that he knows a thing or two concerning the scoring of runs.

SUPERIORITY TOO OVERWHELMING

By Neville Cardus

A newspaper report of Bradman's 132 in 90 minutes against H. D. Leverson-Gower's XI at Scarborough, 1934.

W YATT COULD HAVE HAD the new ball before luncheon today if he had wanted it; a captain usually has tentative plans laid for all emergencies, but it was unlikely that Wyatt was prepared for this one. The chief cause of the abnormality, in fact the only cause, was Bradman. Farnes, bowling at a good pace, seemed to be in-swinging the new ball. Brown edged a short one past his leg stump and soon after played on; Bradman tried to drive a half-volley wide outside the off-stump with a horizontal bat and barely dug it out of the wicket with the inside edge. He stood away to hit another splendid ball from Farnes and just snicked it off his leg stump. At the other end Bowes swung a ball away from his drive and Sutcliffe either just got to it or just failed, the ball going extremely low and wide to his left. With his score still under twenty Bradman gave a chance that Wyatt dropped, off Farnes. Wyatt and Bradman are the only persons who can give any opinion about the merits of this chance; it was straight to Wyatt, in the gully, between his legs a foot from the ground, but it was no mis-hit; it was a cut from the centre of the bat, and there ends the list of Bradman's delinquencies.

His excellences were multifarious and unique; he drove Farnes's fastest half-volleys past mid-off for four; he would stand back to Nichols and if Nichols turned from the off put him to the on boundary, and if from the leg through the covers. Verity he stretched down to and pulled to the on boundary twice in an over, with an extra-cover boundary thrown in. Nichols, changing ends, left the slips open. Bradman tapped him through them; it was much easier than hitting, and the ball went down to the boundary just the same. Furthermore Bradman was nursing a sore right hand, which gave him a lot of trouble. After the first excitement this sort of thing becomes slightly monotonous. A bowler bowls, Bradman makes a stroke, not a single fieldsman moves, and the ball is returned from the boundary. The essence of any game is conflict, and there was no conflict here; the superiority on one side was too overwhelming. Bradman was 50 in 38 minutes and 100 in 80; then he started running out to Verity, and either drove him high to the on boundary or along the ground past cover. He hit him for 19 runs in an over, and scored 32 in ten minutes before he was stumped. Just as he begins his innings Bradman will, occasionally, show uncertainty for ten minutes, sometimes for only two or three balls. Bowlers must get him out then, otherwise he will bat until he feels inclined to go. There is not the slightest doubt that had he wished he could have continued to play quietly—that is to say, at a mere 80 per hour—and made 200 long before tea.

SYMPATHY FOR AN IDOL

From an editorial in the Sydney Morning Herald, *29 September 1934. The editorial was inspired by Bradman's sudden and serious illness with an appendicitis at the end of the 1934 tour of England.*

IT MAY TRULY BE said that in both his homeland, and in the country which is the home of the game he has enriched with his skill, everybody, young and old, has heard with intimate sorrow of the grave illness of Don Bradman. A new admiration is added for his brilliant display in the last matches of the Australian tour in England by the knowledge now that he played his great innings in the fifth Test with a large blood clot on the muscle of his right thumb. His old trouble of excessive bleeding when injured adds to the anxiety felt when it was announced that he was operated upon hurriedly for appendicitis in an acute stage. The statement by Sir Douglas Shields, the eminent surgeon attending him, that 'the boy is very ill, and will continue to be for a long time' caused consternation in Sydney yesterday, although the surgeon added, 'there is definitely no cause for alarm'. Arrangements have been made for transfusion of blood if necessary. Bulletins are issued regularly from his sick-bed in tribute to the widespread public concern over his illness. King George and Queen Mary have telephoned from Balmoral expression of their solicitude. The fight for recovery by this idol of cricketing enthusiasts on both sides of the world is of first-class international interest; and there could be no more remarkable token of the great name he has made in the sporting entertainment of legions of British people. As the London Press declares, Bradman has captured the imagination of the British public, besides the Australian, as perhaps the greatest batsman in the annals of cricket, especially when account is taken of the moral ascendancy he has asserted on the field.

For some time Bradman has been playing under grave difficulties a game made the more strenuous from popular expectation from him of superlative performance. It is clear now that he has been overstraining himself, and that constitutionally he has been running risks of which most of his admirers knew little or nothing. It seems equally clear that, whatever the risk, Bradman had to carry on at the high pitch demanded by the idolising populace—so tyrannical a thing is pre-eminence in the sporting field. The time has come, in fairness to him, to abate that high demand. The risk has been run for too long. Now that Bradman is called upon to pay the penalty for it in this dangerous illness, the sympathy for him will be the greater from appreciation of the gallantry with which he responded to the call for popular entertainment and the exactions it laid upon him. His youth adds a pathetic touch to his illness, for the famous cricketer, who has made such splendid batting history, is still only twenty-six years of age. The laurels which the Australians won on their recent tour indeed turned to ashes temporarily for every Australian at the news of the stricken condition of this outstanding national champion in the game. He has won more than admiration; he has won the public heart. It hardly requires saying that the period of anxiety which, the cables inform us, must continue for a week, will hold the attention of every Australian. Bradman has been idolised for his maintained brilliance and his almost superhuman skill. All hearts will go out to him the more because his admirers realise at last that he is not superhuman at all, and that in the cause of satisfying public demands upon him he has exceeded the limits of what was fair to his own physical capacity.

THE THREE 'HOURS'

By Thomas Wood

From Cobbers, *1934.*

SHE [SYDNEY] IS, AS the wits point out, three hours ahead of anything else that matters in the whole of Australia, in spite of all that the clocks can say—Our Harbour, Our Bridge, and Our Bradman.

OUT OF THE PUBLIC EYE

By R. S. Whitington

From Cricket Caravan, *1950. Whitington played for South Australia under Bradman's captaincy in the 1930s.*

BRADMAN CAME TO SOUTH Australia for his own good and private reasons. We were perfectly happy to treat him exactly as we found him and to give him all the loyalty he showed he deserved. I was then still but a youth and was even prepared to idolise Bradman the man, just as I had idolised Bradman the cricketer. Hadn't I spent Saturday evening after Saturday evening vainly trying to convince my father, a dyed-in-the-wool Trumper fanatic, that Bradman was the greatest batsman in history? But Bradman the man was not so easy to idolise as Bradman the batsman. He decided, so far as I was concerned, to remain encased in a shell that any oyster would have envied. Getting through that shell proved a major work and might be compared with a Jewish attempt to enter the Moslem Dome of the Rock in Jerusalem. With Don it was a case of so far and no further for me.

I played for the same district club as Vic Richardson and was known to be one of his closest friends, but Bradman never became very trusting. He either did not realise or did not care that he had a potential idoliser at his elbow, albeit one who could not idolise with his eyes shut.

An incident which occurred in a lane running off Adelaide's King William Street one night about this time, however, was both illuminating and significant. We were standing in the semi-dark lane outside the exit from a cinema-theatre during the interval between films. The lane was almost deserted, most of the audience having either remained in their seats or used the main exit at the front of the theatre. Just as we were both moving back into the stalls, two young men, joking to each other and roaring with unrestrained laughter, approached along the lane. Rarely have I seen two people, who were obviously completely sober, quite so overjoyed with life. To my amazement one of the men proved to be Bradman. Bradman with someone he trusted, and out of the public eye, could clearly be as friendly and unreserved as anyone could wish.

As we went on tours together he gradually began to relax a little and, partnered by Charlie Walker, he would take me and Mervyn Waite or Ron Hamence on at sessions of auction bridge. Once, when the Sydney-Brisbane Express was delayed on a stifling night at Casino, Walker, Waite and I even persuaded him to share in a bottle or two of ice-cold beer with us but it took a mighty lot of persuasion. During my four years with the South Australian team, that was about the only occasion when I ever felt completely at home in Bradman's company. He became quite human after about two glasses. At other times there always seemed to be a veil of awkwardness between us. Bradman, in fact, in some strange way, always made me feel as if I were back at school. Many other cricketers and non-cricketers have told me they had exactly the same feeling in Don's presence, although he has relaxed considerably in recent years.

DUEL WITH O'REILLY

By Jack Fingleton

An account in the Sydney Sun *of Bradman's 212 in 202 minutes in the Bardsley-Gregory Testimonial match at Sydney, October 1936.*

FOR SOME YEARS NOW many New South Wales cricketers sat at ease in the pavilion and lazed away the hours while Don Bradman had piled up his centuries, double centuries and triple centuries in the middle of the field. It was not until yesterday afternoon that those of us who had played on the same New South Wales side as Bradman realised just how lucky we were in past years.

The Victorians, South Australians, Queenslanders, the Englishmen, the South Africans, and the West Indians have all been through it, and yesterday Don gave us, his former team-mates, our first practical demonstration of how hopeless it is to quell him when he is in the mood. There could never have been more interesting cricket in the history of the game than that bitter battle for just on an hour yesterday between two Australian cricketing immortals.

Names linger in cricket for years and time adds to the lustre of individuals and performance, but there in the flesh yesterday, each pitting his remarkable genius against the other's, were the two outstanding exponents of all that is great in modern batting and bowling. If memory is correct, the only subsequent time O'Reilly and Bradman had been against each other was when they played as lads in a final in the Bowral district. The story runs that Bradman was thrice dropped off O'Reilly before he got to 20. Bradman then went on to get 200.

Yesterday, years after, he got his usual double century. He sent the enthusiastic crowd into ecstasies as only Bradman can; he gave the fieldsmen sore feet; made the lads on the board work as they only work when Bradman is on the job; he made strangers friends as they slapped each other on the back in the thrill of his glut of boundaries; he sent thousands home as soon as he got out and doubtlessly made many late for appointments last night, for nobody dared leave the ground while he was cutting berserk—but before all this was possible Bradman had to play himself through a very hectic period with O'Reilly. Bradman made a very shaky beginning, which was not remarkable for he has had only net practice in which to find form, but he was just finding his batting feet when O'Reilly came on.

'This chap is a marvellous bowler,' said Bradman once as he was wiping his forehead. 'I have never before so enjoyed a duel with any bowler. It is fight all the way.'

Bradman gave O'Reilly every respect for a long time. For us in the leg positions it was most interesting to watch how he kept down deliveries which we have seen curl up in the air off the bats of other players. It was a thrilling battle and if Bradman triumphed in the end as he has triumphed over all other bowlers, it was not until he had brought all his genius to bear to ward off O'Reilly.

'Have you heard that new song for bowlers?' said McCormick once as he watched the ball being picked up from the boundary.

'No, Ernie,' said Don. 'What is it?' 'You're driving me crazy,' said McCormick as he caught the ball and went back to continue his hopeless task.

DON, DON, LAY THE WILLOW ON

Anon.

From a Sunday Sun *and* Guardian *cricket supplement, November 1936.*

Don, Don, lay the willow on;
there was none like you before you;
there'll be none when you are gone.

Come and bat again before us
till the arching sky that's o'er us
rattles with the mighty chorus:
'Don, Don, Don!'

WORTH RISKING THE WEATHER

By Ray Robinson

From an essay reproduced in After Stumps Were Drawn, *1985.*

BRADMAN HAD A PALPABLE distaste for playing on wickets sticky enough for him to expect the ball to rear. Few batsmen, if any, relish batting in such conditions, but none showed his aversion more plainly. Bradman's unrivalled skill normally allowed him to do almost as he liked. He was so accustomed to absolute monarchy that a rebellious wicket or a treasonable bumper robbed his batting of authority more than it did humbler batsmen not unacquainted with struggling for runs. He seemed as unhappy as a managing director would be pedalling a bicycle to work after years of having been ceremoniously delivered at the office door by limousine . . .

Because of this, Herbert Sutcliffe, England's opening batsman in 54 Tests, always made a point of adding 'on good wickets' when he described Bradman as the finest batsman of the day. Frank Woolley, Kent's incomparable left-hander, even went to the length of choosing a World XI in his book without giving Bradman a place, because of doubt about his ability on sticky wickets. To me, it would be safer selectorship to put Don in and chance the weather.

No Bradman, no cricket

By Keith Dunstan

From The Paddock That Grew—The Story Of The Melbourne Cricket Club*, 1962. Dunstan writes here of Albert Cuttriss, a long-serving official at the MCG.*

He [Cuttriss] has no doubts about the best time for cricket—this was the Bradman era of the nineteen-thirties. He remembers particularly the third Test match in 1936, the time when Bradman made his 270 and had his record 346 sixth-wicket partnership with Jack Fingleton. Bradman batted all the fourth day and that night he was still not out. Despite the fact that the fifth day was a working day the crowds flocked back. Albert says half the bicycles in Melbourne must have been at the ground that morning. In those days it was possible to check one's bike for threepence a time, and the staff had a terrible time coping with them. So the crowd came expecting a fantastic score from Bradman of 300, 400 or more. But he was out very quickly. Then as soon as he was out, although it was before lunch, half the crowd left. No Bradman, no cricket, as far as they were concerned.

BRADMAN MAD

By William Pollock

From So This Is Australia, *1937.*

AUSTRALIA IS BRADMAN MAD. You hear his name all day long in the mouths of men, women and children in the cricket season. Everything he says or does—or is supposed to say or do—is seized upon. 'Bradman is news,' an editor said to me. 'If he cut himself shaving it would be a front-page story.'

There are rather fewer people in the whole of Australia than there are in London, and most of them idolise their little champion of cricket. And the Don copes with it splendidly. He might so easily be an insufferable young man with a swollen head.

Actually, however, he is friendly, he smiles quickly, he is generous about other people, he has an alert mind and a level head. Don is a go-getter in business as in cricket. He is with Harry Hodgetts, of the Board of Cricket Control, in stockbroking in Adelaide. He works hard and is well off. I have heard people say he is worth £10,000. I don't pretend to know. He is fond of music and can play the piano. He is a good dancer. He reads a good deal, particularly history and travel. He talks intelligently on all sorts of subjects. He is practically a non-drinker and a non-smoker.

In talking to a learned doctor about his batting, I asked, 'What makes him so quick with his bat?' Said the learned doctor: 'Afferent and efferent nerves. They are the nerves which control our body actions. The afferent nerve telegraphs from eye to brain, the efferent nerve from brain to limbs. In my opinion, Don Bradman's efferent and afferent work quicker than most people's.'

Don drinks a little ginger beer and 'a nice cuppa,' as they call tea in Australia.

'Why don't you have a beer?' I said to him one evening. 'Good for you.'

'No, thanks. Haven't had more than six glasses of the stuff in my life, and don't like it,' he said. Occasionally he takes a glass of sherry.

It is an extraordinary experience to see Don coming in to bat in Australia. The crowd become nearly hysterical at the sight of him, and directly he gets off the mark you'd think he had given away a million pounds. One thing I noticed about him is that he walks out to the wicket much more briskly than he used to. The last time he was in England he walked in very slowly, apparently taking time to get his eyes accustomed to the light. Here he almost marched in. He has speeded up.

Is his pre-eminence good for Australian cricket? I wonder. When he is out hundreds of people at once start to leave the ground. They have simply come to see him. It is surely not a good thing when the individual—any individual, whether 'W.G.', Ranji, Jessop, Hobbs, or Bradman—becomes bigger than the game. Cricket must always be greater than its players.

Bradman, married to a pretty and attractive wife, lives in Kensington, outside Adelaide. He has built himself a charming house big enough to have its billiards room; yet he makes next to nothing—*directly*—out of cricket. He gets £30 for playing a Test match. When he plays in England he makes about £600 out of the tour. So in four years his cricket brings him in roughly £750. Indirectly, of course, it is cricket which has put him where he is, financially as well as famously.

And he is probably the greatest gate attraction cricket has ever known—a far greater money-spinner at the turnstiles than were 'W.G.', Ranji, Jack Hobbs. Nearly £30,000 was taken at the gates in the third Test in Melbourne. I should say that Bradman drew at least £2,000 into the ground when there was a prospect of him batting.

Yet all 'the King of Australia' (as he is called) gets is, say, £5 a day—which is precisely what Sievers, Ward, Rigg—others who do not draw a penny to the gates—are paid. It is all slightly absurd. What would happen if Bradman thought he would go on strike and not play unless he were paid, say, a thousand pounds per Test? The Board of Control would throw a fit and run round in circles—but they would have to pay up. The crowds would not come if Bradman were not playing.

One thing I have learned in Australia is that cricket is no longer a team game there; it is a 'star' game where gates are concerned. Four years ago it was Larwood who drew the crowds; this time it was Bradman. Don is the one and only real star attraction. People who know nothing about cricket go to see him bat, women in particular.

Now, I don't counsel Don to go on strike for more money—heaven forbid—but it does occur to me to wonder what would Babe Ruth or Bobby Jones or Alex James or Fred Perry have thought of £750 in four years for playing their games? I rather think they would have laughed and laughed and laughed. It is all nonsense to pretend that big cricket is something apart—something that should somehow be independent of money. It just isn't. The idea behind the Tests is to get as much money as possible. Without the Tests, first-class cricket could not live either in Australia or in England.

I am not Bradman's publicity man, but I will say this: Australian cricket is at the moment very largely dependent upon him. He is away by himself as the man who draws the money. He is the star entertainer of Australia—a far more widely popular star than Harry Lauder, who did an hour's broadcast there for, it was said, a fee of £500. And so, if they will excuse me, it is childish of other Australian cricketers to resent the crowd appeal of Bradman. They may not, some of them, like it very much, but they are largely dependent on him in cricket's fight against all sorts of counter-attractions.

I think I met only one person in Australia who could not talk about Bradman—a young woman. 'I'm afraid I don't know anything about him,' she said. Perhaps it was a pose.

CHEERING NEWS

By Bernard O'Reilly

In February 1937, acting on a hunch, mountain bushman Bernard O'Reilly set off into the rainforests of the McPherson Range in search of a Stinson airliner which had disappeared with seven people aboard eight days before. This is his account, as told to a Sydney Morning Herald *reporter, of how he eventually found the wrecked plane and two survivors, both near death.*

I SAW A BURNT clearing and the wreckage of a plane. As I came to the edge of the clearing I saw two men, one lying on the ground and the other sitting up. When they saw me one of them called, 'Come down here. We want to shake hands with you'. The other man said, 'Me, too'. I hurried over and shook hands with them. Then there was silence for a second. We were all too excited to speak. One of them broke the silence saying to the other, 'We will be able to have that drink at the Australia after all'. 'What's the score?' was the question one of them asked. I told them that Bradman was 165 not out and it seemed to cheer them immensely.

GRACE RECALLED

By Daniel Reese

From Was It All Cricket? *Reese was a prominent New Zealand cricketer in the early 1900s.*

IF BRADMAN'S STATURE WAS small, his bat was full width! His slow walk to the wickets did not prepare one for the change of atmosphere that occurred the moment he took strike.

My first glimpse of the new champion was on the Melbourne cricket ground when he was playing for the Australian XI against the Rest of Australia. When batting his whole attitude was one of eagerness for runs. The bowlers tried harder, the fieldsmen became keener, the public sat up and watched. The off theory that for years had been left alone was now dealt with as it had been twenty and thirty years earlier. His cut behind point, his hitting the ball between the fieldsmen, was the same as that of the Grace I had seen at Crystal Palace. Soon he was scoring half as fast again as the previous batsman had done. It was a delight to see him scoring freely off bowling that other batsmen found difficulty in playing. I found myself comparing him with the champions of the past. I saw flashes of the genius of Grace and Trumper, but his technique was the technique of Grace, and his scoring strokes, also, more like those of 'W.G.' Like Grace, he was busy—busy all the time—and runs came from his bat at a rate that made the score mount rapidly. Cricket could never be a dull game when Bradman was batting. Although Bradman has a wide range of strokes it is mainly his placing that enables him to score at such speed. Imagine this in a Test match when he scored a century before lunch, another before the tea adjournment and still another before stumps! Grace twice scored 300 runs in a day against the best bowling in England, and Trumper got a similar number in a county match in 1899, while Macartney has scored a century before lunch, but since then no other player, till the arrival of Bradman, has scored as fast and kept it up for so long. He has not the poise and graceful style of Ranjitsinhji and Trumper, but has all the mastery of strokes and machine-like precision of Grace.

The hold that Bradman had on the people's interest is to be seen in an experience of a New Zealand friend of mine who, when visiting Australia in 1936, saw a Test match at Melbourne. He noticed a woman, sitting next to him in the pavilion, take out her knitting and begin intently watching the stitches as she turned the heel of a sock. Presently my friend said to her: 'Aren't you going to watch the cricket?'

'Oh, Bradman's out,' was the prompt reply!

MINTIES DO THE TRICK

An advertisement for Minties, 1937.

The bells of England bellow
Big Ben becomes unstuck
Policemen shout, the Guards turn out
When Bradman makes a duck!

But why should Don be dismal
Or beat with grief his brow?
Why curse a kick?
The cure is quick
One packet of Minties does the trick—
And second innings—wow!

CENTURY IN THE GLOOM

By Ralph Barker

From Ten Great Bowlers, *1967. Bradman's innings of 103 which Barker describes here was largely responsible for Australia's narrow first-innings lead in the third Test, 1938. Bill O'Reilly took 10 wickets in the match, bowling Australia to a five-wicket victory.*

BRADMAN HAD HAD TWO previous Test Match innings at Leeds, and his average there was 319. Now, as he sat on the pavilion balcony with his pads on, watching Fingleton and Brown open for Australia, England's apprehensions can be imagined. 'Everything depends on you,' said Hammond to his bowlers, and they responded well, picking up a wicket before close of play when Wright came on at 28 and bowled Brown with his first ball, a leg-spinner that kept low. B. A. Barnett appeared as night-watchman, and Australia ended the day at 32 for 1. England's situation, however, still looked desperate.

Next day, on a dull, misty morning, England were frustrated by that most irritating of cricket phenomena, the night-watchman who keeps his lamps burning next day. Barnett, of course, was a useful player, a left-hander, unstylish, but sound in method. He often looked in trouble against Verity, as did Fingleton, but this pair added 55 runs before Fingleton, who had hardly lifted his bat all morning, was bowled by Verity trying a short-arm hook, 87 for 2.

Bradman, who came next, was applauded all the way to the wicket, the whole Yorkshire crowd standing for him to a man. He too began scratchily against Verity. He didn't middle the ball at first, nearly played on and nearly spooned a half-volley to mid-off. After breaking his duck he sliced Wright luckily for three, but then settled down.

The light became steadily worse, yet Bradman was batting now with almost ridiculous ease. Twice in successive balls he drove Bowes through the covers for four. Barnett completed his 50, but five minutes before lunch he slashed at Farnes and was caught behind by Price. Lunch was taken at 128 for 3.

All through lunch the cloud built up to the west, enveloping the ground in a murky thunder haze and threatening rain. Australia were only 95 behind with seven wickets to fall, but England had the runs on the board and rain would be to their advantage. When play was resumed the light was still bad, and it quickly became sepulchral. Bradman batted without a cap. Hammond used Farnes and Bowes, hoping to pick up a wicket before the inevitable appeal came against the light. McCabe had his off-stump knocked out of the ground by Farnes, playing back when he should have gone forward, but still there was no appeal. 136 for 4. Badcock played all round a ball from Bowes, and that was 145 for 5. No one could see the ball in the murk—no one, that is, except Bradman.

Why in heaven's name didn't he appeal against the light? No one could understand it. No Test match in living memory had continued through such an eclipse. Australian wickets were tumbling. Yet Bradman was working to a tactical plan. He knew what he was doing.

Bradman had convinced himself that his side would get more runs before the rain came, even in semi-darkness, than afterwards on a wet wicket. He had not forgotten Verity at Lord's in 1934. He was seeing the ball well enough himself, and he backed himself to go on seeing it, to make enough runs to pass England's first innings total virtually on his own. Then if it rained it would be England who would be caught.

This for Bradman made tactical sense. It was a gamble, but Bradman was prepared to gamble in this match, for strategic as well as tactical reasons. The stakes were high. Since he wasn't sure he could win at the Oval, he had to win here. No one would have guessed from Bradman's demeanour that he was aware of the chance he was taking. One mistake by Bradman and Australia could be out for 150. Yet he seemed almost unnaturally unconcerned. Between overs he was chatting with the England players, laughing and gesticulating, treating the situation as a huge joke. It was no joke for the man at the other end—nor, of course, for Bradman.

The man at the other end was now Lindsay Hassett. While Hassett, striving desperately to stay there, suffered agonies of indecision, Bradman went on quietly and effortlessly building up the Australian total. He cut, he drove, he deflected, he even went down on his right knee to sweep. Even in this nocturnal atmosphere he reached 50 in 85 minutes. Hammond, forced to rest Farnes and Bowes so as to have them fresh for the new ball, due at 200, used Verity and Wright. The Australian score crept to within 28 runs of the England total. Then Hassett was caught at slip by Hammond off Wright. 195 for 6.

Waite came in and spoke to Bradman on his way to the wicket. But Bradman's instructions were firm. There was to be no appeal against the light until England took the new ball. Soon the score passed 200,

Hammond signified his intention of bringing back Farnes and Bowes, and Bradman appealed against the light. It was no more than a formality, and the players left the field. Curiously enough, as soon as they disappeared the light improved dramatically. Tea was taken, and twenty minutes later the players were back.

The new ball was taken on the restart. Bradman edged Bowes through the slips for four, but otherwise he was as sure as before. He protected Waite from the new ball, farming the bowling, and the partnership had overtaken England's score and added 37 runs before Waite was caught behind off Farnes. 232 for 7. Bradman was 97 not out, and in the next over he reached his hundred. Of all his innings in Test cricket this was surely the most astonishing. One doubts if anyone else in the game's history could have played it. None of the other Australians could play their shots at all. Yet he reached his hundred in two and three quarter hours.

THE HAND THAT BOWLED BRADMAN

By Bill Andrews

From The Hand That Bowled Bradman, *1973. Here, in the preface to his memoirs, the former Somerset all-rounder explains the origin of the book's unusual title.*

M<small>Y LIFE HAS BEEN</small> peopled by great cricketing names—and great characters. This book is about most of them. They include the peerless Wally Hammond, who, I suspect, vetoed my one real chance of a Test place, and Don Bradman, who figures in the title of this book. At Taunton in 1938 he gave me his wicket. He took a blind swipe and I bowled him. Hence the light-hearted greeting I've used ever since when meeting someone for the first time, 'Shake the hand that bowled Bradman'.

Perhaps I should add that he had scored 202 at the time.

OUT OF THE ORDINARY

By Walter Hammond

From Cricket's Secret History, *1952.*

I WAS FORCED TO admire the cool way Don batted. On one or two occasions, when he was well set, and when he saw me move a fieldsman, he would raise his gloved hand to me in mock salute, and then hit the next ball *exactly* over the place from which the man had just been moved. Reluctantly I had to admit once more that he was out of the ordinary run of batsmen—a genius!

THE BRADMAN CLASS

By C. P. Snow

From a chapter on the British mathematician G. H. Hardy in Variety of Men.

IN 1911 HE [HARDY] began a collaboration with Littlewood which lasted thirty-five years. In 1913 he discovered Ramanujan and began another collaboration. All his major work was done in these two partnerships, most of it in the one with Littlewood, the most famous collaboration in the history of mathematics. There has been nothing like it in any science, or, so far as I know, in any other field of creative activity. Together they produced nearly a hundred papers, a good many of them 'in the Bradman class'. Mathematicians not intimate with Hardy in his later years, nor with cricket, keep repeating that his highest term of praise was 'in the Hobbs class'. It wasn't; very reluctantly, because Hobbs was one of his pets, he had to alter the order of merit. I once had a postcard from him, probably in 1938, saying: 'Bradman is a whole class above any batsman who has ever lived: if Archimedes, Newton and Gauss remain in the Hobbs class, I have to admit the possibility of a class above them, which I find difficult to imagine. They had better be moved from now on into the Bradman class.'

THE KING DELAYED

By Bert Oldfield

From an article in the Sydney Morning Herald, *15 March 1938.*

WHEREIN LIES BRADMAN'S GREATNESS as a batsman? Granted he has a quick eye, fleetness of foot, uncanny anticipation, and unlimited patience, but behind these obvious qualities lie a will and mind that govern all his movements. His development of stroke play and self-control as he progressed in the game was to me amazing. I have seen him, when dismissed for small scores, quietly sitting in the dressing-room, like a student pondering the cause of his mistake, and thinking out effective methods of overcoming the error. He has always been a keen critic of his own defects and this, no doubt, is the secret behind all his greatness and success.

At Lord's, during the Leeds Test match of 1930, the late King George was viewing the match from the committee-room. So interested was he that when reminded of an important engagement in London he declared he would not leave the ground until Bradman had completed his century. This Bradman did very soon, and after the King's departure went on to compile 334 out of Australia's record total of 729 for six wickets.

That same evening as we drove back to our hotel at St Pancras, street urchins clambered on to the running-board of Bradman's car just to catch a glimpse of him, and to greet him with their shrill tributes.

On one occasion, after Bradman had made a mere 80 odd, I saw a newspaper poster in London which read: 'Bradman fails.' This reminds me of the poster which greeted his downfall at Leeds after his record innings: it contained only these two words: 'He's Out.'

STRANGE BUT TRUE

By Jack Ingham, sports editor of the Star, *1938.*

IT IS STRANGE, BUT I think true, that all the time, day and night, somewhere in the world someone is talking about Bradman.

THE BRADMAN FACTOR

By Richard Cashman

From Cricketer, *1982.*

CRICKET BOOMED IN THE 1920s and the 1930s and most of the record Test and Shield crowds date from this period. The emergence of superstar Don Bradman was primarily responsible for the new interest. I have found that Bradman's presence at the crease doubled Sheffield Shield crowds and was almost as significant in Test cricket.

Bradman qualified as an umpire while only 25 and in later years, as here, occasionally stood in minor matches in Adelaide.

Bradman invariably attracted a gallery when he batted in the nets.

Scenes from a road-safety film.

Golfing at Burnham Beeches, Buckinghamshire, in April 1948, two days after arriving in England. The two spectators in white shirts are team-mates—Sid Barnes, left, and Bill Brown.

Bradman introduces his players on arrival in England in 1948.

From left they are Keith Miller (obscured), Ernie Toshack, Ron Hamence (obscured), Ron Saggers, Ray Lindwall, Sam Loxton, Neil Harvey, Doug Ring and Lindsay Hassett.

Bradman poses at Southend with Essex's captain, Tom Pearce, on 17 May 1948.
Two days earlier Bradman had led a slaughter of Essex's bowlers, scoring 187 of the 721 runs amas.
by the Australians in one day.

Bradman reverses his hat for the camera. His companion is Sam Loxton.

Bradman at first slip on the 1948 tour, a fielding position he rarely occupied.
The batsman is England's Bill Edrich, the wicketkeeper Don Tallon and the crouching fieldsman
Colin McCool.

It is possible to accurately assess a Bradman factor in cricket because he played at a time when—with the exception of the bodyline series—bat dominated ball.

It is reasonable to assume that, given the good wickets and very large scores, most spectators came to see the great batsmen of the era rather than the bowlers. And Bradman was the star attraction. He defied even the depression which put thousands out of work and many more on the breadline.

The calculation of the Bradman factor is based on Shield matches at the SCG and the MCG from 1930–40 because precise daily figures are available at almost every centre. I have chosen Shield figures in preference to Test matches because international cricket was more occasional and other variables intrude, such as the bodyline series and the presence of rival English superstars.

Analysing the Bradman factor was simple. I compared the daily crowds when Bradman was involved in 74 days of Shield cricket at the SCG and the MCG as a New South Welshman (1930–34) and as a South Australian (1935–40): the average attendance on the 41 days when he batted was 14,557, whereas the average when he did not bat was only 7,627. Therefore the Bradman factor amounted to 6,930, an additional 91 per cent. Bradman usually occupied the crease on at least two days of a match, and the additional spectators would amount to 13,680.

Looking at the impact of Bradman in another way it can be seen that when he played for New South Wales (up to 1934), the New South Wales vs Victoria clash remained the top draw of the season and was played in the prime crowd-drawing periods of New Year in Melbourne and the Australian Day holidays in Sydney. The matches drew on average 50 per cent larger crowds than the equivalent matches against South Australia (New South Wales vs South Australia, SCG and Victoria vs South Australia, MCG). But from 1935, attendance at the South Australian matches almost doubled the average game attendance in the New South Wales vs Victoria contests. 'The King' had arrived in Adelaide.

It should be stressed that Bradman alone may not have drawn all the additional 6,930 spectators who came to the ground when he was batting. Some may have come for other reasons. Some may have turned up to witness the Bradman vs O'Reilly duels at the SCG after 1935 which the bowler sometimes won. However, there can be no doubt that the great majority of the additional 6,930 were attracted by Bradman alone.

There are countless stories told by contemporary players about how disconcerting it was for the batsman following Bradman—once the Don was dismissed many of the crowd filed out. Len Darling, who says he fielded for almost 5,000 of Bradman's runs, tells the story about how he was about to catch Bradman on the boundary at the SCG—after Bradman had chalked up another century—and how the spectators, greedy for more Bradman runs, yelled at him to drop the catch. Administrators appreciated the crowd-pulling capacity of Bradman and he figures prominently in match advertisements. The Queensland Cricket Association began its *Courier Mail* match notice of the 1931 Test against the West Indies with the statement that 'Don Bradman will be playing in the third Test . . .' It later added that 'Brisbane spectators will have their first opportunity of seeing him since his wonderful performances in England, and of showing their appreciation.'

A Shield advertisement in 1936 featured a banner headline, 'Bradman', along with his picture. It was only further down and in much smaller print that 'Q'ld vs. South Australia' was mentioned.

The dramatic impact of Bradman on match attendances can be further illustrated by three examples. In one New South Wales vs Victoria clash at the SCG (4–8 November, 1932) a large Friday crowd of 9,694 saw Ponsford score an impressive 163 not out in a Victorian total of 6–306. On the second day Ponsford went on to score 200 in 275 minutes but was eclipsed by an 'amazing' innings of Bradman in which he scored 238 runs in 200 minutes. The crowd on the second day, 24,658, was more than two and a half times larger than that of Friday. Normally normal Saturday crowds exceeded Friday crowds at the time by half.

Bradman played a quite different innings in the match between South Australia and Victoria at the MCG from 1–4 January, 1936. When he went into bat on the first day his side was 1–8 and he held them together with a responsible innings: by the end of the day he was 229 not out and his team, 5–349. This innings was watched by a large New Year's Day crowd of 23,546 and a good crowd attended for the next day (Thursday) of 16,035 to watch Bradman go on to 357.

With South Australia in command and no prospect of a further Bradman innings, interest in the match on Friday and Saturday plummeted with attendances of 3,488 and 4,450.

Perhaps the most spectacular example of the Bradman factor was the game between Victoria and South Australia at the MCG from 29 December, 1939–2 January, 1940 when there were 'back to back' crowds of more than 30,000.

On Friday, 29 December, 12,292 spectators witnessed good batting by Victoria which led to a big score of 475 on Saturday. With the prospect of Bradman batting on Saturday 30,288 came up and by stumps on that day he was 52 not out. Another bumper crowd of 30,837 came on Monday, New Year's Day, and were not disappointed when Bradman progressed to 267 runs in 340 minutes. Consecutive crowds of such dimensions are unique in the history of the Shield for there have only been six daily crowds of more than 30,000.

HARD HITTING

By Frank Woolley

Woolley, a champion England batsman in the 1920s, gave this appraisal of Bradman in his book The King of Games.

[He is] THE KIND of genius batsman who arrives about once every twenty years or so on purpose to show us which really are the best bowlers. Absolutely untaught, Bradman's success seems to make of coaching a waste of time.

Though he often plays with a cross bat, Bradman is the grandest living example for youngsters to copy in one particular. He really *hits* the ball. Such vicious striking at the ball as his is, and always has been, rare. I have never seen fiercer.

As in the case of all geniuses, he exercises some kind of hypnotic influence over the bowler. Otherwise they could not fail to more persistently attack his off stump with the going-away ball than any of them do. No batsman can cross-bat that one for long.

SQUASH CHAMPION

A newspaper report of the final of the 1939 South Australian squash championships, won by Bradman. His opponent Don Turnbull was a former Davis Cup tennis player.

AUSTRALIA'S CRICKET CAPTAIN, D. G. Bradman, last night defeated the former Davis Cup tennis player, D. P. Turnbull, by three games to two in the final of the amateur squash racquets championship of South Australia at the Amateur Sports Club. The standard of play was considered by competent judges to be equivalent to the best Melbourne amateur standard, and after the match Turnbull said he thought that both he and Bradman would like to go to Melbourne for the Australian championship, if possible. Bradman made two sensational recoveries during the match, in which the prolonged rallies kept the spectators at a high pitch of excitement.

Displaying remarkable agility, and driving with perfect length down the walls, Turnbull took the first two games 9–0, 9–4. Although Bradman played much better and placed his shots more accurately, Turnbull's agility gave him a lead of 8–3 in the third game—within a point of the match. At this stage Bradman displayed admirable coolness. Stroking flawlessly and scoring many points with delicate drop-shots, he evened the score, and forced Turnbull into errors to take the game 10–8. Turnbull continued to make errors, and Bradman romped through the fourth game 9–3 to even the score at two games all.

Bradman and Turnbull excelled themselves in the final game, and the score went to five points all. With a service ace and two winning drives, Turnbull led 8–5, but he then missed a sitter to give Bradman the service. At this stage Bradman made another amazing recovery. Forcing Turnbull on to the defensive with accurate placements, he evened at 8 all, and then forced Turnbull into errors to win the game and the championship. The match lasted an hour. Scores:—Bradman d. Turnbull, 0–9 4–9 10–8 9–3 10–8.

Apart from his cricket, and now his squash fame, Bradman has a golf handicap of 3, and is described by Turnbull as 'the makings of a very good tennis player.'

MODEST EXIT

By Arthur Mailey

From an article in the Sydney Sunday Telegraph*, 1940.*

I SAW HIM ON one occasion in England climb down a fire escape in order to dodge a crowd of admirers at the front door of the hotel. Woodfull's team had won the Ashes and one would have expected that when Woodfull passed through the doors the crowd would have disappeared. So little notice did they take of the Australian skipper that he might have been a waiter. They wanted nobody but Bradman. I told a rather aggressive lady that it was useless to wait, as Don had made his exit down the fire escape. 'You're fooling me,' she screeched. 'I know he hasn't left the hotel, and even if he has I'll wait till he comes back tonight.' That was that.

MORE REALIST THAN ROMANTIC

By H. S. Altham

From The Heart Of Cricket*, 1967. Altham, one of the most revered figures in English cricket, wrote this article originally for the* Cricketer Spring Annual *in 1941, against a background of world war.*

WHEN THE FIRST CONTINGENT of the Australian Expeditionary Force join their comrades in the field, I have little doubt that one of the first and most frequent questions addressed to them will be 'Is Don Bradman as good as ever?' Even in the middle of Armageddon, the little man has retained 'headline value', and 'Bradman—0' is still more sensational news than the usual 'Bradman Again!' to the tune of a double century. How is it that amid all the stresses and distortions of our distracted world, we still can feel not merely interest but a pulse of happiness and reassurance when we read of a man playing a game thirteen thousand miles away? I will court the sneers of our 'brittle intellectuals' and say that it is mainly, I conceive, because we believe in that game as a cement of good-fellowship, sanity and fair dealing between men and peoples, as embodying within its code and its traditions much of what we are fighting for. Moreover, the bare legend of a day's play in Adelaide or Sydney revives for so many of us countless happy memories of our own: it may be of that evening in the 'St George and the Dragon' when we and our friends of the rival and vanquished village, over tankards of 'immortal vintage', 'tired the sun with talking and sent him down the sky'; or of a sun-baked day at Lord's, when, in shirt-sleeves with a paper over our heads we watched Walter Hammond in all the majesty of his power and grace; or, more distant but no less precious, of the moment when, in the new and slightly embarrassing glory of a pair of batting gloves, we opened the innings for the Under Eleven team of our preparatory school. And of this game, with its happy associations and its reflection of so much that we hold worthwhile, Don Bradman is the unchallenged champion.

It is idle, if alluring, to compare the champions of different epochs: we may wonder indefinitely how H. L. Doherty would have fared with Budge, or Harry Vardon with Henry Cotton: whether Alex James in his prime would have bewildered the brothers Walters in theirs, whether Ronnie Poulton's swerve would have been checkmated by the closer defensive tactics of a modern international. Would 'W.G.' have been really bothered by the googly and the legside field, and how would Hammond have fared on the old fiery wickets of Lord's in the seventies? Such questions cannot be answered, but we may with a feeling of absolute security assert that in no age and at no game has any man more dominated his contemporaries than has Don Bradman in the dozen years—and they are no more—of his first-class career. How many runs on a good wicket would England barter for the surety of seeing Bradman's back twice disappearing into the pavilion? What odds would any man lay, when he reaches a century, against that hundred going into two? How much of Test match history in those dozen years can be assigned to him and him alone? Figures can lie, but in cricket, taken in the large, they tell the truth, and in his case defy all argument. In that period twenty-three matches have been finished, England winning 13 and Australia 10: and in nine out of those ten Bradman has made over 100, in six of the ten over 200. It has been the same in all his cricket from Test match to second grade in Australia: no one in the game has approached him for consistency over anything like the same period. He has already far outstripped in aggregate all other Australian batsmen: Trumper, Macartney, Clem Hill and Joe Darling, Sidney Gregory and Warren Bardsley are all as 'The Field' to Eclipse.

To total 1,000 runs in a domestic season in the Dominion is a tremendous achievement: only Ponsford and Kippax have done it more than once—in each case twice. Bradman has done it every season except one since he first appeared.

What then, is the secret of this astonishing phenomenon? Let us consider first the physical equipment. Bradman is a small man and were a stranger to meet him standing still in ordinary clothes he would notice nothing remarkable about him except a pair of exceptionally high shoulders, an unusually resolute jaw and a keen pair of eyes. But see the same figure in flannels and in action and the first secret is not far to seek. For here is obviously a perfectly co-ordinated body, balanced on feet as neat, and at the same time as strong, as any professional dancer's, which ensure maximum speed and accuracy of movement: add to this that flexibility of hip which is a hall-mark of nearly all great games-players, great power of forearm, wrist and (often forgotten) hand, and you have some idea of the machine that turns out the runs. Machines need looking after and Bradman has always known how to keep his not merely, it would seem, in good running, but in racing trim. But greatest of all his natural assets is a speed of reaction which, I believe, scientific tests have proved to be quite abnormal; perhaps only with Ranji was there so small a time-lag between conception and execution, and this is the secret of his stroke play whether in defence or attack. He sees the ball sooner, watches it longer, and can play the stroke later than anyone else. Remember, too, that in his case each stroke decision is regulated by a singularly acute cricket brain and a, by now, immense batting experience.

It would be illogical to expect in a man of his build the effortless ease of stroke play which one associated with Frank Woolley or the power of Walter Hammond's driving, though in all conscience there is power enough; nor can he rival one of the greatest of English batsmen—George Gunn—in giving the impression that he has 'all day to play his shot in': the tempo of his batting is staccato. But the power and versatility of his stroke play are astonishing; unlike the vast majority of his contemporaries he can fight a war on two fronts, for he seems equally at home with an off-side or leg-side attack: he can hit the ball through the covers with equal facility off the front or back leg, and he is a brilliant cutter, both square and late; but it is on the other side of the wicket that his mastery is most impressive. He is the finest hooker in the world and can direct this stroke at will anywhere from wide mid-on to fine leg with the vital, and very rare, security of hardly ever lifting the ball, whilst to bowl even a fairly accurate length on the line of his leg-stumps or legs is to ask for punishment; here, perhaps, his peculiar genius is most pronounced, in his ability to force the ball through any inviting gap, generally off the back foot, meeting it very near his body, and with a combined thrust of the forearms and flick of the wrists played with a perfection of timing that makes a utilitarian stroke into a work of art. Allied with this great variety of stroke play there goes an extraordinary facility for placing the ball, and only very accurate bowling and the most skilfully adjusted placing of the field has any chance of keeping him even moderately quiet on a good wicket. In his earlier years, and even now when the whim takes him, he could and can go the pace of a pure hitter, and for a time in the early part of the 1934 tour he seemed practically to have selected that role for himself: then I believe an almost stern remonstrance from Woodfull sobered him, with the monumental result that we all remember, and since then, though his stroke play could never be anything but remarkable, runs rather than strokes appear to have become his main objective.

For the extraordinary consistency with which he pursues that aim we must look beyond the mere technique of a superlative defence coupled with outstanding physical fitness and a stamina that sustains him through the longest day. If I may borrow terms from another sphere, Bradman is not a romantic but a realist: he finds his satisfaction in achievement rather than in method; he is not tempted, as Jack Hobbs often was, to try dangerous strokes simply because the mere making of runs by ordinarily secure means had begun to pall, or to regard a mere century as the signal for 'chancing his arm', either as a concession to his physical nature or from the feeling that made Michelangelo want to give up painting in favour of sculpture, 'because it was too easy'. He will always play to the clock and the state of the game and very rarely fails to take drastic toll of a tiring attack during the last ninety minutes of a day's play; but, other things being equal, he is content to go on his way from his first century to his second and from his second to his third with the same deliberate speed, unwearied, unexcited and, above all, undiverted.

It is sometimes said that 'Bradman cannot play on a sticky wicket': that is nonsense. With his natural gifts he could not help being good under those conditions, when the ability to move the feet quickly and play a delayed stroke accurately mean so much: in the Leeds Test match of 1938 the ball was consistently on top of the bat, but he made his century as usual and that century settled the match, whilst in that absorbing game, in which all Yorkshire to this day believes they were robbed of victory by rain, he played Verity, on his own admission, as well as he ever remembers being played.

Another statement that I have sometimes heard made, in a sort of vague disparagement, against Bradman is that he is 'inhuman'. If this means that he is uniquely immune from the ordinary frailties of the cricketing flesh, he certainly stands condemned, for he does not tire, he does not relax, and even on the days when he is, for him, palpably out of form, a long score remains more probable than a short one. But if it implies that he lacks personality or the capacity to enjoy the game himself and make others enjoy it, it is ludicrously false. His immense vitality, for one thing, gives it the lie: one cannot be bored with a man who is so tremendously alive every moment he is on the field. But it was finally and utterly disproved by his captaincy of the Australians in 1938. No one can have been surprised at his tactical shrewdness on that tour, but I doubt whether anyone was quite prepared for the personal ascendancy which he established over his team. I do not think I have ever admired anything on the cricket field so much as his leadership through those heartbreaking days at the Oval in August: his own fielding was an inspiration in itself, and as hour succeeded hour with nothing going right and the prospect of the rubber receding over a hopeless horizon, it was, one felt, his courage and gaiety that alone sustained his side. And when the tragic accident came, the game was over, the balloon was pricked and his team was a team no more.

I have written much more than I meant: much more, indeed, than my friend the Editor asked me: more perhaps than he will see fit to publish, and I have caught myself wondering whether a sense of proportion in time as well as space has not been left out in a school-master's 'arrested development'. But if Falstaff in a tavern in Eastcheap 'babbled o' green fields', may we not find comfort in remembering our own Arcadies? I am the happier now for having seen 'W.G.' bat and Kortright bowl, for having fielded to 'Ranji' and Archie MacLaren, and for having been comprehensively bowled by Colin Blythe. But, as I have written in another place, 'In the many pictures that I have stored in my mind from the "burnt-out Junes" of forty years, there is none more dramatic or compelling than that of Bradman's small, serenely-moving figure in its big-peaked green cap coming out of the pavilion shadows into the sunshine, with the concentration, ardour and apprehension of surrounding thousands centred upon him, and the destiny of a Test match in his hands.'

EACH TO HIS OWN

By G. H. Hardy

Hardy, the celebrated British mathematician, made this reference to Bradman in his 1941 book, A Mathematician's Apology.

I WOULD RATHER BE a novelist or a painter than a statesman of similar rank; and there are many roads to fame which most of us would reject as actively pernicious. Yet it is seldom that such differences of value will turn the scale in a man's choice of a career, which will almost always be dictated by the limitations of his natural abilities. Poetry is more valuable than cricket, but Bradman would be a fool if he sacrificed his cricket in order to write second-rate minor poetry (and I suppose that it is unlikely that he could do better). If the cricket were a little less supreme, and the poetry better, then the choice might be more difficult: I do not know whether I would rather have been Victor Trumper or Rupert Brooke. It is fortunate that such dilemmas occur so seldom.

AN ARTIST, BUT NOT FOR ART'S SAKE

By R. C. Robertson-Glasgow

From Cricket Prints—Some Batsmen And Bowlers 1920–1940, *1943.*

IN THE POPULAR VIEW, Bradman is the batsman of colossal scores, a machine that turned out runs as other machines turn out screws or sausages. As to fact, this view is right; but the holders of it are likely to miss the underlying truth that Bradman was that rarest of Nature's creations, an artist without the handicap of the artistic temperament, a genius with an eye to business. In the commerce of cricket he was the best salesman that the game has yet seen.

THE LEGEND

By Ray Robinson

From Between Wickets, *1946.*

FULL JUSTICE HAS NEVER been done Don Bradman, outstanding batsman between two World Wars and, maybe, since the Wars of the Roses (We know that Nelson had a good eye and Marlborough was never at a loss in the field, but evidence is lacking whether either of those lesser heroes could hook from outside the off stump).

If the countless columns and chapters published about Bradman were placed end-to-end they would stretch, on a still day, from the pavilion end to Puckapunyal, and would reach beyond the bounds of credibility. To begin with, no writer of schoolboy fiction would have dared to credit his hero with performances so astonishing: a hundred in his opening first-class match; 236 in his first match in England; first visiting batsman to score 1,000 before the end of May; 131 in his first Test match in England; 254 in his first Test at Lord's; 105 before lunch and 309 in one day at Leeds a fortnight later (all before he turned 22); and so on until in his 190th first-class match he scored his 93rd century.

His successes are enough to make a United States Air Force communiqué seem like an understatement. Around these astonishing deeds is being woven the Bradman legend, the legend of the cricketer who, in the year the war began, was given 21 lines in *Who's Who*—only eight fewer than Hitler, and 17 more than Stalin.

There is much in the contention that no history is so true as the legend, the people's impression of a man or event, which is handed down and survives, unencumbered by precise detail or cold, obscuring fact—some anecdote, fable or even a phrase which, though inexact in itself, is more revealing than whole sheets of verified data. Drake is, rightly, better known for the tale that he finished a game of bowls before tackling the Great Armada than for his outstanding feat of seamanship, circumnavigation of the world. Many who know little of the lives of the great composers, and are more familiar with the *Footlight Serenade* than the *Moonlight Sonata*, have been struck by the wonder of a Beethoven creating music after he could not hear a note.

The legend of W. G. Grace, founder of modern batting and 43 years a first-class cricketer, owes much to a bushy beard which played no part in adding even a snicked single to his scores, and to his artfulness in fooling umpires—all the more comic because he didn't need to.

The legend of Don Bradman, though it will hinge on his unprecedented run-getting, will not be fashioned from score-sheets, averages and aggregates alone. If that were so, it would be too impersonal—the sort of thing that someone who never saw him could put together. It would lack enough flesh and blood to live. Embalmed with decimal points, it would be entombed between the covers of books, to be exhumed only when some later champion rivalled or surpassed the records. The living legend will be a fusion of reminiscence, a montage from the mass impressions of those who have watched Bradman, admired his skill, marvelled at him and been puzzled and shocked by him.

What has been written about Bradman will have some influence on this. But most of it leaves an impression wholly preposterous: it leaps from crag to crag, with no more than a passing glance into the valleys and rarely a peep into the ravines. This is partly because of the urgency of the efforts of the Press to serve cricket piping-hot from the pitch. Even reports that are not read until next morning have to be lodged by a deadline that leaves little time for rumination. Another reason is that some newspapers entrust cricket reporting to men with no more qualification than that they write about football in winter, or have become known to the public as boxing or tennis critics, or have proved their flair for sport by beating the news editor at darts.

One of London's largest-selling dailies published a front-page story of Verity's triumph against the Australians on the Monday of the 1934 Test at Lord's, with never a word about the state of the wicket after heavy rain in the night. Unless those who read that account had watched the match or had seen another newspaper, they were left to guess an answer to the seemingly-insoluble riddle of how a bowler who had taken only two Australian wickets for 113 in the preceding Test, a fortnight earlier, had suddenly developed the knack of getting 14 for 80 in one day.

Anyway, regardless of writing against the clock, and blind spots here and there on the Press benches, cricket was not invented merely so that a Bradman, a Hammond or a Hutton could play it. When a great crick-eter falls below his customary standard, or is on view only briefly, the spotlight moves on to whoever are the heroes of the day. Few would want it deflected from the action of the play for an autopsy of an innings that died of natural causes.

Then there have been a few Australian lily-gilders who, over-zealously observing the newspaper rule about catering for the public's inclination for hero-worship, have avoided or played down anything about Bradman that they imagined might impair the build-up (which never needed bolstering).

It is the cumulative effect of all this emphasis on success, with so little counterweight, that presents an unreal picture of Bradman as something superhuman, not of this world. Like a trick mirror at a seaside fun park, it distorts him to the point of giving the impression that, unlike mortals, 'tis in him to command success—excepting only the occasional twists and turns of the luck of the game, which are beyond the control of even a batsman above human fallibility.

The future student of cricket history may easily be set wondering why Don ever got out—unless it were from boredom with run-making—and what could have gone astray to prevent his scoring 100, 200, 300 or more every time. Many who have seen him only a few times and know him only as a small, alert figure in flannels or a smiling face in a photograph, probably wonder the same way.

Bradman has been over-simplified to the public, like Hitler, Petain, blitzkrieg, non-aggression pacts, and other notabilities and events which superseded him in the headlines. It has all been made to look so easy for him, as if he were a cricketing counterpart of those Hollywood film stars who are never called on to do anything except smile, burst into song and canoodle comely leading ladies.

That is why Bradman has not been done full justice. Many a time it has not been a pushover for him. The impression that he is an unemotional gatherer of easily-won triumphs is false. He is far from being like a piece of mass-production machinery, without the hopes and anxieties, the exultations and despairs, that others feel. To understand him properly, you have to get down from the peaks to the lower levels of his career. Chief result of this mountaineering is to heighten the wonder of his deeds and to discover that he is an even more remarkable batsman than is commonly thought. It has given me a firmer-based esteem for his qualities than could be built on a foundation of blind hero-worship or local patriotism. When isolated happenings, sometimes unexplained, are fitted together they make a pattern which leads to a truer valuation of his unparalleled achievements, too often taken for granted.

TOSCANINI OF CRICKET

By G. F. McCleary

From Cricket With The Kangaroo, *1950.*

His FIGURE MUST BE familiar to many who read these lines. The first impression he gives is of perfect physical fitness. His muscles are beautifully co-ordinated and instantly responsive to the dictates of the brain. It is a pleasure to watch the movement of that strong and supple body. The next impression the spectator receives is that he is in the presence of a highly-competent person. It is not necessary to be a cricketer to realize as the Don takes his place at the wicket that he is a man who knows his job. You have the same feeling when Toscanini walks on to the platform. He inspires confidence. He would inspire confidence if you did not know who he was. How confidence before performance is thus inspired is one of the mysteries of personality; but there it is.

At the wicket he plays with consummate ease and assurance. Usually he begins quietly; he makes no haste to get runs, though on occasion he gets going at once. But he soon shows that a batsman's job is not merely to keep in but to score runs for his side. He has complete command of every stroke, and when he hits he hits hard. All his strokes are a delight to the eye, but perhaps the most fascinating is the late cut; he plays the ball as if he loved it and is sending it to the boundary for its own good. Bowlers are changed, but it makes no difference to the upward progress of his score. As one notes what the Don's bat does to the ball one wonders why he ever gets out.

A VISIT TO BRADMAN & CO

By Sydney Deamer

From an article in the Sydney Daily Telegraph, *October 1946.*

THE BRADMAN HOME IS three miles from the office of Don Bradman and Co., and although he owns a car, Bradman travels to and fro by tram, arriving at 9, and departing at 5.30.

There is a subdued stable atmosphere about the office. It reminds one of a family solicitor's place, except that it is tidier, lacking the scent of book dust, and the sprawl of 'papers' tied in pink-tape. The outer office is serviced pleasantly by a well-groomed young business man, and there is a shelf of neatly arranged financial papers for the use of visitors.

Bradman sits at a panelled inner office facing the door. The sanctum is carpeted and quiet, and the desk immaculate. The only two pictures I noticed were a large photograph of a Test team, and a colored photograph of the two children—both good-looking and more plump than their father.

Bradman was letter writing when I went in. It was the first time I had met him alone, and I was interested to compare my impressions with those of the cricket writers.

They had warned me that he was not an easy man to interview— not even easy to reach. I found this understandable, because on the way to the appointment I read a placard outside all the news-stands declaring: 'Mrs Bradman Spills the Beans.'

It was the placard of a crime-sporting-gossip sheet. The sheet was anxious to know if Bradman had definitely made up his mind whether he would be available for the forthcoming Tests or not. Bradman was unable to say—at the time he did not know himself. So the author of the piece which had inspired the placard had seen Mrs Bradman in what he called an 'unguarded moment,' and had got her to 'spill the beans.'

The 'beans' amounted to a very small row—merely that Bradman would love to play for Australia—no definite statement except that 'Bradman himself could not be interviewed . . . remained detached, unapproachable, uncommunicative . . . his only comment that he did not want to be pestered with posers about his cricket future, and when stirred out of his silence he made only acid reference to inquisitive people who should mind their own business.'

So that when I saw Bradman I was not surprised that he was guarded and cautious, particularly as, to his knowledge, he had not met me before. But he is not a difficult man to interview once with him. He will either tell you what you want to know or he won't. And when he decides to give information he gives it with the precision of a well-trained Staff Officer.

He is obviously not a spontaneous, spacious man. He keeps himself well reined-in, and finds it easier to do so, because he is not very imaginative. But he is no boor. If he does not laugh easily he can smile, and, without being affable, put a stranger at ease.

Nevertheless, Bradman is not a 'hearty' man. Repeatedly he reveals what can be fairly called the 'official mind.' I got the impression that wild horses could not drag an indiscretion from him.

A MISSED ENCOUNTER

By Ernie Toshack

From a newspaper interview, 1984.

WHEN WE [NEW SOUTH WALES] went over to play South Australia after the war Ray Lindwall said, 'I'd like to have a crack at the little fella', and I said so would I. But Bradman didn't play. When we saw him get that 187 in the first Test in Brisbane, Ray looked at me and I looked at him. Ray said, 'I'm pleased now that I didn't have to bowl to him', and I said, 'Yes, if we had, neither of us might be in this Test'.

THE IKIN INCIDENT

By Walter Hammond

From Cricket My World. *The incident Hammond describes occurred during the first Test of the 1946–47 series and long remained a cause of controversy. It seems most of the English fieldsmen thought Ikin had taken a fair catch, but the Australian batsman at the other end, Lindsay Hassett, as well as the umpire, thought it was a bump ball. Bradman, 38 years old and trying to re-establish himself in Test cricket after an eight-year wartime lay-off, went on to make 187.*

AUSTRALIA'S FIRST WICKET WAS down for 9 runs—and Bradman was walking out, small and tight and tough, but, most of us thought, more than a little nervous. If we could get him, quickly, just this once, it might mean that the Ashes were ours; for a sharp set-back after such a lot of ill-health and absence from the game must surely set the pace for future games.

I said a word or two to the bowlers, and made sure the field was just so. Bradman was taking centre—the player who learned how to see a ball by batting a golf-ball with a stump, up against a rough brick wall, and never letting the rebounding pellet drop to the ground.

'We've *got* to get Don out!'

How often, in Tests, has that echoed through the heart of every opposing player, tensing him to extra keenness, stretching his abilities to the edge of the impossible. We all realized it as we gathered round his wicket like crows; Bedser and Voce realized it, with nothing whatever in the wicket to help them, Bedser reminding one of Maurice Tate with somewhat the same late swing and the hostile readiness to knock the bat flying if the batsman's watchfulness flickered, and Voce pegging away at his nasty going-away ball that had tumbled Don's castle on earlier tours.

Against them, we saw the spectacle, at first, of a Bradman unarmoured and unarmed, being forced into awkward strokes, fumbling when he had time in hand, his brown face tense and strained, full of little nervous gestures. He did not start with his old divine right, flashing at the ball like one who drives beasts with a whip; he was unhappy, ill at ease, unable at first to see the ball properly at all.

The Brisbane crowd, terribly loyal, were yet unable to hide their apprehension for their idol. The applause was erratic; there was no shouted persiflage for once. I was told that two men fainted among the spectators on that hot morning, but I doubt if the heat had anything to do with it.

Bedser, sweating with eagerness to take Don's wicket for a 0, sent up a wicked one—and Don snicked it quite involuntarily, like a schoolboy, through the slips. If my arm had been a little longer . . . but the red streak was out of reach. Bedser took the ball again, set his jaw, wheeled his arm strongly over, the bat thudded—and the ball hooped up in front of short-leg, again just a foot or so from scrabbling hands.

Don's lips tightened into a line, and Bedser's jaw-muscles showed as he ran up to deliver the next ball—but the Umpire's voice frightfully shattered everyone's concentration—'NO-BALL!'—and Don came out like a tormented tiger and hit hard. Next moment, he was running pantherine down the pitch to open his score, after more thrills than we had hoped for or he had dreamed of.

Our bowlers kept at him, forcing him back on the defensive, hedging him in, surrounding his quick-moving feet with pitfalls and gins. The Bradman of old was gone; this tight-lipped batsman was all at sea in his timing; once, and then again, he snicked the ball through the slips just that fast, and that distance beyond our outstretched fingers, that made the catch impossible. And he looked hunted!

We felt our hands twitching, and our feet tensing for the jump, every time Don put his bat towards the ball; and he looked about afterwards as though he was not sure which of us would have him. At this stage, our out-fielding was as good as I have ever seen it, with the ball coming in like lightning, and never a fumble.

Don scored ones and twos, and an unsure four or two. Slowly and shakily, he got into double figures, while Barnes, rattling up runs now and then, was almost ignored by all present. I think Barnes himself felt that this was unflattering.

He began to hook balls no one should have hooked, made a few boundaries, and then Wright's eye rested steadily upon him, and I saw Wright's hand curl lovingly in the delivery of a trap ball. Barnes joyously clouted it, but the ball spun off the bat, and Bedser, fielding at forward square-leg, so nearly got it that the crowd's groan was only changed to joy half way through, when the ball trickled to earth. Even then, Barnes did not learn; two balls later, the same trick spun the ball the same way, and this time Bedser got his palms under it, and they had lost 2 for 46.

Hassett walked out, looking very neat, and everything depended on the next half-hour's attack.

Bill Voce was still inspired. I watched him tempting Bradman, and saw Bradman's unhappy eye as he, who had taught the world's bowlers to be humble, watched the bouncing ball and wondered whether he could smite it with the majesty of old. Bill came up again, lion-hearted, and slung down that awkward going-away ball—and Bradman slashed at it, irritated beyond endurance—and Ikin, at second slip, shot into the air like a released spring, and had the ball in his hand. Ikin waited for Bradman to leave, but he did not move, looking down on the ground.

'OWZATT?'

The appeal rocked the ground, and for an agonized fraction of a second, the umpire's silence seemed to imply doubt. Then he slowly shook his head, his lips pushed together, his brows frowning.

Ikin looked incredulous. We all thought it was a certainty, and at the negation, my heart turned over. *The ball had flown shoulder-high.* Don's eyes flickered, whether with surprise or shock I could not tell. And then, like a released tide, came the roar of relief and approval from the crowd. Bradman had scored 28. If he had gone out then, history might have been written differently. But cricket is full of such 'Ifs'—and our job was to get on with the game.

I think the pause for luncheon, the old familiar chatter and jokes, and a hearty meal, did Bradman a lot of good. Early in the afternoon, he looked round the field as if he were slowly awaking from some unpleasant dream. Bill Voce was bowling, and his next ball was swept to the leg boundary without hesitation or ado. The next went whistling through the covers. The old Bradman had risen from the dead, and I knew we were 'for it'. His 50th run came after just two hours' play; he followed it with a cut through the gully that was just typical Bradman, and the crowd, which had been afraid to lift up its voice, breathed in heavily and then let fly! For the first time, Don smiled. At the other end, Hassett was helping himself to neat little cuts from the joint, very primly and properly.

The Bradman century went up just after the third hour of play, and it looked then as if nothing devised by the hand of man could stop him. I had been ringing the changes among the bowlers, but none of us had the measure of him, and that was the plain fact. The younger Voce might have done it, or perhaps an older and wilier Bedser; I might have done it myself once upon a time, but that time was not now. So the flashing drives and cuts continued, and he had 162 at the end of that eventful first day.

Dressing room nerves

By Keith Miller

From Cricket Caravan.

THE FIRST TIME I played in the same side as Don was in the Brisbane Test of November 1946. 'Braddles' seemed very happy with all the members of his side. The fact that most of them were unbaptised to Test matches did not seem to concern him. I have always believed Don to be happier with men younger than himself than he was with fellows of his own age and brigade.

I remember that I watched Don closely before he went out to score his 187 in that Test. I had always imagined that he would be supremely confident while waiting to bat, but that is not so. While padding up and waiting his turn Don was just as keyed up as any other player. I have always found him to be so. Indeed, on that occasion in Brisbane, a day so vital to his cricketing future, he was even more tense than younger members of his side. But he was a phenomenal marvel as a batsman. He had every copybook shot and some four or five of his own. He controlled his hook-shot as I have never seen any other batsman control it. When he hooked a ball he could almost choose the picket it was going to hit along the boundary. Most batsmen just hook and hope; some of them may even pray—during and after the stroke . . .

Signing bats in London, 1948.

Watching the play with his team, Old Trafford, 1948.

Another batting session over. Bill Brown is the other batsman.

Visiting friends in Lancashire, 1948.

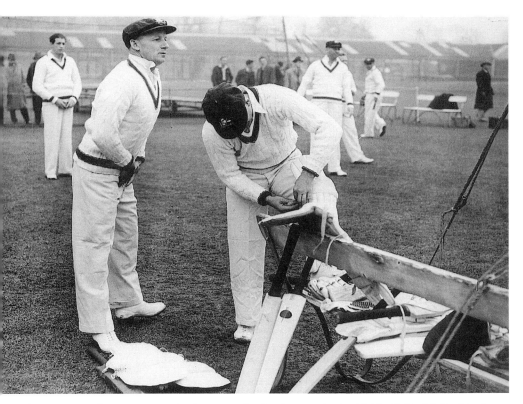

Bradman removes his protector and other gear after batting practice in 1948. Colin McCool is the batsman padding up and Ernie Toshack, at left, the player waiting to bowl.

Bradman meets the Duke and Duchess of Gloucester in England in 1948. Until the previous year the Duke had been Australia's Governor-General. The other players are (from left) Ron Hamence, Colin McCool and Doug Ring.

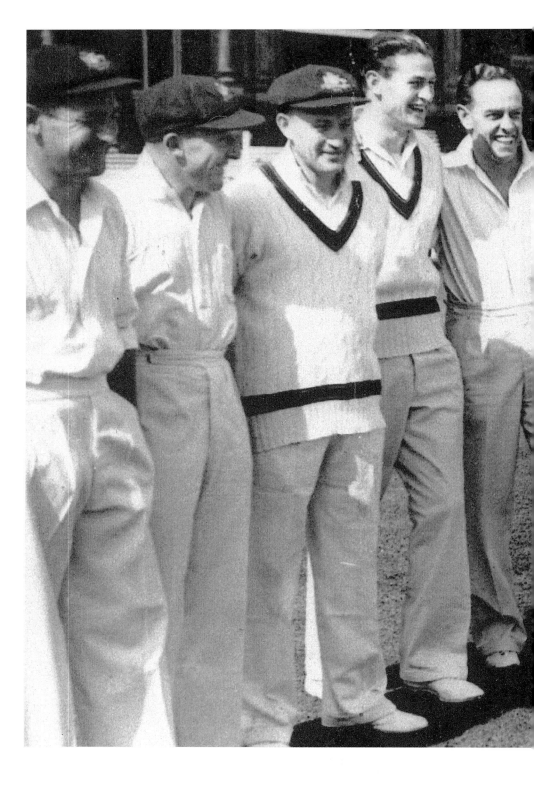

Bradman is wished a happy 40th birthday by his team on the final day of the match against the Gentlemen of England, one of the last fixtures of the 1948 tour. In this, his final appearance at Lord's, Bradman scored 150.

'Auld Lang Syne' at London's Savoy Hotel, 1948.

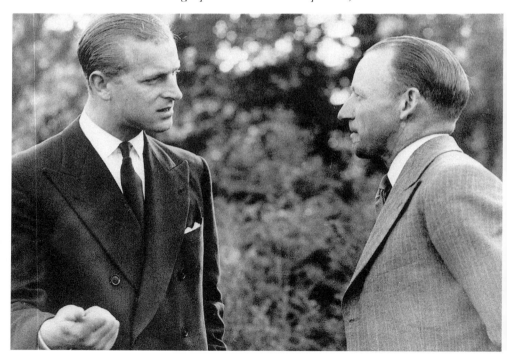

With a young Duke of Edinburgh, 1948.

The Don's last match in England—at Scarborough in September 1948. He and Sid Barnes resume the innings. Bradman made 153.

Bradman at his testimonial match in Melbourne, December 1948.
Arthur Morris is the team-mate behind him.

Don has always set his men a perfect example so far as his demeanour on and off the field is concerned. I have yet to hear him question an umpire's decision even in the dressing-room. Indeed, we sometimes would get very annoyed with him for not sympathising with us when we thought we had suffered from bad decisions. Don always blamed himself for his own dismissals and never had any excuses to offer. When Alec Bedser was thriving on his famous leg-trap and had trapped him three times running, 'Braddles' used to come in and say to himself, 'Aw gee, I can't make head or tail of what I should be doing.'

I believe Don's almost lifelong friend, 'Johnnie' Moyes of Sydney, sent him a cable about this time, saying, 'Why don't you stand back and force them past mid-on?' To this Don replied, 'Don't you think I know, but I'm getting too old to see them in time.'

A GOOD CHOICE

By Fred Trueman

From Ball Of Fire*, 1977.*

IT WAS SAID AUSTRALIA had helped pick the England team for years. The classic case was when Don Bradman went on about Doug Wright being the finest leg-spin bowler he had ever played against. They kept picking Doug and Bradman kept knocking double centuries off him.

A WEEKEND SPOILT

By Alec Bedser

From Our Cricket Story, *co-written by Alec Bedser and his twin brother Eric. This is Alec's account of how he bowled Bradman for a duck in the fourth Test at Adelaide, 1946–47.*

I BOWLED TO A short leg field as the ball was swinging a little. After receiving eight balls Don was bowled with the ninth, a wonderful moment indeed for me. There was a deathly silence all round the ground, and Don had walked quite a distance from the wicket before the crowd could bring themselves to believe their idol was out for a 'duck.' Then there was a sharp roar of shocked surprise followed by a murmur of excited chatter.

Afterwards Don was good enough to tell me, and he has since written in a similar strain, that this ball was the finest ever to take his wicket. 'It was delivered,' he said to me, 'on the off stump, swung very late to hit the pitch on the leg stump, and then came back to hit the middle and off.' All very satisfactory to me, but not to Don. It is the type of ball that can easily miss the stumps instead of hitting them.

The next day being Sunday, in company with Jim Langridge and Eric, I went to the beach at Glenelg, and while we were lounging contentedly on the beach a boy came up to me. He was not, as I first assumed, an autograph hunter, for he said in a hurt voice, 'You've spoilt my weekend. I could hit you. Why did you bowl out Don Bradman for a duck?'

I sympathised but nevertheless wished I could perform the feat more often. Apparently the boy's mother had taken him a long way to see Don, who was the object of all his youthful hero worship, bat for the first time. I don't think I have ever seen a youngster bursting with such indignation.

A truth witnessed

From Christian Renewal, *St Pancras Parish Magazine, Chichester.*

Bradman is a living witness to the very important truth that men are not equal.

Advice second-hand, 1948

By Neil Harvey

A story told in an interview, 1982.

I was 19 years old. The second youngest was 26, Sam Loxton. I kept getting out cheaply in the first six or seven games. I wasn't really game to go to Bradman to talk to him. He was a superstar. He would have killed anyone now or in the future. I asked Sam, my room-mate, to ask Don what I was doing wrong. The question went to Don via Sam. The answer came back via Sam. The answer was: 'I can't tell him anything because he can bat, but if he keeps the ball down he can't get out.'

Twelve bishops for a Bradman

From a newspaper, 1948.

One of the best yarns that His Lordship the Bishop of Tasmania told at Synod of his experiences during Lambeth Conference in England was that of the Canterbury Cathedral choirboys. With the customary cussed inquisitiveness of their species, the boys, while appearing to the congregation to be singing as cherubs in their angelically immaculate-white surplices, quickly recognised some of the Australian Test team members among the congregation. They therefore hastened to the west door of the Cathedral after the service to obtain autographs of any Lambeth Bishops, but especially of the Test team members. The Bishops observed that there was a good deal of swapping of autographs going on among the choirboys, and they learned to their amusement the humbling fact that the Canterbury Cathedral choirboys' assessment of their value was that 12 bishops' autographs were regularly traded for one of Don Bradman's.

DOMINANCE WITHOUT PARALLEL

By E. W. Swanton

From Sort Of A Cricket Person, *1972.*

THE ARRIVAL OF BRADMAN was the most significant cricket event of my early days as a journalist, and indeed his first tour of England coincided with my promotion to the ranks of Test reporters. In the winter of 1928–29 Bradman made his bow for Australia in the first Test against England at Brisbane. Though his beginning was no more propitious than that of his side (and he was actually dropped for one match), by the end of the series he was established in company with Archie Jackson as a white hope of Australian cricket.

Of these two, Jackson, the stylist, was the hot tip; but it did not take Don Bradman long to change the rating. By the end of the first week of the tour I had seen him tot up 421 runs for once out: 236 at Worcester, followed by 185 not out on the old Aylestone Road ground at Leicester. Rather ill-luck he had at Leicester, for rain cut short the prospect of another double hundred when it was there for the taking.

Twice more at least in that month of May rain interrupted the Don's progress when his hungry eye was on the chase, the first in circumstances which give a revealing glimpse of his mentality as a young man. Percy Fender had been covering the MCC tour of Australia a couple of winters before, and was now combining the captaincy of Surrey with a good deal of cricket-writing in the *Evening News*. When it came to assessing the Australian prospects, that shrewdest of critics published his view that D.G.B. might be too unorthodox in his method to be a great success on English wickets: what served in his home conditions would not necessarily do here.

Unfortunately for Surrey this dictum had not escaped the little man's attention. He was about as quick in detecting a critical press comment of this kind as he was in spotting the googly—and just about as ruthless in dealing with it. So the Australians came to the Oval, and Don advanced to the wicket with a special glint in his eye. By 6.25 on the first day the score was 379 for five, and he was still enjoying himself with 252 against his name. He had been batting for just under five hours and Fender's analysis read—21–1–75–2. It was at this point that the rain came, to his great chagrin for, as he says, 'Percy George was just getting his length and I was just getting my eye in.' He would assuredly have taken fresh guard on the Monday, but, alas, there was no further play in the match.

I mention the other rainy occasion in May 1930 because it had a sequel. Don was batting against Hampshire at Southampton on the 31st of the month, and in search of the 'Thousand in May' (or, to be quite accurate, by the end of May, for some of them have had innings in April), which to this day has been reached by only six men. When it began to rain as he approached the target, Lionel Tennyson good-naturedly kept his side in the field, so that he and they all got a wetting, until it was reached.

Years after, Bradman being now captain, Lionel during a Lord's Test

Match went up to the Australian dressing-room and sent in his name. The reply came back that Mr Bradman was engaged and was sorry he could not see Lord Tennyson for the moment. There the matter would have ended, with Don probably making a later effort to seek out his caller, had not an Australian columnist heard of the incident and cabled back to Sydney a story of how Bradman had insulted an old England captain. Note it was an Australian journalist, and not a cricket-writer. The thing was promptly cabled back to London, and so made quite a stir in both countries. The matter of the generous gesture at Southampton was recalled. On the face of it Don had been impolite, or at best heedless to an older man of distinction to whom he owed some obligation.

The truth behind the facts, not hitherto told, is this. Lionel, having lunched far too well, went first to the England room and spent some time there. Don knew this, was apprised of his state of health, and decided he did not want his team to meet the great man in these particular circumstances. With one eye on the field and one ear cocked towards another visitor who was present, he sent his message.

Can one blame him? This was a Test Match, with all its attendant tensions, and there has always been a strict code (besides notices and doorkeepers) protecting the privacy of the dressing-room, which, normally, Lionel Tennyson would have respected as well as anyone else. But, of course, Bradman was very widely blamed on the facts as they were printed, and the really galling thing from his point of view was that, when interviewed, he could not give the valid explanation.

There is an ethical aspect to the affair. It is beyond question that the journalist in question did Bradman an injury. But did he write his story knowing the full facts or only the bare details within the dressing-room? As a member of his profession I prefer to believe he did not know all.

One might analyse the story a little further. Bradman does not expand readily, and since his first headlong rush to fame has been generally wary of the press, until individual writers gain his confidence, when they find him extremely helpful and considerate. Apart from his own performance on the field, he has accordingly suffered, from time to time, criticism to which a more extrovert nature might not have been subject—for instance Lionel Tennyson, hail-fellow-well-met with everyone and a universally popular cricketer. He was, incidentally, as Bradman is, a good friend to me, and I am sure that none of those who knew him will think the worse of him for my having told this story whole and in perspective. He is not the first old Test captain to have fallen victim to the hospitality of his friends on a cricket occasion, nor will he be the last.

The story has been included both out of belated justice to Sir Donald Bradman and also as an illustration of what mischief can be done by the publication of a certain sort of story. It is often loosely said of some paper, by the sort of person who aims for a cheap laugh by denigrating 'the press', that it is only interested in scandal and dressing-room gossip. Generally a close examination will show this to be a half-truth at best, and when such stuff is given prominence it is hardly ever the work of the cricket-writer.

Those who cover big cricket, and especially the cricket correspondents travelling with teams abroad, see and know about plenty of incidents that might be blown up into lively off-field stories. But they very rarely write them, recognizing that so long as he does not commit a public scandal the player is entitled to some private life, even on an international tour. Cricket's repute has certainly suffered since the war from lurid off-the-field disclosures, but this seamy type of journalism has been rather pathetic 'ghosted' stuff, appearing under the names of a few famous players who have been tempted by four-figure sums to reveal all.

Back now to the Don's triumphal progress in 1930. I was subbing in the office when the first Test was played at Trent Bridge—it is the first and last time I have missed a Test Match through being at the office end. Anyway his share of a fine game won by England was 8 and 131. The Lord's Test I did see and report in a secondary manner: the first Test I ever wrote about and in several respects the best.

There was a press annexe in those days at ground level among the public seats under the Grand Stand balcony, and from this angle (between cover-point and extra) I watched and enthused, suffered and hoped, as Australia crushed the English bowling, but not the spirit of the English batsmen whose second innings effort came near to saving this wonderful game. I can readily summon the sights and scenes of those four days in the sun: the peerless stroke past cover-point with which Woolley despatched his first ball for four; Tim Wall's catch right down on his boots, standing nominally in the gully but actually half-way to third man, that brought Frank's marvellous 41 to an unlucky close; 'Duleep' cutting and glancing on that first day; the little old King, with grey bowler, big button-hole, and high walking-stick, shaking hands with the players in front of the pavilion; Hammond pouching a slip catch off the very first ball afterwards; the Don's unhurried entry into the sunlight; his swift advance down the wicket to hit the next one, from White, full pitch up to the Nursery Clock-tower; the board at close of play showing Australia 404 for two, last man (Woodfull) 155, number 3 155 not out; Bradman's further relentless plunder on the Monday; the wry joke of an improvised '7' having to be found for the Tavern scoreboard before the declaration at 729 for six; Hobbs being bowled out of the rough round his legs by Grimmett; Woolley smacking him for four, only to find that he had brushed the stumps with the back of his pad; Chapman apparently 'farming' Grimmett during his partnership with Allen and carting him lustily every so often into the Mound Stand; the excitement when Robins's spin on the dusty fourth afternoon for about half-an-hour raised feverish expectations; the splendour of the Maharajah Jam Sahib of Nawanagar, otherwise 'Ranji', in full Eastern dress, jewels flashing from his tunic and turban, holding a sort of levée behind the pavilion.

This, by the way, was the reputed occasion that prompted the immortal Maurice Tate to mutter, hand over mouth in his own unique, confidential way: ''Cor, see Ranji—looks a veritable 'Indoo, don't 'e?' An incontrovertible comment if ever there was one.

I must beware, by the way, of becoming enmeshed in detail of past matches or this book will run to an unconscionable length. If a reader wants to know more, the assumption must be that he has *Wisden* within reach. So, though with regret, let us leave Lord's for Leeds and that phenomenal first day. Or rather, for the eve thereof. Scene: the crowded Queen's Hotel lounge. From the other side of it, M. Tate espies me, signals, and those vast feet bring him clumping over. The young reporter is flattered at such recognition. Thinks: 'scoop perhaps?' Maurice puts hand to mouth while many watch and unburdens himself of the following confidence: 'We must beat these beggars this time.' I suppose I nod knowingly, feeling I am now really in on the tactics of the game. There was never a readier conversationalist than Maurice.

Twenty-four hours later, this time in the foyer, I come in the company of Vic Richardson and young Stan McCabe. We have shared a taxi back from the ground, and on the way they have been saying, 'Well, we ought to be good for a drink from the little fellow tonight!' But now here is the Don saying to the girl behind the desk: 'I'm going up to my room. Will you please send me a pot of tea?'

Meaning glances pass between the other Australians, as 'the little fellow', heedless of any atmosphere, makes for the lift. In 1930 he was withdrawn, shy of the vast publicity that followed him, teetotal. Besides, by the third Test Don and an Australian journalist were already composing his life-story—and that could be done only in the evenings. He was a man pursuing a goal with single-minded dedication. The idea of a relaxed drink with some of the team would, in 1930, hardly have occurred to him.

Did Don dictate another chapter of his book that evening at Leeds? I would not put it outside the scope of his energy—but consider how he had spent the day. He came in to bat in the second over of the morning and by lunch he had made 105. In the afternoon he added a further 115, and at close of play, against an English attack consisting of Tate, Larwood, Geary, Tyldesley (R), Hammond and Leyland, he returned, unbeaten still and seemingly as fresh as he had started, his share 309 of Australia's 458 for three. So toppled the Anglo-Australian record of 'Tip' Foster made at Sydney in 1903–04. His brilliant 287 had been scored in seven hours, that is to say at a rate of 40 an hour. Yet here was Bradman making upwards of 50 an hour off his own bat, for hour after hour, all along the ground, with scarcely a hint of risk and no more false strokes than could be counted on the fingers of one hand. (In fact, in contrast with his 254 at Lord's, which was chanceless, he here offered three very difficult catches, the first when he had made 141.) After a further hour next morning he was out for 334.

When the Headingley field is close-cropped and shiny, runs come there more quickly than in most places, for the Test pitch seems to be the highest point of a very shallow upturned bowl. The ball flows off the bat from whatever angle just slightly downhill. I can see fat Dick Tyldesley now at mid-off, narrowly failing to cut off a firm defensive stroke, turning and chasing the ball which rolls tantalizingly a few yards ahead of him, neither gaining on the other until the ball hits the rope a second or so in front.

It was after his Headingley experience that someone made bold to ask this sturdy son of the Lancashire soil his opinion of Bradman. He took the matter personally and is said to have tersely replied 'he's no damned good to me'.

Don was not much good to any English bowler in that triumphal summer of 1930, though it was in Lancashire that I did see him twice toppled cheaply, once by an expatriate Australian, once by a Scot. At Aigburth early in the tour Ted McDonald, sinuous and sinister, knocked his stumps all awry. The next occasion was of much greater moment, the fourth Test at Old Trafford, England having been saved by rain in the Third.

To the England team at Old Trafford came Ian Peebles, aged 22, an Oxford undergraduate who had made a highly unusual entry into big cricket, having been drafted into the 1927–28 MCC side to South Africa on the strength of one first-class match (Gents and Players at the Oval) and the fervent recommendation of 'Plum' Warner. When the Australians had come to Oxford in May Don, then in full cry for his thousand runs, had not enjoyed a prolonged look at this promising exponent of leg-spin and googly, having been bowled by a near-shooter by H. M. Garland-Wells for 32.

Now Ian, in his first Test in England, faced the run-machine with one important psychological advantage. At Manchester, strange to say, it had rained. The wicket, as all agreed, was in no way spiteful. It was, however, a slow turner, and the Don had made all his 728 Test runs so far in the dry. His first ball from Peebles, a perfectly-pitched leg-break, nearly bowled him. He struggled to 10, whereupon Hammond, of all people, missed him at slip. Then he edged another leg-break and this time there was no mistake: it was c Duleepsinhji b Peebles 14. The weather easily won this fourth Test, but at least, if only temporarily, the spell of Bradman's invincibility was broken.

Ian was at his best in 1930, before persistent muscular trouble in his right shoulder took the zip out of his leg-break. He had a beautifully smooth, rhythmical run-up and high delivery, great power of spin, and that perceptible dip at the end of the flight that made it difficult to judge the length. The best batsmen thought they were 'there', and found to their cost that they weren't. He had come south when only seventeen to learn the art of bowling from Aubrey Faulkner, of whose School of Cricket he acted as secretary. Faulkner kept Ian so hard at it that he taught himself to bowl left-handed to ease the strain on his right shoulder. He could wheel down practically anything, and I once took a slip catch off him bowling left-arm at a brisk medium-pace, in the second innings, after a one-day game had finished early. To this extent, I suppose, he was an even more versatile bowler than Gary Sobers.

Don Bradman set the seal on a prodigious season in the fifth Test at the Oval where he made 232, and brought his tally for the rubber to 974, a number unapproached in a series either before or since. Yet having got this far his sights were set firmly on the thousand. Suddenly he was given out caught behind off Larwood, it is said on a lone appeal from mid-on. Don was not amused. The story went that the umpire concerned explained that he thought on reflection he had made a mistake in his favour a hundred runs or so earlier, but that was no doubt someone's flight of fancy. At all events Larwood and Tate bowled 113 overs between them for this wicket and that of the number 11, Percy Hornibrook. Peebles had one of the more extraordinary analyses in Test cricket: 71–8–204–6.

Perhaps I should pause a moment here to attempt some brief evaluation of Don Bradman's astonishing achievements in 1930, and this can surely best be done by answering the questions: What was the bowling standard against him, and how did his record compare with others? As to the first, well, England could call on the identical attack (all of them already mentioned) which had retained the Ashes 4–1 the previous year in Australia. In addition there were such prolific county wicket-takers to choose from as Nichols, Goddard, Dick Tyldesley, Voce, Robins, Peebles and Freeman. Neither the English bowling nor their out-cricket generally could be described otherwise than as of good Test quality. As to the second, Bradman for seven completed innings averaged 139. The next figure in the Australian list was Woodfull's 57. The wickets certainly were for the most part good and easy-paced; yet no one else on either side achieved anything remotely approaching Bradman's devastation.

Old Trafford apart—and perhaps excepting, too, one dangerous spell after rain by Larwood at the Oval—Bradman batted his way through the series with an easy dominance to which I have experienced no parallel. The stranger seeing him for the first time must have noticed the exceptional quickness of his reactions, his speed between the wickets and the lithe fitness that enabled him to take the longest innings in his stride. He was small-boned, dapper, his power of stroke deriving from strong wrists and an exquisite sense of timing. To give a physical example from the present generation is not easy. He was about the height of John Edrich, but lacking his chunkiness; a shade bigger all round than the Nawab of Pataudi. Perhaps Doug Walters comes nearest to him in build and height.

You saw all the strokes, the off-drive less frequently than the others. The precision and the variety of his cutting specially struck one. He was a most delicate glancer, and adept at playing the ball off his body at all the on-side angles. When he hooked he got into position so quickly that he could hit the ball early with a downward thrust of the bat aiming in front of square-leg. A stylist? Not indeed in terms of such contemporaries as Walter Hammond, 'Duleep', or McCabe. The bat was more of a sabre than a pendulum. But if perfect balance, co-ordination and certainty of execution be accepted as the principal ingredients of batsmanship, we who watched the Don in his early manhood will not hope or expect ever to see its art displayed in a higher form.

England lost the fifth Test by an innings and the Ashes duly returned to Australia. Bradman had set fresh standards and opened up new horizons. But at the Oval another thing had happened which was more significant in the long run than the winning and losing of the series. During a long stand for the fourth wicket between Bradman and Jackson it rained, and when play was resumed Larwood made the ball fly.

The contrast between the play of these two young batsmen at this point is vividly clear still in my mind. While Jackson stood his ground and offered defensive strokes of classical straightness, Don exceeded even his own normal great speed of foot, improvising brilliantly and keeping his body well clear, one side or the other, of the rising ball. Whether or not he was happy that afternoon against Larwood's speed, with the short ball flying shoulder high and more, he did not look as though he was. In one or two minds the suspicion registered, and with it the thought that here might be a way of cutting the phenomenon down to size. The accident of the rain falling when it did, of Bradman happening to be batting—though the odds about that were pretty short, to be sure—and of Larwood being on hand to exploit a pitch that was soft on top and hard underneath: the combination of these circumstances sparked an idea that in due course led to the scourge that became known as bodyline. Though no one can have recognized it at the time, this Oval scene of 1930 marked the end of an era so far as Test cricket was concerned.

FIVE KEYS TO SUCCESS

By Trevor Bailey

From The Greatest Of My Time, *1968.*

I SAW THE DON in 1934 and in 1938. My hero did everything that was expected, amassed runs quickly and with almost clinical efficiency. Of course, the only series in which his batting was brought down to ordinary standards was when he faced Larwood and Voce in the notorious bodyline tour, but even then he comfortably headed the Australian averages with 56.50.

It was not until 1948 that I played against him. He came to this country as captain of an exceptionally powerful Australian team who steam-rollered their way over England and the counties with the speed and efficiency of a German Blitzkrieg. I bowled against him then on three occasions, for Essex, for Gentlemen of England, and in the Hastings Festival. He was past his prime, but he scored 187, 150 and 143 and supplied me with three very good reasons for placing him as the finest batsman I have ever bowled against. I did have the satisfaction of claiming his wicket on one occasion—but it was only with a long hop after he had decided he had plundered sufficiently!

Why did he score so many runs? There were five main reasons: the first was the inevitability in the way he dealt with the bad ball. He did not merely hit the loose delivery and hope it was going to the boundary, he despatched it there. A particularly fine example of this occurred in the Essex massacre at Southend, when the Australians made 721 runs in the day. The Essex captain, Tom Pearce, decided to put on our second leg-spinner, Frank Vigar, for a psychological first over immediately preceding the luncheon interval. The result was catastrophic, as Don helped himself to six consecutive fours. I was originally stationed at mid-on, but, though I finished at deep midwicket the result was exactly the same, another boundary. All six were perfectly executed, along the ground and obvious fours before they had even left his bat.

Secondly, the Don saw the ball earlier than most people and this, combined with his exceptional reflexes and footwork, meant that he was in a position to play shots that nobody else attempted. Don himself provided me with one of the most revealing examples of this when for once, after a fine dinner, I managed to induce him to talk about his own batting, something which he does rarely. He recalled a match in Australia when a fast-medium seamer called 'Ginty' Lush was bowling at him with the wicket-keeper standing up. The Don suggested that in the interests of safety it would be wiser for him to stand back as he intended to flick one backwards and a nasty accident could occur. Normally, he did not indulge in such batting flippancies, but the fact that he could contemplate, and execute, such a stroke against an accomplished bowler in a first-class game underlined his genius. Also, as a young man he could cross-bat a short ball from a really fast bowler along the ground between mid-wicket and mid-on. In other words he was able to *pull* them early from outside the line, or in front of his face, rather than getting inside the line to *hook*. He was so very quick on his feet that he was probably the most difficult batsman to contain there has been; indeed the speed of his footwork enabled him to hit many balls to the boundary on the full toss which a normal cricketer would have had to play from the crease. When confronted with the problem of bodyline which was both physically dangerous and tactically successful, he attempted to solve the dual threat by stepping to leg and cutting some of the short deliveries into the vacant areas on the off side. When one considers the exceptional pace of Harold Larwood and Bill Voce, one realizes just how quickly Don had to move his feet to be in a position to execute such a shot.

Thirdly, Bradman possessed superb powers of concentration and regarded a century as a springboard for bigger things.

Fourthly, he possessed a fine defence. Nobody can make as many runs as he did without being basically sound. He certainly lifted his bat to third man, which helped when playing cross-bat shots off the back foot, but nobody brought it down straighter, when playing defensively back as well as forward—that, after all, is the vital thing.

Finally, Bradman believed in reducing the number of chances of losing his wicket to a minimum and so generally kept the ball along the carpet. A six may be an exciting shot, but if the timing is not perfect a catch can easily result.

One interesting facet of his batting was the way he so often scored faster than he appeared to be doing. In one match to my amazement the scoreboard announced his 50, while I was convinced he was no further than the early 20s. I still marvel at the 300 he made in one day of the Test match in Leeds in 1934. Admittedly the game was not 'closed up' so much in those days, but it remains a wondrous feat of batsmanship.

Last innings

By Neville Cardus

Cardus's description of Bradman's duck in his last Test innings, 1948.

Bradman had a wonderful reception, and then, with the crowd still in its emotion at the thought of Bradman playing his last Test, Hollies bowled his first ball short and it was played easily back. The next had no such straightforwardness—'a sinful ball', someone said. It was slower, curving voluptuously, floating alluringly; and Bradman, at full stretch forward, still could not cover the spin and was beaten and bowled. An immoral act of Hollies, some of the crowd thought. After applause for the wicket, the end of a remarkable over was acknowledged. A momentous day ended with misty sunshine and the serenity of Morris in a lovely innings. Whether Bradman bats again or not, his team promises a proper farewell for him.

Tears in his eyes

Eric Hollies' account of his famous dismissal of Bradman in 1948, as quoted by Arthur Mailey.

I sent down a leg break first ball, then a googly, which bowled him. But I don't think Don saw it properly. He seemed to have tears in his eyes.

An American perspective

By James A. Michener

From Return To Paradise, *1951.*

In the 1920s one of the world's most remarkable sportsmen appeared in a small Australian town. He was Don Bradman, cricket's Babe Ruth, Ty Cobb and Joe DiMaggio rolled into one. He mesmerised the opposition. Sometimes he batted for days, scoring double and triple centuries.

He was knighted by the King for having practically murdered English bowlers. But they got even. In the 1930s they developed two bowlers of super speed who heaved the ball right at Bradman's head. When he tried to defend himself with his bat, the English captain posted half his team in the infield. And Bradman popped up.

This outrageous sportsmanship was indefensible—wasn't cricket, you know—but there was no rule against it. The Ashes deteriorated into a public brawl. At Adelaide, the English were razzed worse than the Giants are booed at Brooklyn. Books were written and there was some talk of dissolving the Empire.

Ready for more

By Ian Peebles

From Talking Of Cricket, *1953.*

Bradman's superlative genius brought about a fundamental change in tactics which persists to this day, even if no present batsman quite equals his power of aggression. He first showed how matches could be won by sustained and aggressive batting with no more than adequate bowling. No throwing his wicket away at 100 or 200—there was still work to be done on a demoralised attack. Many batsmen have since acquired this outlook and insatiable appetite for runs, but none have had the appalling range and power of stroke to put the opposition to rout at the given moment. In the last hour of the day, where the opportunity for victory is so often made or surrendered, most batsmen, especially moderns, 'shut it up'. Not so Bradman, who, like Napoleon, sent for his seven-league boots and took full toll of his opponents' disorganisation. At the end of the day he would be ready for more. 'Nice bit of practice for to-morrow,' he said cheerfully on return-ing to the dressing-room at Leeds, 309 not out. He not only gave his bowlers runs to work on, he gave them time.

THE DON KEPT ON WALKING

by Neil Marks

IN THE 1950S NEW SOUTH WALES was the dominant force in first-class cricket, winning the Sheffield Shield eight times in 10 years. So strong were they at the time that it was not uncommon for a four-day game to be completed in three days or less, with 'the Blues' winning by an innings. One such game occurred in Adelaide in 1955 when New South Wales played South Australia.

The match finished soon after lunch on the third day and after stumps were drawn the two teams came together in the winning team's locker room to drink beer and to talk as cricketers are inclined to do of the game just completed, of games long gone, of characters of cricket now dropped, retired or dead, of umpires who couldn't tell an LBW from a batting glove, of fillies good enough to win at Fleming-ton and of fillies that they happened to be taking out that evening.

The yarning was in the time-honoured tradition of cricket, going back to days of Spofforth and sure to continue long after the days of Warne.

In the winning team at that particular game were two young colts beginning to make their name, Brian Booth and Warren Saunders. Not wishing to imbibe too early in the day (in Booth's case, not wishing to imbibe at all), the two youngsters decided on a game of tennis. So they walked around behind the grandstand to the Memorial Drive Tennis Club, borrowed some balls and a couple of racquets and began a 'boots and all' singles match on one of the perfectly prepared grass courts that then abounded in this magnificent sporting area of Adelaide.

Saunders and Booth were both excellent sportsmen. Booth would represent Australia in hockey at the 1956 Olympic Games and both were A-grade tennis players. The first set was a tough affair and every point was hard fought. With the score standing at 4—all, 30–15, on Booth's serve, Saunders noticed a man walking along the path that ran beside the courts. As the figure drew closer, he realised that it was none other than Sir Donald Bradman. Suddenly the young up-and-coming opener realised that he had a chance to impress the most powerful man in world cricket.

Saunders braced himself for the next serve, which forced him wide to his forehand, yet with natural anticipation and skill he managed to return cross court. Booth, though, knew before his opponent played the shot where the ball was heading and played the perfect drop shot over the net with Saunders well out of his ground—a certain winner. Not so! Saunders wasn't renowned for giving in easily and, what's more, he knew that 'The Don' was watching. He charged towards the ball which was just about to bounce for the second time and somehow managed to get his racquet underneath it, lobbing it over Booth's head. Booth turned and chased it, and with his back towards his opponent deftly returned it under his arm. Saunders chopped it off at the net. Booth lunged forward and lobbed it back. Still at the net, Saunders leapt high and smashed the ball at his opponent's feet. With the dexterity of a ballet dancer Booth blocked it back. Saunders hit for the open spaces, Booth returned it once again with a blinding forehand volley which with timing and power Saunders volleyed back—passing Booth down the backhand line. It was a rally that would have had the spectators at the centre court of Wimbledon jumping to their feet and spilling their strawberries and cream.

Bradman had not stopped but he had slowed his walk as he witnessed the rally. The point finally decided, the two combatants looked over at the man who averaged 99.94 in Test cricket and who, in his day, was also an A-grade tennis player and scratch golfer. The two players, knowing that they must have impressed the champion, greeted him as he walked past . . .

'G'day, Sir Donald!'

The greatest living Australian raised his hand in a gesture of salutation and remarked, 'I'd have thought that you two would be better off practising your cricket'.

And The Don kept on walking.

MASTER OF ALL

By A. A. Thomson

From Cricket: The Golden Ages, *1961.*

BRADMAN'S LAST TEST INNINGS at the Oval was one of those comic-pathetic episodes that could only have happened in England. The rubber had already been won and the fifth Test, at this stage, was his to do what he liked with. He was cheered all the way to the wicket in profound admiration. He was cheered all the way from the wicket in profound sympathy. In between he was irretrievably bowled second ball for a duck. It was an unplayable ball, but afterwards the bowler, that fair-headed finger-spinning humorist, Eric Hollies, may well have carried it on his conscience for years.

In Bradman's cricket career, a pathway of almost unbroken personal success, what was one nought among so many centuries? I cannot think it worried him greatly, except that he would have wished to give so appreciative a crowd some final offering to appreciate and it was not in his nature to be satisfied with less than one hundred per cent of achievement. His failures were absurdly few and he looked on them neither regretfully nor philosophically, but as sharp demands for their future avoidance. If he found himself guilty of a bad stroke, he would cut it surgically out of his repertory as a specialist might cut out a gangrene. But I am thinking of one of his failures which he may have simply regretted. Each of his four tours to England opened at Worcester on the lovely ground in the loop of the Severn. On that perfect stage, under the shadow of the great cathedral, Bradman scored 236 in 1930; 206 in 1934 and 258 in 1938. In 1948 there was a sad falling-off from the Bradman-Worcester standard. He scored only 107. It is just possible that, in his serious way, he has worried about this; not from run-gluttony, but from tidiness, for next to his steely determination, his strongest characteristic is an orderly mind.

His parallels with Grace are many. He was a marvel, a wonder, a nonesuch, and he made his own legend; he had no bristling beard or burly figure or alarming presence to build up the impressive image: only his strength of character and his unmatched skill. Each of the two men had a core of relentlessness in his nature; W. G. may have been more genial, but then nobody ever dared put him in a mood not to be genial; he could quell the rebel with one look. W. G. made all the records as cricket grew and expanded under his hand. Bradman broke nearly every known record and set up more records that will never be broken. As W. G. towered above his contemporaries, so did Bradman above his own, and he did not dominate duffers. He played for twenty years and the batsmen whom he excelled ranged from the 'unbowlable' Woodfull, the prolific Ponsford and the brilliant McCabe to Morris, Barnes and the mercurial Neil Harvey. Against him were ranged batsmen of the quality of Hobbs and Sutcliffe, Woolley and Hammond, Hutton and Compton; and who were the bowlers off whom he scored his myriad runs? They included Larwood and Tate; Verity and Bowes; Allen and White; Peebles and Fames; Bedser, Yardley, Laker and Hollies. He was human and therefore not infallible. Bowes once bowled him first ball and Hollies second ball. Bedser beat and bowled him more than once and had him caught three times in succession by Hutton at fine leg. Bradman eventually became master of all of them, but his mastery was all the greater because those with whom he strove were in their various ways masters in their own right.

Wilfred Rhodes bowled against him in 1930 in what was Rhodes's last, and Bradman's first, season in English first-class cricket. Twenty years later Rhodes told me: 'I once saw him come in and put his first ball straight back past the bowler for four; and the second, and the third. He did it without getting his eye or anything. Yes, maybe Jack Hobbs second and Victor Trumper third, but Bradman first, without a doubt . . .'

There were some who said that Bradman could not bat on wet or sticky wickets. Hedley Verity (and I wish he were alive to repeat it) simply denied this. Even after 'Verity's match', he could say: 'Bradman was a great batsman on any wicket.' Bradman is an Australian; for him cricket was always meant to be a game played on a plumb wicket under a blazing sun. If he had played every day, say, in our county cricket, enjoying and suffering the infinite variety of English turf and English atmosphere, he would have adapted himself to the conditions (or, preferably, the conditions to himself) and would have become as much a master on bad wickets as were Tyldesley, or Sutcliffe or that odd genius, Edgar Oldroyd. His distaste for the bad wicket was not that he could not cope with it, but that it prevented cricket from being the rich and spectacular game that it ought to be.

To those who say that Bradman was a mere run-getting machine, I would reply that this is the age of the beautiful machine and that no machine was more nearly perfect. I would also reply, no doubt illogically, that Bradman was no machine, but was, and is, a very human person. R. C. Robertson-Glasgow, whom God preserve, said of him: 'Bradman was that rarest of Nature's creations, an artist without the handicap of the artistic temperament . . .' That was a true saying. Bradman has his troubles, with periods of indifferent health, and with the hurts that envy and jealousy can inflict upon the man on the pinnacle, but he never suffered from the egoism, hard-boiled or soft, that is nine-tenths of the artistic temperament. He made runs as a millionaire makes money. But who, seeing the power, the daring, the fluency, the untamability of his batting, could deny that he was a supreme artist?

Since retirement his contribution to cricket has been as an administrator. In that capacity he has had the reputation of being a hard man. But why not? As a captain, the friendly and talented Norman Yardley said of him that there was only one thing that he enjoyed more than beating you by an innings and two hundred runs and that was beating you by an innings and three hundred runs. Again, why not? It is not right only to half-want to win. In the delicate negotiations between the countries of the Commonwealth on the delicate question of 'throwing', he has conducted himself with his own kind of shrewd fair-mindedness. What will happen we can only hopefully conjecture, but if things go wrong, it will not be Bradman's fault. Honest folk cannot honestly agree about what constitutes a 'throw', but Bradman has at least done his best in his own country to help to keep the problem on fair and sensible lines.

It is not given to every man to be universally loved, as Trumper was loved by Australians, George Hirst by Yorkshiremen and Hobbs by all to whom the name of cricket means anything at all. The quality of complete integrity is more valuable to its owner and the world than natural likeability, though some men have them both—Trumper and Hirst had and Hobbs has—in abundance. A man of strong character willing to fight for what he thinks right and wholeheartedly determined to achieve the objective he pursues will not court easy popularity, and through this may lose many 'popular' votes. But he will gain a respect which will increase and will at last become absolute. That respect Sir Donald Bradman has and will retain.

There is a final anecdote, mildly (or wildly) apocryphal, which tells how Yorkshire took Don Bradman to its otherwise flinty heart. The last ball of the Headingley Test had been bowled and the winning hit made. As Bradman, with his partner Harvey, strove to reach the pavilion, the spectators surged on to the field and the police fought a battle of sheer physical strength to clear a passage for the victors. As Bradman, crushed in on all sides, approached the pavilion gate, he found his way barred by an old man, a typical Yorkshireman of the old school, who was visibly suffering under deep emotional stress. His expression clearly showed his schizophrenic state. Here was the enemy, the villain of the piece; here was the man who had torn England (a part of Yorkshire) to tatters. But he had done it by strong captaincy, of which a Yorkshireman must approve, and by batting so magnificent, so apocalyptic that it took the breath away. Bradman was wonderful. Bradman was the devil incarnate. A tear rolled down the man's cheek. He raised his hand. His lips moved. There was only one word in the national vocabulary that could express, in all its fine shades, the heights, the depths, the absolute, the *ne plus ultra*.

'Ee,' he cried passionately. 'Ee, yer *boogger*.'

'I LIKED THE BLOKE'

By Colin McCool

From Cricket Is A Game, *1961.*

BRADMAN, OF COURSE, WAS way out on his own. He was the
killer. Yet he has been chipped and chivvied and knocked by his
colleagues and critics more than any other player in the game. Maybe
he was too successful, too dedicated for the ordinary human palate.
Whatever the reason he has become the number-one target for vitriol
whenever any has been flying about.

I didn't play in a Test on the Australian tour of England in 1948. As
a result, scores of people, well-meaning, have come up to me and said
sympathetically: 'You must have got on the wrong side of Bradman.'

But I didn't, and it is almost embarrassing for me to point out that
Bradman never let anything but form influence him when he was
picking a team. There was no dirty intrigue to keep me out of the side.
I simply wasn't playing well enough. In any case, you can see from the
results that the fellows he did pick weren't doing too badly!

I might as well come out straight and admit that I liked the bloke.
As far as I was concerned he was fair, just and very human.

You can't say that of everybody in this game of cricket.

When we got back home after the 1948 tour, and the team was
breaking up, Bradman came up to me and said: 'Thanks for everything.
You've been a brick.' Not many captains would have said that to a man
who had played such a small part in keeping the Ashes. In fact, the
more I remember Bradman the more I remember his warmth and
understanding.

There was the time I was the shock selection for the Australian tour
of South Africa. It was clear from the party that I was included to get
runs as much as anything else. I was still getting over the surprise when

a letter arrived from Bradman saying: 'You are capable of making as many runs as anyone else in this side. Remember that, and make every post a winner.'

FALLIBLE, BUT STILL THE BEST

By Bill O'Reilly

From Cricket Conquest, *1949.*

BRADMAN AS USUAL DOMINATED the show. But Bradman was eighteen years older than he was when he first bludgeoned his way to immortality against the flower of English bowling in 1930. A Bradman, you may say, is a law unto himself. That may be, but if he could attain such success in 1948 against the English Test array, what would that young gentleman of 1930 have done against it, when he had the enthusiasm and all the other splendid attributes of youth at his disposal? That Bradman was a relentless young fellow who not only got big scores but took a fiendish delight in pulverizing the attack. Pity help the bowler who had managed to give him a torrid time during the early part of any one of his innings. He remembered any indignity that he had been forced to accept and he exacted retribution in profusion when he was in full sail later in his stay at the wicket. He had an insatiable appetite for runs. It seemed that run-getting was his ingrained method of self-expression and not lacking any of the innate tendency of self-assertiveness, he expressed himself long and loud. There was no escaping the Bradman bat when it was charged with the responsibility of smashing down all opposition. Off-theory bowling to a packed field was chicken feed to him, whereas the packed on-side field set for the leg-theory bowler was as nought. I have seen him step wide of his stumps and hit the leg-theory merchant past point where there was no fieldsman at all, and the off-theory bowler must often have wished that he had twenty fieldsmen instead of ten. That was the pre-war Bradman.

Not once since cricket has been resumed has 'the little fellow' taken up the whole stage as he did before. He was still a fine batsman undoubtedly, but the 'killer instinct' had gone completely. He, at most times, appeared quite human—if there is truth in the old adage 'to err is human.' Almost without exception each innings of the tour was marked by a well-defined period of uncertainty at its initial stage. Bradman's performance in collecting so many runs on this tour was worthy of the great player that he had been. Even though his eyes and legs worked ever so much slower than they had been used to do, his fundamental knowledge of the game carried him through. The point I am driving at is this. If the Bradman of 1948 could still carry off the batting honours for the 'best Australian team ever,' then two reasonable inferences can be arrived at. Firstly, the English bowling was below its best standards, and secondly, Australia possesses no budding Bradman. Where would the present Bradman have finished in comparison with the 1930 Bradman if it were possible to have had the two of them on this tour? That is a hypothetical question which I believe every cricketer of 1930 onward will try to answer.

THE SUPREMELY CAPABLE MAN

By John Arlott

From Gone To The Test Match, *1949.*

IT IS, SO IT SEEMS, pleasant to be an Australian and to feel that you have a stake in Don Bradman. Whether it is as pleasant to be Don Bradman is doubtful.

It is impossible to discuss Bradman the cricketer without first recognizing Bradman the public figure. More people are interested in Bradman, but not in cricket, than are interested in Bradman *and* cricket. Because he is Bradman, he is constantly singled out from his team-mates. If he attempts to step back into the line of the team, the person who has approached him is offended. If, with normal courtesy, Bradman accepts the advance as a gesture of well-meant admiration— then he widens the gap between himself and his fellow-players. He is news on the field and potential gossip off it.

I have been with Test cricketers in public places when, if they were recognized—and often I think they were not—at least no one molested them. I have seen Bradman's meal in an hotel dining-room constantly interrupted by bores and boors, and I have seen him accosted by four separate strangers in the twenty yards from the dining-room to the cloak-room in his hotel. He must wear the public mask constantly, for he is rarely left alone. When he is alone he must devote himself to his mail—if only to sort the single important letter from two hundred which importune for his autograph, his presence at a garden-party or his opinion on a matter in which he has no interest. Most public figures have a covering shield of secretaries to protect them from annoyance and to deal with the backwash of obligations entailed by publicity. Bradman must contrive this organization for himself. He has contrived it successfully, as Don Bradman will contrive most things he sets his mind to. He is the supremely capable man. Satisfied with the terms of his employment, he would make the perfect executive. He prefers, however, to make his efforts on his own behalf. He has been single-minded as a cricketer, a business man, a musician and as a public figure; and has succeeded as each. He was given, and has maintained, a good average body and a good average brain; he has directed them with that rare perfect single-mindedness which makes for the attaining of objectives.

Because he is 'a success', because he is a public figure, because he is

Bradman, he has missed much of the best of cricket. He has never been a temporary failure among other temporary failures, never shared with ten others, neither appreciably greater nor appreciably less than himself, that sympathy and mutual delight in temporary success which the other cricketer knows. He has never played a game at Bath or Melton Mowbray or Basingstoke where players outnumber spectators, and a batsman who is out may take off his pads and saunter unmolested, hands in pockets, round the ground to the marquee for a quiet drink. Horace Hazell can throw his boots and flannels into a bag and catch the bus to Bristol; may talk to the man in the next seat unrecognized, or, if he is recognized, is recognized as 'Horace,' a pleasant chap and one of us. But your Bradman must hurry to a car and hide himself from the crowd that pickets his hotel.

An old-hand county batsman, tired of a match going down to a draw on the third day, can 'have a swish' and get out and catch the early train home, or can say, 'Don't send me in, skipper—give one of the lads a chance and put me down number ten, my feet are sore.' But when Bradman rests for one match of an arduous tour of England, the local spectators are hurt and they adduce fifty 'good' reasons why Bradman *ought* to have played. If he moves himself down in the batting order he 'insults our players'. If he throws his wicket away, he has robbed ten thousand people of the conversational gambit, 'When I saw Bradman make his hundred at —.' A county player can fail to score double figures in four consecutive innings, and even the *Dullshire Gazette* will not say much about it, being busy with his colleagues who have done well. But if Bradman plays three low innings in succession, then his 'bubble' is 'pricked,' or there is a sinister rumour . . . It is all so futile, so bad for cricket, so bad for Bradman.

Rising forty, which is veteran age for an Australian cricketer, he came to England in 1948 for his last tour. 'Is he still the Bradman of old?' was the question. Of course he damned well wasn't. Any man in possession of all his faculties *must* develop and change in ten years.

D. G. Bradman of the 1948 Australian team was a great batsman in his 1948 right. He scored hundreds, brilliant hundreds, hundreds which could hardly have been more appropriate if he had stage-managed them. Because he was an older man, eighteen years older, than the Bradman of 1930, he was less hungry for records. He was concerned to make runs for his side, no doubt he found it pleasant still to make a century. He could still annihilate almost any bowling on a friendly wicket. But some of the old fierce single-mindedness which urged him to go on breaking record after record was gone. The quality of his single-mindedness had not weakened, but the will to that particular single-mindedness was blunted by maturity and a wider consciousness, a different *general* aim. At forty some of the strokes of the early twenties are no longer business cricket: like Hobbs, Bradman, with cricketing maturity, discarded those strokes of youth which had demanded the extremes of the eye and speed of youth. Yet Bradman in 1948, forty years old, was still playing strokes impossible to any other cricketer in the world. He stood at the crease perfectly immobile until the ball was on its way to him, then his steps flowed like quicksilver out of trouble or into position to attack. He could still pull the ball outside the off-stump accurately wide of mid-on's right hand to avoid a packed off-side field. He still played the ball off his back foot past mid-off before that fieldsman could bend to it. He still hit through the covers with the grace of a swooping bird. He could cut and glance, drive, hook and pull, and he could play unbelievably late in defence. He often made a shaky start—the shakiest starts of all before his biggest scores. Those who had never seen Bradman bat until 1948 saw a great batsman: those who knew his batting between 1930 and 1938 saw a new greatness, a greatness owing more to the brain. He could grow tired now—naturally, as any who have spent more than a few minutes 'in the middle' would expect. There were times when, as the ball came slowly to him in the field, with the batsmen not attempting a run, he stooped like a very tired man. But let speed be essential in a stop and throw, and he moved with most of the old dancing alertness—never more than during his last Test at the Oval.

As a captain he did the right thing almost automatically, for the idiom of the game has become his native language. High-shouldered, shirt collar turned up to the chin, cap pulled well on, he walked backwards to his position in the field as the bowler walked to his mark. His eyes moved alertly as a blackbird's, and he would stop the game while, back cautiously turned to the batsman, he passed his latest intelligence to the bowler. He set the defensive field with true Australian mastery. He nursed his bowlers wisely and received magnificent service from his fieldsmen.

Never since his teens has Don Bradman known a quiet game of cricket. Every innings he has played for twenty years has been potential big news. This deprivation and this burden have not been suffered without effect. On the rare occasions when he was not actively engaged on cricket or social or business matters and his face could fall into repose, he wore a tired look. But at a word he was alert, birdlike, wearing his slightly twisted grin, making the wry remark accompanied by a smile, an automatic smile to remove any possible offence. When any word a man says may qualify for both publication and misinterpretation, conversation becomes an art indeed, but ceases to be a pleasure.

From late April until late September 1948, in England, Donald George Bradman played cricket, captained a cricket team, made speeches, was polite to bores, ignored the spite of those who grudged him that he had earned, kept his temper and consolidated a great public reputation. He gained more of respect than of envy from those who sought to understand.

Salute from America

A New York Times *editorial, March 1949.*

Probably few Americans would recognise a googly bowler if they saw one, or be able to distinguish an over from a boundary hit. But they could hardly fail to recognise that Don Bradman must have been quite a cricketer when they read in their newspapers that he had been knighted by the King.

Australia's retired Test match star is one of the great batsmen of all time. He is one of the few British cricket players who have been so honored. If not the only one who has been knighted strictly on the basis of his playing skill.

Sir Donald has often been called the 'Babe Ruth of cricket'. It is not a bad comparison, except that throughout the British Empire cricket is much more truly the paramount national game than is baseball in the United States.

We have other sports that compete for public favor. There is no other king but cricket in the British lexicon. As long as there is an England there will be cricket grounds somewhere in the fore ground.

Bradman was the unchallenged shining light for almost 20 years. We salute Sir Donald with admiration but without any regrets that we cannot match his title with a sports knight of our own. We like our kings uncrowned.

BRADMAN NO MORE

By R. C. Robertson-Glasgow

From Wisden Cricketers' Almanac, *1949.*

DON BRADMAN WILL BAT no more against England, and two contrary feelings dispute within us: relief, that our bowlers will no longer be oppressed by this phenomenon; regret, that a miracle has been removed from among us. So must ancient Italy have felt when she heard of the death of Hannibal.

For sheer fame, Dr W. G. Grace and Don Bradman stand apart from all other cricketers—apart, indeed, from all other games-players. The villagers used to crowd to their doors when 'W.G.' and his beard drove through their little main street. Bradman, on his visits to England, could never live the life of a private citizen. He couldn't stroll from his hotel to post a letter or buy a collar-stud. The mob wouldn't let him. There had to be a car waiting with engine running, and he would plunge into it, like a cork from a bottle. When cricket was on, Bradman had no private life. He paid for his greatness, and the payment left some mark. The informal occasion, the casual conversation, the chance and happy acquaintance, these were very rarely for him, and his life was that of something between an Emperor and an Ambassador. Yet, for all that, there remained something of that boy who, thirty years before, had knocked a ball or ball-like object about in the backyard of a small house in New South Wales. He never lost a certain primitive and elemental 'cheekiness,' and mingled, as it were, with his exact and scientific calculations, there was the immortal impudence of the *gamin*.

But, above all, Bradman was a business-cricketer. About his batting there was to be no style for style's sake. If there was to be any charm, that was for the spectator to find or miss. It was not Bradman's concern. His aim was the making of runs, and he made them in staggering and ceaseless profusion. He seemed to have eliminated error, to have perfected the mechanism of stroke. Others before him had come near to doing this; but Bradman did it without abating the temperature of his attack. No other batsman, surely, has ever been able to score so fast while at the same time avoiding risk. He was, as near as a man batting may be, the flawless engine. There were critics who found surfeit in watching him. Man, by his nature, cannot bear perfection in his fellow. The very fact that something is being done which had been believed to be impossible goads and irritates. It is but a short step from annoyance to envy, and Bradman has never been free from envy's attacks. So, when, first in 1930, he reeled off the centuries, single, double and treble, there were not wanting those who compared him unfavourably with other great ones—Trumper, Ranjitsinhji, Hobbs, Macartney. And Bradman's answer was more runs. Others, perhaps, *could* have made them, but they didn't. No one before had ever been quite so fit, quite so ruthless.

It was a coolly considered policy. Cricket was not to be his hobby, his off-hours delight. It was to be his life and his living. A few hundreds here and there for Australia and State—what use in that? Others had done it, would do it again. He did not mean to be just one of the stars, but the sun itself. Never was such ambition achieved and sustained. Never was the limelight directed so unwaveringly on one man in one game. To set such a standard was unique. To keep it was a miracle.

But the sun itself has degrees of splendour; and, whatever the numbers may say, Bradman was never again quite so incredible as in England in the summer of 1930. Like all great artists, he knew how to begin. So he made 236 at Worcester and 185 not out at Leicester. Then, with a mere trifle of 78 against Yorkshire he relented into rest. At Nottingham, in the first Test, he was set fair to win the match for Australia when R. W. V. Robins bowled him with a googly. It is a freak of chance that in both his first and last Test matches in England he should have fatally mistaken a googly for a leg-break. It is also reassuring to mere mortality. In that first

Test he scored 131. This was a *hors d'oeuvre* of the feast to follow. At Lord's, in the second Test, he made 254, and the innings only ended with one of those catches that set A. P. F. Chapman apart from the other England fieldsmen. Then, at Leeds, he scored 334.

George Duckworth, who was keeping wicket for England, rates this innings as the greatest he ever saw. Archie Jackson, that glorious and ill-fated batsman, had opened the Australian innings with W. M. Woodfull. Off the fifth ball of the second over from Maurice Tate, Jackson was caught at short-leg. Bradman joined his captain. The first ball that he received from Tate whizzed just over his off-stump, and Duckworth, believing that Bradman must be bowled, let it go for byes. Then the show began. Bradman never hit in the air. Boundaries sprang from his bat with murderous precision and calculated profusion. Larwood, Tate and Geary—no mean trio—were helpless. A new machine was at work. A new standard of ambition had been set. At Manchester, Ian Peebles induced Bradman into error to the leg-break. But Bradman returned to himself with 232 at the Oval in the fifth Test. In the five Tests he had scored 974 runs at an average of 139. Statistics cannot record the number of runs he carried with him to each innings. But, in a country of great fieldsmen, he stood out pre-eminent. His gathering and throwing approached perfection. Only in catching, probably owing to the smallness of his hands, he was no better than the next man.

Then, after he had taken his pleasure of the South African bowling in Australia, came the first eclipse. A new style of attack, popularly known as bodyline, with the great fast bowler Larwood as its spearhead, was launched on the Australians in Australia by D. R. Jardine. This is no place for discussing the ethics of the matter. Technically, Bradman found no satisfactory answer. He met it, certainly, with a virtuosity of footwork possible to him alone. But his average in eight Test innings sank to a mere trifle of 57, including a score of 103 not out.

When Bradman next came to England, in 1934, there was no

Larwood against him, and no Voce. He resumed his mastery. In the Leeds Test he scored 304; at The Oval 244. But, whereas in 1930 he had annihilated doubt, there were now certain qualifications. He was found to be incomplete against that great left-hand bowler, Hedley Verity, on a sticky wicket. At Lord's, in the second Test, he lost his head, if one may use such a phrase of such a master of calculation and coolness. Perhaps it was attributable to his uncertain health. But too much emphasis has been laid on this failure. Verity himself did not agree with the popular generalisation that Bradman 'couldn't play on the bad ones.' And he knew. But it should be said that, with the exception of Larwood in Australia during the 1932–33 tour, Verity was the one bowler who battled with Bradman on something like level terms, even on the truest of pitches. Besides this failure at Lord's in 1934, another man, one of his own team, contributed to some dimming of the Bradman glory. That was W. H. Ponsford, of Victoria. He was playing in his last Test series against England. Most of his records, once seemingly unassailable, had been stolen by Bradman; but now Ponsford, one of the greatest players of spin bowling that ever batted, ran level with his rival, and actually beat him in the matter of Test average by a decimal point.

Already Bradman had proved his power to live on a pinnacle of success. Now, against G. O. Allen's team in Australia, 1936–37, he was to show that he could return from failure. He started downright badly, and the vultures that await the fall of the great hovered expectantly. But he disappointed them, and, by the end of the tour, he was once more the authentic Bradman. In 1938, his third visit to England, he came as captain. Henceforward, in Tests, except for one innings of 234 at Sydney, he was to deal in single centuries only. It was a concession to old man Time.

Where does Bradman stand as a captain? Such a question opens the way to opinions which, even when gathered from those who played with him from day to day, cannot be reduced to any certain conclusion. On the field he was superb. He had seen and weighed it all. Shrewd and tough, he was not likely to waste anything in dreams or mercy. No one ever saw Bradman not attending. Cricket, to one who made and kept his way from hard beginnings, was a business, not a pastime.

He made mistakes. He took only three regular bowlers on to the field for the last Test at The Oval in 1938. For him, as for Australia, the match was a disaster. Bradman, when bowling, fell and injured his leg. England scored 903 for seven wickets; Hutton 364. Both these totals are Test records. Bradman was unable to bat, and Australia lost by the record margin of an innings and 579. How different from the scene of ten years later, when Lindwall went through the England batting like a steam drill. But, all in all, Bradman was the supreme tactician.

On the personal side, his success was more doubtful. Great captaincy begins off the field. True leadership springs from affection even more than from respect. Bradman certainly earned the respect. But, by his very nature, he was bound to have admirers rather than friends. Stripped to the truth, he was a solitary man with a solitary aim. It was what the man did rather than what he was that invited obedience. There are humorously affectionate stories about most great cricketers; intimate, if somewhat apocryphal tales about them; of what Dr Grace said when Ernest Jones bowled a ball through his beard; of Patsy Hendren's reply to a criticism from the Sydney 'Hill'; of what Johnny Douglas uttered when second slip floored a catch. But there are no funny stories about the Don. No one ever laughed about Bradman. He was no laughing matter.

During the War, disturbing rumours reached England about his health; and, whatever truth there may have been in them, certainly the England team under W. R. Hammond found Bradman uncommonly near to being a sick man. But, happily, he recovered. So did his batting. Not without luck, surely earned, he first groped, then rushed, his way back to normal. Enough of the old skill returned for him to score 187 at Brisbane and 234 at Sydney.

There followed his last visit as a Test cricketer to England. As a batsman he no longer flamed high above his fellows. He was now no more than a very fine player, and it was arguable that both S. G. Barnes and A. R. Morris were stronger factors in the quelling of bowlers. But Bradman's fame, if possible, increased. Next to Mr Winston Churchill, he was the most celebrated man in England during the summer of 1948. His appearances throughout the country were like one continuous farewell matinée. At last his batting showed human fallibility. Often, especially at the start of the innings, he played where the ball wasn't, and spectators rubbed their eyes. But such a treasury of skill could spare some gold and still be rich. He scored 138 against England at Nottingham, and, when it much mattered, 173 not out at Leeds.

Most important of all, he steered Australia through some troubled waters and never grounded on the rocks. Returning home, he received the first Knighthood ever given to a playing cricketer.

Bradman's place as a batsman is among the few who have been blessed with genius. He was the most wonderful run-scorer that the game has yet known, and no batsman in our own time has so highly excited expectation and so rarely disappointed it.

FLAWLESS BRADMAN

By Sir Robert Menzies

From The Measure Of The Years, *1970.*

THE GREAT DON BRADMAN, as I have said on other occasions, defies all rules or definitions. As he is a human being, he must somewhere have had a weak spot; though bowlers found it difficult to discover. The immense *authority* of his batting, the complete justice with which he dealt with each ball on its merits and dispatched it on what seemed to be its predestined errand have made him the undisputed master batsman of my time. Century followed century with almost monotonous inevitability. We could find no fault in him. Yet perfection itself has a sort of sculptural quality. One begins to yearn for a little artistic aberration which would make mere mortals feel less awed, but possibly a little happier.

BOUNDARIES AT DINNER

By Ben Travers

From 94 Declared. *Travers was a guest at the Bradman home while following the England team in Australia in 1962–63.*

I WAS THE GUEST of Don Bradman at a dinner party at his house—an exclusive dinner-party, since the only other guests were Arthur Mailey and Bradman's two fellow selectors, one of whom was Jack Ryder. I was regarded as a privileged and reliable auditor of their discussions on this, the second evening of the Test, and I was given the opportunity of taking stock of Don as cricket's legislator rather than its supreme expert. His success in both capacities tends to obscure the fact that he possesses a brain which would have got him anywhere in any walk of life. His personality and manner have something akin to his batsmanship: 'Try me. You won't get by me. In fact, I'll probably hit you for four.' In conversation with anyone so decisive and sharp-witted, it is often a pleasure to be hit for four.

ADVICE TO GOOD EFFECT

By Adrian McGregor

From Greg Chappell, *1985. The incident McGregor describes here took place in 1967–68.*

BEFORE THE STATE TEAM began their eastern States tour a sterner hand stepped in to resolve Greg's on-side hitting. Sir Donald Bradman, having failed to convince those worthies, Chester Bennett and Jack Dunning, to curb Greg's on-side habit at Prince Alfred College, took matters into his own hands. Sir Donald was chairman of selectors for the team and he and co-selector Phil Ridings used to visit the South Australian dressing-room just before play each day for a cup of tea. Bradman, always private in preference to prolix, commanded such a presence that few of the young players dared approach him. Greg watched him, noticed that he was not tall, wondered how he had dominated the bowlers as he did but sensed, 'He had something . . . he was different.'

This day Greg was signing bats on the autograph table by the dressing-room door when Bradman passed. 'Good morning, Sir Donald,' said Greg, holding a bat for something to do with his hands. Bradman stopped and replied, 'I'd change that grip if I were you.' Greg asked what he would suggest. Bradman advised him to hold it as he used to, with the vee between the thumb and the forefinger of both hands pointing straight down the back of the handle towards where the handle spliced into the blade. 'That's the way I used to hold it and I think that's the best way to hold it to be an all around the wicket player,' he said. 'The grip that you've got now is very good for the on-side, but you'll never be a good off-side player with it.' Greg thanked Sir Donald for his interest. Bradman pressed his point. 'It's going to take you some time. Practise. It will feel uncomfortable because you've been doing it the other way but if you persevere you'll become comfortable.' Sir Donald started to walk away and then turned and said, 'I've given this piece of advice to one other player who used to play for South Australia—he didn't take the advice and he's no longer playing for South Australia.'

Greg grabbed two players from the dressing-room. 'Come on, come and bowl to me.' He batted in the nets for half an hour using the new grip, moving the back of his top hand around from the front of the handle. 'Within 20 minutes I started to feel comfortable and I couldn't have gone back to the other way,' said Greg. 'I used it that day.' With such good effect that Les Favell was able to write soon after, 'He is hitting the ball through the covers with a full swing of the bat and still retains his on-side strokes.' The strokeplay had been born which 16 years later would bring him his twenty-fourth and last Test century and would provoke Richie Benaud to eulogize on television:

> *Beautiful stroke. What a marvellous way to bring up 100, with a classic cover drive that we've seen so often over the years from this great player.*

MIND POWER

By Colin Cowdrey

From The Autobiography of A Cricketer, *1976.*

ONE OF THE LESSER known facts about Bradman is that soon after he retired from decimating bowling attacks all over the world he became severely stricken by the golf bug. One day, after a particularly bad round, he returned to his home on the outskirts of Adelaide, sat in a chair and quietly announced to his family that he was now going to become a scratch player. Lady Bradman, a delightful person with a rare understanding of the outrageous quirks of games players, immediately realised that this was going to mean another upheaval to her house-hold. Working and meal-time routines would have to be radically rearranged and conversation would now be dominated by such earth-shattering themes as the overlapping grip and the dynamics of the downswing. Lady Bradman reckoned that it would take the little dynamo about two years and, as always, she was right. Sir Donald rose at five, worked feverishly on his papers, breakfasted absolutely on schedule, drove off to attend to the affairs of his companies with deter-mination and then, at the appointed moment, headed for the golf course, there to slave for hour upon hour at his woods and irons. His handicap duly plunged to scratch and by the expiry of his self-imposed time-table Don Bradman was one of the finest amateur golfers in Australia. He had mastered one game; he did not enjoy being mastered by another. If only he had been fifteen years younger Gary Player and Peter Thomson would have felt the lash of his tail.

The quite ruthless ability to drive himself, to concentrate utterly, to exhaust any problem he regarded worthy of his attention, to waste no time on fools and frivolity, to live his life to meticulous schedules, made him the remarkable cricketer he was and the extraordinary man he is. If he begins to expound on rose-growing, Australian wine, building a swimming pool or the local rateable value it is worthwhile listening because he does not venture opinions unless he is master of the subject.

I have never quite lost the awe of him I acquired when my father hustled me on deck in the Mediterranean, on my way home to school from India, to see the ship in which Bradman was passing. But by the time I returned to Australia for my fourth tour, this time under the captaincy of Mike Smith in the winter of 1965–66, I had got to know him quite well. We exchanged Christmas cards and the occasional letter and, in Australia, I had visited his home fairly frequently. We also played golf together on his home course at Kooyonga, Adelaide, where he embarked on every round as though he were driving off for the World Match-Play Title.

In those friendly games he would be most helpful, advising which was the best line to take to the hole, where the hidden hazards were down the fairway, which were the difficult greens and why.

His brilliance at ball games made him a fine lawn tennis and squash player but I had the great pleasure, on that tour, of introducing him to a game he had never tried before—real tennis. He had seen the court at Lord's and was aware that there was another court in Melbourne where I played occasionally. I promised to take him for an introductory game when he arrived for the Test match and one Sunday morning he collected me at the Windsor Hotel, an alert little figure in grey flannels, white shirt and scarf. He was visibly excited.

Real tennis, with its origins back in the French monasteries of the fourteenth century and a bemusing vocabulary of its own, is a highly complex game. Directions like 'laying a chase on the hazard side' are beyond most people's comprehension until they have been on a court for several long sessions but, during our knock-up, Bradman questioned everything and let nothing pass until he understood it fully. Several times he became quite impatient at my apparent inability to explain all the implications of a certain rule in a single sentence. In those moments he looked like a school-boy who could not understand why bridge is not as simple as snap.

But so penetrating is his mind that by the time we began playing a game he understood every tactical situation perfectly. And that was not all. What staggered me was his fantastic speed about the court, racing from one corner to another to retrieve a ball which a man half his age would have ignored. Bradman at the time was fifty-seven and had already suffered one heart attack.

It was that morning, on that court at Melbourne, that I understood why Bradman was probably the greatest cricketer that ever lived. I was aware not of a man but a machine whirring at my elbow. He was conscious of no mortal thing outside those walls. His concentration and determination were absolute. Here was a man, at an age when most men would have been living out their past glories in a rocking chair, aggressively storming a new challenge. He was a power house.

In Australia they used to be proud of 'Our Bridge, Our Harbour and Our Bradman'. He is universally respected but, among people who know him and millions in Australia who don't, his image is not one of a glamorous, popular idol. This may seem curious in a country where winning is in itself a philosophy. I think the explanation is that Bradman's insistence on getting to the heart of any problem as swiftly and directly as possible leaves little time for frills. It is not his way. He has not time to waste on what many would regard as the natural courtesies in argument. Whereas another man might preface his disagreement with 'Well, perhaps one could take a slightly different view to that . . .' Bradman would cut the preamble to 'No, you are wrong because . . .' He is entitled to be dogmatic because he does his homework, and is invariably well briefed.

He can only cram so many activities into his life by observing the strictest personal regimen. He rises at five a.m. and goes to bed at midnight. Every moment of those waking hours has to be used to a purpose. In earlier days he would guard his time and plan it as meticulously as a Prime Minister. When talking to him there is usually a theme for discussion, a point to pursue, a problem to solve. It is not difficult to see how, when he turned his attention to stockbroking, he was successful. Indeed, over dinner with the England team one night, Sir Robert Menzies said that in his view Bradman knew more about certain aspects of Australian finance than any other man in the country.

Inevitably he is at his most dazzling on the subject of cricket. He has the sharpest cricket mind of all the cricketers I have met. His knowledge is so extensive that I can quite understand the difficulties he occasionally faced in his capacity as chairman of the Australian Board of Control. There must have been other members who found it hard to keep up with him and, indeed, to tune in on his wavelength of thinking.

I regard it as a tragedy for cricket that in a game beset by problems so much of this brilliant talent has been so pathetically wasted. While the hub of everything revolves around Lord's, Bradman has been in the branch office in Adelaide. Of course, his influence has been considerable over the years. I cannot think there had been any major change without his view being sought. How much more could he have done for cricket had he been able to come to London each year. Every summer at Lord's there is an international conference at which Australia is represented. Only twice in twenty-five years has Sir Donald been present.

His method of dealing with the ugly throwing problem in Australia illustrated well the way in which his splendid brain and driving force could have been put to wider use. The irony here is that when he was concerned solely with selection of Australian teams he picked bowlers who later, it transpired, had suspect actions. That's how difficult the throwing problem was. But when he became chairman of the Australian Board we had all learnt a lot more about it and he sought to put things right. He accepted his responsibilities and recognised throwing as one of the main evils in the game. He decided that it should be eliminated as quickly as possible. His approach was the familiar one of giving it his undivided attention for some eighteen months. He collected reports on throwing, wrote reports on throwing, had films taken of every bowler in Australian State cricket, sent to England for films of many of the players in county cricket and in the end compiled so much information on the subject that he could give an excellent four-hour film lecture with his ancient hand-cranked projector. Armed with all the evidence, he assailed every administrator and umpire in Australian cricket with the new-found facts of his case and won the day. Throwing was banished from all levels of the Australian game in two or three years. It was a wonderful achievement.

It was fortunate that G. O. Allen was at the helm of English cricket over this period, guiding the decision making. They had been good

friends over the years and in the days before the telex and easy tele-
phone communication this rapport and alliance was important.

Gubby was one of Douglas Jardine's fast bowling battery in
1932–33, Larwood, Voce, Allen, Bowes and Tate, in the assault which
came to be known as bodyline. But, as they drew up their plans, Gubby
made it quite clear that whereas he would give the captain all he had,
bowl as well and as fast as he knew how, with an occasional bouncer
too, he was quite adamant that he would have no part in the new
strategy devised in the main to snuff out Bradman's domination.

Gubby captained Middlesex, played for England against Australia in
1934 and led the MCC team to Australia in 1936–37, something of a
making-good operation after the cracks Jardine had opened up four
years earlier. By happy coincidence, Bradman was captain of Australia
and largely responsible for turning a deficit of two into a three-two win
to Australia. But it had been a successful tour in the widest sense, and
Gubby, who had been the youngest man to sit on an MCC Committee was later chairman of Selectors, became President of MCC and for
the last ten years has been Treasurer. His retirement this year is a severe
blow and I doubt whether we can ever hope to find the same calibre
of person to give as much time as he has done. Both the Don and
Gubby Allen have really given the best part of their waking hours to
the welfare and advancement of the game.

The Don, it might be said, is an outstanding and unusual man. If he
thinks something is worth doing he gives it all he has. I once wrote to
him when we were setting up a trust fund for the dependants of a man
very close to the English cricket scene who had died suddenly at an
early age. I merely asked for a little advice about the possibility of
investing some of the trust in Australian shares. His reply was typical.
Instead of a letter I received a priceless portfolio of investment information, meticulously detailed and immaculately presented. How could
it have been otherwise?

To have met and come to know Don Bradman is one of the real

privileges arising from my cricket travels to Australia. He came nearer to mastering the art of batsmanship than anyone. He had astonishing fleetness of foot, sharpness of eye and timing, but it was his mind that powered his success.

A GHOSTED OUTLINE

By Frank Keating

From an article in the Guardian, *2001*

I NEVER SAW HIM BAT. But, in a way, I did manage the next best thing. When he was 70, I was in Adelaide following Mike Brearley's England Test side. One mid-morning, nervously, I telephoned the great man in the city suburbs. 'Sorry,' he replied firmly, 'if I gave you so much as a half-minute interview—even to the *Manchester Guardian* of Neville Cardus—I'd insult and infuriate a few thousand previous fellows I've refused down the years.'

I piled on boringly into a laborious rehearsed question. He listened in courteous silence before interrupting. 'Sorry, I really must go. My friends are hooting outside. They've come to pick me up to play a round of golf.' That was my cue. I hared into my hotel lobby and hailed a cab. 'The Kooyonga golf club and step on it.'

I was in a bush furtively pretending to look like a butterfly collector when he emerged in baggy grey flannels from the clubhouse with his three buddies and approached the first tee.

At a distance, I followed them surreptitiously round the dunes and bunkers, so I saw Bradman's drive, and his iron play short and long, his chips and his sand wedges, and his putts—his 'forward defensive'. With a satisfying clunk, of course, he middled every single shot and every ball flew straight and true and fast. So on that memorable morning I did

The new knight. Sir Donald in 1949 with the Governor-General, Billy McKell.

The renowned harmonica player Larry Adler visited the Bradman home in 1961 and played a duet with Sir Donald at the piano.

As a Test selector and senior cricket administrator, Sir Donald remained a frequent flyer long after his retirement.

His last match. In 1963, aged 54, Bradman was persuaded by the Prime Minister,
Robert Menzies (left), to lead the Prime Minister's XI at Canberra against the touring England side
led by Ted Dexter (right). Bradman was out for four.

At home, 1967.

Sir Donald as a guest broadcaster for the ABC at the cricket.

Sir Donald with his old bodyline foes, Harold Larwood (left) and Bill Voce, at the Centenary Test in Melbourne in 1977.

With Viv Richards, another great batsman in the Bradman mould.

Sir Donald records his Bradman Tapes series with Norman May in 1988.

Back to Bowral. Sir Donald and Lady Bradman at the opening of the Bradman Museum at Bowral in 1989. The businessman Ron Brierley, one of the museum's early benefactors, is at left. Courtesy of News Ltd.

Although Bill O'Reilly and Sir Donald never resolved their personal differences, the old bowler, now confined to a wheelchair, made the trip to Bowral for the opening of the Bradman Museum, where he and Bradman (above) had their last meeting. Courtesy of News Ltd.

twig the ghosted outline of his cricket, the physical demeanour of his strokes, the deportment of his batsmanship—though having seen the outlines, of course, I had to imagine the hangman's mercilessness with which those cricketing strokes had so cruelly treated the bowlers who toiled as he reaped his incredible harvest.

THE PENALTY OF SUCCESS

By David Frith

From Wisden Cricket Monthly, *November 1980.*

AUGUST 27 WAS THE 72nd birthday of Sir Donald Bradman, the greatest run-getter in cricket history. It was also the day on which one of Fleet Street's most colourful and polished sportswriters chose to discredit him—through the expressed opinions of nameless contemporaries—in a rather tasteless rebuke for his absence at the Test Centenary gathering in London. 'His contemporaries shake their heads,' wrote Ian Wooldridge in the *Daily Mail,* 'implying that the Don . . . is averse to sharing anything, limelight not excluded.' Then came an analogy with 'Patton's lust for glory', and a 're-enactment' of Keith Miller's 'deliberate' duck at Southend in 1948, when the Australians made 721 runs in a day against Essex.

Of the 77 players missing from the official Test Centenary group were fourteen who were unable or unwilling to travel from Australia and fourteen Englishmen who were also absent from the celebrations from start to finish. But Bradman was singled out for criticism, as he has been for half a century for such misdemeanours as receiving presents from admirers that he did not put into a players' pool, for travelling separately at times, and for keeping his own company. A big and not very attractive club could be formed by disgruntled journalists who have sought and been refused an interview. For many of them, notwithstanding their apparently A1 powers of imagination, it has clearly been impossible to visualise what it must be like to be the most sought-after.

Perhaps an explanation is in order. Sir Donald Bradman has approached the autumn of his life with the same degree of meticulous organisation he has shown as boy, batsman, captain and businessman. He has gently wound down his affairs. He has been troubled by physical ailments, some merely irritating, like the knee which hampers his golf, some of acute concern, such as diverticulitis. The health of his son and daughter has been a constant source of anxiety. But even above and beyond that has been the ill-health of his wife, Jessie, who has miraculously survived open-heart surgery and periodic relapses in recent years.

Few couples have been as devoted as this during their 48 years of marriage. Earlier this year Lady Bradman was eager to journey to England with her husband for the Centenary celebrations. The trip could only have been conducted in conditions of near-total privacy, and there would have been mutual anxiety throughout, whether together or separated. The prospect militated decisively against the venture. That is why there was no Bradman at Lord's. It had nothing to do with glory. He has had his share of that. He has frequently been slated for shunning it.

As for Miller's personal protest at Southend, Bradman could hardly have ordered him to put down his playing cards and go to the wicket, for he himself was batting at the time, entertaining the 15,000 crowd hugely with an innings of 187 in just over two hours—his only innings against Essex in four tours of England. Miller, who would hardly have been playing cards in the dressing-room if his captain had been present, lost his off stump to a ball from Trevor Bailey which Robertson-Glasgow described as 'a very good ball'. Moreover, he needed some runs, having made only 36 in two weeks.

No appetite for the slaughter? There can be nobody who knows anything about Keith Miller who doesn't admire him enormously as cricketer and man. But when the fancy took him he could kill bowlers with the best of them. Only a fortnight earlier he had mauled Leicestershire with 202 not out. On the next tour of England he scored 220 not out against Worcestershire and 262 not out off the mighty Combined Services. And in the famous 1948 Essex match he did his bit in dismembering the county with 3 for 14 at the start of their first innings. The match was over by the second evening.

It has been said often before; we say it again: Don Bradman scored far too many runs for the comfort of some.

BRADMAN STILL ALIVE, 1980

By Roy Fuller

An excerpt from the English poet-novelist's autobiography, Vamp Till Ready.

CHRONOLOGY HAS MISTED UP, like that scene in *Bonnie and Clyde*. In 1938 I saw Bradman squatting in the outfield at Lord's, plucking a blade of grass to chew, humming to himself. My thought was: I must remember this for posterity. But here I am at sixty-eight, Bradman still alive—reported in *The Times* this very morning as saying that Vivian Richards is the best on-side player he has ever seen.

BRADMAN AND VIV RICHARDS—A COMPARISON

An observation by Sir Leonard Hutton, quoted in the press, July 1984.

THIS CHAP RICHARDS IS very good, very good, but Don was better. Don played straighter. He never hit the ball in the air. Richards hits the ball in the air and therefore has to have a little bit of luck to get away with it. They don't all go for six, you know.

SPLENDID SIMPLICITY

By Murray Hedgcock

Hedgcock told this story against himself in a letter in 1986.

BRADMAN WAS IN LONDON in the late seventies for a Lord's Taverners shebang of some sort, and there was a press launch at the Hilton where we all (hacks, veterans, everyone) queued up respectfully at the finish for autographs. When I introduced myself, I asked: 'When are you going to write any more books, Sir Donald—or was *The Art Of Cricket* your magnum opus?' Whereupon he squinted up at me and in that buzz-saw voice commented: 'Magnum opus? I don't even know what that means'—which seemed a splendid, simple way of cutting into a touch of pretension on my part.

SPORT'S FIRST SUPERSTAR

By Michael Parkinson

From an article in the National Times, *1983.*

A FEW YEARS BEFORE I was born, my father, a Yorkshireman who did not believe in untoward displays of hero-worship, once walked 30 miles to see Don Bradman bat. Upon his return he faced a family who clearly believed he had a slate loose. Who, in their right mind, would waste that much precious shoe-leather to see a cricket match? My father went to his grave unrepentant. Retelling the story—as he did many times—he'd say, 'But I saw HIM bat and they didn't.'

I still envy my father that memory. I never saw Bradman bat in the flesh, but growing up as I did in a household controlled by the aforesaid pilgrim I was aware of his name and his reputation long before I ever knew where Australia was. For a kid in a pit village to be breastfed on the Bradman legend, 12,000 miles away from where it started, is a clear indication of Bradman's unique position, not just in cricket but in all of sport.

It is a demonstrable fact that no single athlete has either so dominated or changed a sport as Bradman did. In modern times you could argue that Mohammed Ali gave a new dimension to heavyweight boxing and certainly changed a few opinions about the fight game. Undeniably George Best, with his brilliance and his glamour, paved the way for a new breed of soccer superstar. But they, for all their extraordinary gifts, were aided and abetted by an international network of media expertise. They were manna from heaven to a public brainwashed into anticipating a new hero every minute.

Don Bradman's singular achievement is that he became sport's first superstar in an age when word-of-mouth was the alternative to today's action replay.

SUI GENERIS

By Alan Gibson

From an article in the London Times *in 1980, commemorating the 50th anniversary of Bradman's first innings in England.*

BRADMAN, IN THE LENGTHENING perspective of cricket history, will surely be seen as a spectacular irruption. Grace in his early years was as dominant among batsmen, but Grace drew upon an orthodox tradition, magnified it, and otherwise left it much as he had found it. Bradman, from the start, played in his own way, never quite orthodox, but so successful it could not be called unsound, and never changed it, though he adjusted it as experience indicated and age required: never quite classical, never quite romantic. It might be said of him, in an altogether more complimentary sense than of the Bourbons, that he learned nothing and forgot nothing. He had no progenitors. He founded no school. He left no successors. The only other great batsman of whom this might be said is Ranjitsinhji, but Ranji's career to Bradman's was a shooting-star to a comet. Bradman was *sui generis*.

MODERN MIRACLE

By Bill O'Reilly

From an after-dinner speech O'Reilly made in Sydney in 1986.

THERE'S NEVER BEEN AND never will be in my estimation a batsman so good as that fella. I don't care how many you like to pour into one—all the Chappells, the Borders and so on. Forget them: they're just child's play compared with Bradman, and I've seen them all.

Bradman was a bloke whose ability with the bat was absolutely inconceivable. The Yanks talk about Babe Ruth and all that. To hell with
Babe Ruth. This boy was a modern miracle.

A SENSE OF HIGH ADVENTURE

By Alan Jones

From his foreword to the first edition of this anthology, 1987.

I CAN WELL REMEMBER as a boy being given my first meaning-
ful Christmas present, *How To Play Cricket*, a book by Don Bradman.

Such was the fame of Bradman more than 35 years ago that I
imagined him to be a memory rather than a presence in the history of
Australia.

Then, as my interest in sport quickened, other great Australians
emerged to dominate in some of the illustrious sporting theatres of the
world.

As I grew older still, I felt somewhat cheated that Frank Sinatra,
Joan Sutherland and Marlene Dietrich could go on sharing the active
evidence of their greatness with successive generations. Yet, I could not
see Bradman bat.

My studies of Shakespeare's *King Lear* at senior school level then
taught me, in the tragic words of the Duke of Gloucester contemplating Lear's eclipse, that 'as flys to wanton boys, are we to the Gods; they
kill us for their sport'.

In my inability to live through a Bradman innings, I genuinely felt
the Gods were against me. Age and rationality taught me that the
fortunes of this life are not always distributed by choice, and the quirk
of my birth demanded that I merely reflect on the greatness of
Bradman rather than be witness to it.

But it is an inevitable consequence of experiencing great beauty or happiness to know that our joy and exhilaration are tinged with sadness because we cannot hold or keep them.

Perhaps this is a middle-aged feeling but it is, to some extent, common to all of us. Great music, perfect moments in a friendship, exquisite artistry—all things which move us deeply—seem to be over all too soon.

It's like a tree at the bend in a creek, a shaft of gold reflected in the water; the wind blows, the leaves fall and the beauty is gone. Yet in a sense we know that these moments of greatness do remain stored within us, a strength to us in times of difficulty, an incentive to further greatness.

So it is with the memory and example of 'The Don' . . .

There is more to the artist than the performance. What characterised Bradman's approach was the fact that he seemed to find challenge and adventure in every innings, every ball and every return. And it seems that his cricket awakened in those who watched him the same sense of high adventure which, when one is fortunate enough to witness the artist at work, prevents our everyday lives from becoming drab and dull, the common things from becoming commonplace.

Through a period of economic difficulty and international uncertainty, Bradman's accomplishments seemed never to stop at himself. Indeed, he was a truly international person, whose talent and achievement warmed the hearts of opposing nations as much as those of his own. In such a way, greatness knows no bounds.

Of course, denied in my youth a chance to witness a Bradman innings, my later life has given me a richer prize of knowing the man. Several times have Sir Donald and I sat, talked and reminisced on sporting things. One can't prevent taking away the impression of a man whose accomplishments didn't stop at himself.

It's worse than useless if one is clever, talented, well read or well informed to regard such talents as matters for one's private satisfaction.

I well remember Sir Donald telling me recently that the key to success in Test cricket is to get the runs early and quickly, then the bowlers have time to do their job.

His whole career bears witness to the folly of ultra-conservatism in sport. The sense in which only the taking of risk can secure the ultimate triumph is Bradman proven. Bradman's influence was felt in many cricket lives, just as it, in a small and privileged way, is felt in mine.

I can't help but think what a wonderful Governor-General Bradman would have made, speaking to young and old Australians of the virtues of success; the sacrifices needed to secure it; the modesty required to wear it; and the energy spent in sharing it.

No Weakness

By Bob Wyatt

From an interview in the Sydney Morning Herald, *1987. Wyatt, England's vice-captain on the bodyline tour of 1932–33, had been asked how he thought Bradman would have fared against the current West Indian pace attack.*

I NEVER SAW A technical weakness in Bradman except that he did not like the really fast stuff, particularly if it was lifting a bit, but, then, nobody does. I don't think Bradman would have liked batting against the West Indians, but I think he would have made runs against them.

FLUIDITY OF MOVEMENT

By Peter Roebuck

From an article reviewing a television program about Bradman, Sydney Morning Herald, *1990.*

DID YOU SEE THE Don Bradman tribute last night? To hear him talk was to be struck by his certainty and his rigour. To see him interviewed in 1930 was to catch those glinting eyes and those sharp, hard, yet humorous features as they uttered commonplace niceties and planned their next massacre.

His running between wickets was electrifying and unique, left hand splayed and head high, and here, too, were to be found those muscular, late, whiplash drives through point and his devastating pull off anything fractionally short, a shot demanding nerve, eye and confidence, a signature shot learned by hitting a golf ball against a tank.

Two shots stand out in this feast, a conclusive cut off Harold Larwood which took Bradman to a 100 in 1930 and left Larwood staring for an age and apparently swearing vengeance. Bradman's extraordinary cross-bat smash past Larwood during the bodyline series lingers, too, a stroke played from outside leg stump as a counter attack was launched, a move some considered brave and some cowardly.

Yet it was Bradman's judgment and fluidity of movement which impressed most, his ability to glance or late-cut at will. His footwork, so nimble and darting, was wondrous, too, and allowed him to score off any ball. He seemed not to take runs but to accept them. These attributes made containment impossible, even for a bowler who could pitch on a 10-cent piece. No wonder R. W. V. Robins said of his technique: 'If he can reach the ball he hits hell out of it.'

Born in the bush, hardly playing till he was 16, Bradman was an uninhibited batsman with no worries about left elbows. Genius has been defined as the capacity for productive reasoning against one's training. It was easier for the Don because he never had any training and his spirit was free. Batting was about scoring runs, which he enjoyed doing; style and charm were for sentimentalists. Bradman was a practical man who scored runs, chased wins and glory, and built a nest egg, for he had no qualifications and must live on his wits.

What emerged of this elusive man? Bradman gave little away, and yet clues could be found. His voice is clipped, precise and sharp; it is a hard voice, one untouched by fancy, a mirror to a mind which had 'never let the mental side of cricket worry me. If I made a mistake, nine times out of 10 it was a physical mistake.' No mental mistakes! Such mastery is scarcely human; this was a man capable of absolute concentration, a chilling and smiling killer of bowlers.

BAD NEWS

By James R. Quested of Lightning Ridge

A letter to the Sydney Morning Herald, *1993.*

I RECALL A SUPPOSEDLY true story that my father related to me long ago about an Australian cricket fan who travelled to England to watch Bradman in his heyday and was billeted at an English cricket fan's home. He and the Pom were at one of the Tests and Australia was batting when he realised that he had left his wallet at the house, so he excused himself and went back to the house. On his return he said to the Pom that he had bad news for him: when he went back to the Pom's home he had caught the Pom's wife in bed with the bloke next door. The Pom turned to the Aussie and said he had even worse news for the Aussie. 'How do you mean?' said the Aussie. 'Bradman's out!' replied the Pom.

NO ENIGMA

By Evan Whitton

From an article in the Sydney Sun-Herald, *1994.*

MY VIEW OF BRADMAN was previously coloured to some extent by passages in Fingleton's *Cricket Crisis* and Cardus's *Australian Summer*, both of which I read as a schoolboy, and the Ikin incident of 1946, at which I was present. Fingleton's view of Bradman was not entirely adulatory, and Cardus took the view that he was a hard man on the basis of a remark about the imminent death of his son. I think now he was just an extraordinarily self-contained man, and that he had to be that to survive the adulation heaped on him.

I'm happy to say that trawling through some of the literature has caused me to rather warm to Bradman, particularly as captain in the third Test in 1937 and the fourth in 1938. In the end, I'm inclined to think that he was not an enigma at all, but quite a simple man who had a remarkable capacity to focus on essentials.

IN SEARCH OF BRADMAN

By Michael Parkinson

From an article in the Sun-Herald, *1995.*

I HAVE TRAVELLED LONG and far in my search for Donald Bradman. It started nearly 50 years ago when I rode on my bike the 30 miles to Leeds to see his Australian team slaughter our lot.

Since that first glimpse I have been seeking an audience. I have telephoned, telegrammed (remember?), written, faxed, pleaded, ranted and cajoled. The answer has always been No.

I have offered money, attempted to lure him with limousines and expensive hotel suites, persuaded mutual friends to use their influence, even tried incense and prayer. I still haven't interviewed Sir Donald. Not even got close.

On the odd occasion I have glimpsed him in the distance he vanished before I could reach him, like a mirage. Once or twice I have been somewhere only to be told he had just left. One time the host showed me the teacup he had been drinking from. The liquid was still warm. I felt like an explorer who had just found a fresh footprint of the Abominable Snowman.

Why so persistent? Because he was the greatest cricketer who ever lived and a significant man both in the history of the game and the development of his country. In cricket there have been two towering figures, two people who more than any other wrote the history of the game. They are W.G. Grace and D.G. Bradman. One is still with us and any journalist worth his salt has a duty to try to talk to him.

The other reason is much more selfish. In a lifetime of interviewing people I have talked to most of my heroes.

The two big ones who escaped were Frank Sinatra and Donald Bradman. I got closer to The Kid from Hoboken than I ever did to the Boy From Bowral.

But let us suppose that dreams come true and the interview has been arranged. What do I ask The Don? Well, all else apart, what fascinates me about Bradman is his fame. Generally speaking, being famous is a bit like having measles.

It is a minor affliction and the rash soon disappears. But for some it never goes away. It dictates their life and shapes their circumstance. They and their family are forever on display.

They are isolated by a special kind of celebrity and become icons of their time. Sir Donald Bradman belongs in that category.

I went looking for him on Australia Day in Adelaide. You must admire my stamina. Adelaide is his lair, the cricket ground on the first day of a Test match one of his regular watering holes and therefore offering the best chance of a sighting . . .

How close did I get? Well, eventually I sat at one end of a box and he was 15 people away.

I know. I counted. In profile he looked like a chirpy kookaburra. It was interesting observing people's reaction to his presence.

Some sneaked photographs of him, while others blatantly turned their backs to the cricket and surveyed the great man.

I fell once more to contemplating the kind of fame attached to Sir Donald and began comparing it to Keith Miller's.

In the end it is the difference between being inspected and being celebrated. The trouble with national treasures is that they are often placed behind glass, isolated by protocol, protected by a self-appointed Papal Guard.

Sir Donald remains a remote and lonely figure whose life will be judged and assessed by archivists and historians for as long as the game of cricket is played. Keith Miller will be celebrated in song, joke and anecdote.

As I left the Adelaide Oval on Australia Day I was struck by the thought that any country capable of producing two such gifted and singular men has much to be proud of and great reason to celebrate.

GREATEST HERO

By Charles Williams

From Bradman, *1996.*

IT COMES AS LITTLE surprise to hear that Nelson Mandela, when released from his long period in prison, wanted to know whether Bradman was still alive. Bradman was, and still remains, one of the great Australian heroes; but in the end it can without exaggeration be said that he was the greatest of them all.

ONE SIDE OF THE EQUATION

By Peter FitzSimons

From an article in the Sydney Morning Herald, *1998.*

IN SPORT, MANY ARE good, few are outstanding, a mere handful can be described as great, and only one born and raised beneath the Southern Cross can actually be called a phenomenon.

The Sir Donald Bradman phenomenon is built on far more than the man himself and his fantastical feats with the bat. Its true dimensions can only be properly appreciated when you consider that a sportsman who first came to fame in the 1920s—back in the hazy no-man's land that lies between the wars, when Stanley Melbourne Bruce was prime minister and dinosaurs still roamed the earth—is *still* the most revered figure in the nation 70 years later.

How can this be? Here we are living in an age when people who came to fame last Tuesday will quite likely be strictly passe by this

Friday night, and yet the Bradman phenomenon diminishes not a jot from one decade to next, through the twilight of one millennium and surely into the dawn of the next. Sir Donald has not picked up a bat in anger since the end of the 1948 tour; something like 99.94 per cent of the nation has never laid eyes on him; still fewer have ever seen him actually play bar grainy bits of footage here and there; and yet his legend not only lives, it damn near *dances.*

Yes, the whole thing can sometimes get rather overblown, but for better or worse, the shimmering ethereal figure that Sir Donald occupies in the realms of Australian mythology, floating somewhere there just above Ayers Rock and the Olgas, seems to rest on three columns in the sky.

Numbers: 99.94, and say no more. It is not simply that Sir Donald's Test batting average is better than anyone else's *ever*, forever and ever, amen, it is of course by just *how much* it is better. In many sports, comparing people from different eras and nations is always problematic, because there's no actual easy ready-reckoner as to whether, say, Nick Farr-Jones was or wasn't a better halfback than Ken Catchpole, because so much of their games cannot be measured by statistics—but cricket has no such problem.

The game is made for comparisons and of course no-one can help noticing that when Sir Donald is on one side of the equation, those on the other side tend to look a little pale. For while the game has produced such wondrous batsmen as Neil Harvey, Greg Chappell, Sunil Gavaskar, Sachin Tendulkar, Viv Richards and Brian Lara, not one of them has come close to displacing D. Aylight from second place behind Bradman. In the world of cricket, Sir Donald sits atop a statistical Everest of his own making, and no one else makes it to base camp. In all other sports 'records are made to be broken', as the cliche runs, but in the case of Bradman it was made to be broken against.

Nationhood-wise: Sir Donald is to Australia something akin to what George Washington and Babe Ruth are to the United States, what

Winston Churchill and Sir Francis Drake are to England. It's not easily definable, but so instrumental were the aforementioned in establishing good reasons for their nations to stick their chests out, that they have been accorded something close to secular sainthood. In Australia's case, just as the Anzacs showed what our soldiers could do in the military arena, Sir Donald demonstrated beyond all dispute what one of ours could accomplish in the sporting arena. We not only loved it when the Don scored 334 runs in a 1930 Test at Leeds, we positively outdid ourselves in ecstasy when a London newspaper trumpeted the two grateful words, 'HE'S OUT!', when his innings finally did close— because it was acknowledgment from others as to just how great our bloke was.

The enigmatic nature of the man himself: While many sportspeople who have enjoyed a single hundredth of his fame are seen to have their hands up for every endorsement they can get, would go to the opening of a *wound* and are only too keen to let anyone with a camera into the most personal details of their lives, Sir Donald has generally steered away from all this.

Apart from a mania for endorsements while he was playing, he has never really cashed in since on the reverence in which he is held, and still lives in the same house he bought with his late wife, Lady Jessie Bradman, in 1935. One cannot even begin to fathom what it would now be worth to, say, Ampol or BHP or Nike to have Sir Donald endorse some of their products, but clearly he is reluctant to exchange goodwill for money, and the goodwill extended towards him has never diminished because of it.

A GOD SUBSTITUTE

By Don Watson

From an article in the Australian, *1998.*

IN THE GALACTIC ERA of my growing up we dominated every sport that mattered. We won Davis Cups and Wimbledon, we ruled the pools, we won gold and broke world records on the track. Hoad, Rosewall, Emerson and Laver; Cuthbert, Strickland, Matthews; Fraser, Rose, Konrads; Landy, Lincoln, Thomas, Elliott—what ecstasy it was to be alive and have their sweat mingling with our own!

In cricket, meanwhile, we won many more than we lost and the team abounded with near legends like Harvey, Benaud, Craig, Davidson and Grout. But there was a hole in the galaxy. First Craig was meant to fill it. When he couldn't, O'Neill was thrown into the breach. Later Walters: but, good as he was, Doug wasn't that good. No one was. It wasn't fair. In no other sport were such comparisons made. Only in cricket did the world await a second coming. In cricket no one escaped the memory of Bradman or the shadow he cast.

Of course he was not God, but in a country where sport was a religion and the Ashes like a holy war, Donald Bradman was a God substitute. It makes no sense to call him a great player. Allan Border was a great player. Legend is the wrong word too. Victor Trumper is a legend. Phar Lap, Bernborough and Ned Kelly are legends. Legends have something capricious at their centre—a fatal flaw in their character, a vulnerability to Fate. It's in this, as much as in their ideal qualities, that we see ourselves. Unlike Bernborough, who always left his run to the last minute, and Phar Lap and Ned who died leaving us wondering why and what if, Bradman left us very little to wonder about.

POETRY AND MURDER

By Les Carlyon

From an article in the Age, *1998*

Poetry and murder lived in him together.
He would slice the bowling to ribbons,
then dance without pity on the corpse.
—R. C. Robertson-Glasgow on Don Bradman.

Poetry and murder—words as good as any if you are trying to explain Bradman the cricketer. A young batsman needs a little poetry. If he is to be talked about and eventually chosen to play for his country, he needs somehow to be good to look at, to have dancing feet or a seductive rhythm.

He needs murder in his heart to be able to bat on and on, so that, as a 21-year-old, he is able to stroke and finesse and spank his way to 254 at Lord's and cause Sir Neville Cardus, a contemporary of Robertson-Glasgow's, to write of an innings that was 'cruel in its excessive mastery'.

Cardus had romantic notions about the sport and these sometimes led him to see, in technicolour, things ordinary spectators didn't see, mainly because these things happened not on the field but in some fevered garden where Cardus was on first-name terms with a large number of fairies. Once, after a famous batsman was clean-bowled, Cardus wrote that 'nobody other than a giant of the game could have made a duck so immaculately'.

In 1930, the young Bradman bothered Cardus and other English commentators from the 'fine writing' school. There was no one to compare him to because he wasn't like anyone else. His style wasn't classical. He was self-taught and apparently comfortable with his heresies: a boundary scored with a cross-bat was as good as one hit with a straight bat. Thus, it was decided that Bradman, even though he had amassed century after century, could not be considered canonical.

Yes, he transferred his weight beautifully. And he caressed those late cuts in a way that, when you look at those old films, seems at once delicate and brutal. And he seldom offered chances because as a youngster he had learnt to close the face of the bat. And he always knew where his stumps were and where every fieldsman stood. And, yes, he concentrated like a man facing the gallows. But, damn it, he was still mocking the gods. He had invented his own church.

He wasn't like Grace or Hobbs, or even his gifted countrymen McCabe and Trumper. He was too much the perfect tradesman, ruthless rather than pretty, an 'adding machine' totting up runs as no one had ever done before and with a zest that seemed almost improper.

Which means that to poetry and murder, we should probably add a word like 'verve'. Geoff Boycott had enough murder in his heart to be able to occupy a crease for 10 hours while making 191. The difference is that Bradman pulsated and Boycott merely had a pulse.

Poetry and murder and verve . . . When someone is freakish at sport, we sooner or later begin to search for some trick of technique, some physical irregularity, that 'explains' them. It's the golfer's unorthodox grip, the footballer's outsized hands, the distance runner's lung capacity. We try to reduce it all to physics and acute angles. Yet, most of the time, the answer lies in the mind of the athlete. Most of the time, it has more to do with character than physical proportions.

Like good grammar, correctness of technique will take you only so far. If technique was all that counted, Derek Randall would not have made 174 in the Centenary Test and Muhammad Ali would have been repeatedly knocked out by blows to his exposed and flapping jaw. Nearly all sports freaks have iron in the soul and this is variously called determination, grit, the power to concentrate, the courage to follow one's own voices, self-belief, perfectionism and other things. Detractors may also call it selfishness or ruthlessness.

Whatever it is, it's what George Bush might call the 'character thing'. In his mind, Bradman was always a tough guy. He didn't walk back to the pavilion and say: 'Gee, I was lucky'. With him, hardly anything that happened at the crease had to do with luck. When he broke a world record, it was usually because he had walked out intending to do just that.

With a few plain words, Sir Robert Menzies, another famous cricket writer, probably summed up Bradman the cricketer better than anyone: 'Bradman believed in the virtue of concentrating all his mind on the job in hand.' And maybe Harold Larwood, who bowled Bodyline to the Australians in the 1932–33 series, came close with this: 'They said I was a killer with the ball without taking into account that Bradman with the bat was the greatest killer of all.'

From childhood, Bradman was a competitor, not in the brash style that is now commonplace but in an unusually cerebral way, a loner who had figured it out in private before he was 20, so that he was sure of himself and didn't need to shout as those only pretending to be sure of themselves often need to do. As a schoolboy, he didn't have a batting average because he was never dismissed. At 24, he sat and passed an umpire's exam so that he could be sure he knew all the rules. When, as a 21-year-old, he hit a world-record 452 not out in a New South Wales v Queensland match, it seemed pre-ordained. 'I was completely satisfied,' he said afterwards. 'I had achieved what I had set out to do.'

Here was a young man who concentrated on one thing. Colin Fraser, a Bradman chronicler who grew up during the Depression, once told the Don how his performances had given hope to kids and brought pride to the country. 'I wasn't aware of that,' Bradman told him. 'I was just playing cricket.'

In his TV interview with Bradman a few years back, Ray Martin referred to what many consider Bradman's finest innings: 334 runs in 378 minutes in the third Test at Leeds in 1930. Bradman scored 309 of those runs in one day: 105 before lunch, 220 before tea. When he was caught behind the following morning, after adding another 25, he had made what was then the highest score in Test cricket. He had also made the highest score in a day of Test play (the record still stands) and become the first batsman to make double centuries in consecutive Tests.

And yet Bradman told Martin (and in such a way that you had to believe him) that 'technically' this wasn't his best innings. His 254 in the second Test at Lord's was better. Why? 'Every ball went exactly where I wanted it to go.'

Cardus wrote of Bradman's 'spifflication' of all bowling in that Lord's innings (only Cardus could come up with that one) and so well did Bradman 'spifflicate' the Poms over the next decade that in 1943, after Mussolini had been deposed, a British MP, obviously still traumatised by what he had seen at Leeds and Lord's, declared: 'We have got Ponsford out cheaply but Bradman is still batting.' As Bradman's biographer Roland Perry noted, this did seem flattering to Hitler.

Bradman the perfectionist was always his own toughest critic. 'I saw a lot of cricketers who I thought had more talent than I had,' he once said and went on to mention Stan McCabe. What Bradman didn't say—couldn't say and probably didn't want to say—is that no other player has ever possessed his tough mind, his mixture of poetry and murder and verve.

Cricket throws up statistics the way dogs throw up fleas. To measure Bradman's superiority, one needs to go to just one table, the Test averages. There's Bradman on 99.94 runs, then a massive gap to the other fabled names: Graeme Pollock on 60.97, George Headley (60.83), Herbert Sutcliffe (60.73), Brian Lara (60-odd), Everton Weekes (58.61), Walter Hammond (58.46), Garfield Sobers (57.78), Jack Hobbs (56.94), Len Hutton (56.67), Sachin Tendulkar (54-odd), Greg Chappell (53.86), Javed Miandad (52.57), Sunil Gavaskar (51.12) and Allan Border (50.56). Victor Trumper, 'the perfection of grace' averaged 32.79 against England and 75 against South Africa.

So many champs from so many nations and so many eras—and there's a gap of 40 to 50 runs between Bradman and the field. In his *Farewell to Cricket*, Bradman wrote: 'Figures are not entirely conclusive, especially short-term figures, but it is difficult to avoid their significance if a man produces them year after year against every type of opponent and under all conceivable conditions.'

Quite. Case closed.

A UNIQUE PACKAGE

By Greg Chappell

From an interview in the Sydney Morning Herald, *1998.*

I'D SAY HE HAD very little in the way of self-doubts. There was nothing anyone could bowl at him he didn't feel capable of mastering. He was obviously unique. He was a package of physical and mental talents that apparently have never been found together in another individual.

A SINGULAR MAN

By Gideon Haigh

An article in Wisden Cricket Monthly, *1998.*

THE AUSTRALIAN SPORTING PUBLIC is notoriously fickle, bestowing and withdrawing devotion in a blink, apt to forget even the firmest of favourites within a few years of retirement. Yet the flame of Sir Donald George Bradman, seven decades since he first made headlines, has never burned brighter.

No public appearances are expected for his 90th birthday on August

27: almost a year after the passing of his beloved wife, Jessie, Bradman finds them strenuous. But his continued health will be the subject of front-page encomiums, and feature in evening television bulletins: an annual vigil for some years now. Whatever the tribulations of state, the cricket-fancying prime minister, John Howard, will convey congratulations.

Never mind that the youngest people with clear recollection of Bradman the batsman are nudging 60 themselves, for his feats appear to be growing larger, not smaller, as they recede into antiquity. In the last decade, the cricket-industrial complex has produced a trove of books, memorabilia albums, videos, audio tapes, stamps, plates, prints and other collectables carrying the Bradman imprimatur, while the museum bearing his name at Bowral continues to derive a tidy income from licensing it to coins, breakfast cereals and sporting goods.

A Bradman bat from 1930 changed hands at Phillips in London last year for £20,700, a life-size Bradman bronze at Christie's in Melbourne for $74,750 six months ago. A second collecting institution has opened in his honour at Adelaide's Mortlock Library. There has been yet another reissue of Bradman's 1958 instructional bible *The Art of Cricket* and, despite full-scale biographies in 1995 and 1997, two more books are forthcoming: a compilation of tributes and a volume on Bradman's 1948 side. Sir Donald Bradman has become Sir Donald Brandname.

Mention 'The Don' in Australia and no-one mistakes it for a reference to *The Godfather*. Little bits of his legend can be found everywhere. Australian state capitals boast 22 thoroughfares named in Bradman's honour (Victor Trumper has eight). Australians corresponding with the Australian Broadcasting Corporation do so to PO Box No. 9994: Bradman's totemic Test batting average, a pleasing notion of the Australian Lord Reith, Sir Charles Moses. A newspaper poll last year found that Bradman was the Australian most respondents wanted to light the flame at the 2000 Olympics: at 92, it would be a feat to rank with anything he accomplished on a cricket field.

Australians can count themselves blessed that The Don is still with them. It is 64 years since newspapers, fearful of his prospects after severe appendicitis, first felt the need to set obituarists on him. And Bradman was half his current age when he retired from stockbroking after a 'serious warning' from his physician.

In some respects, however, Bradman himself has been supplanted in importance by Bradmyth. The idea of him is at least as important as the reality. It is odd, but not really surprising, that the best biography of Bradman was written by an Englishman: Irving Rosenwater's superb *Sir Donald Bradman*. And, despite the recent proliferation of Bric-a-Bradman, no-one anywhere has tangibly added to the sum of human knowledge about The Don in 20 years. The most recent Bradman biography, Lord Williams's *Bradman: An Australian Hero*, is a case in point: of 428 footnotes, 244 referred to four titles, two of them previous Bradman biographies.

At one time, it was Bradman who sought Garbo-like quietude, no less than he deserved after more than four decades as a prisoner of his prowess. Nowadays, Australians do just as much to preserve that distance. The last locally-produced Bradman biography—Roland Perry's *The Don* (1995)—had as much substance as a comic strip. The last public interview with Bradman—two hours broadcast in May 1996 by Channel 9's top-rating current-affairs host Ray Martin on the basis of a corporate donation to the Bradman Museum—was what *Private Eye* used to describe as a journey to the province of Arslikhan.

It may justly be asked what more of the Bradman saga begs understanding. The Greatest Story Ever Bowled To is so beguiling as it is: uncoached boy from the bush rises on merit, plays for honour and glory, puts Poms to flight, becomes an intimate of sovereigns and statesmen, retires Cincinnatus-like to his unostentatious suburban home.

But turning Bradman into Mr 99.94 is a little like reducing Einstein to Mr $E=mc^2$. Read most Bradmanarama and you'd be forgiven for thinking that his 80 Test innings were the sum of him. His family is invisible. Precious little exists about Bradman's three decades as an administrator. There is next to nothing about his extensive business career. And no-one, I think, has ever grasped what is perhaps most extraordinary about Bradman: his singularity as a man as well as a cricketer. For the great irony of his beatification is that he was never, as one might imagine, an acme of Australian-ness.

For most Australian boys, for instance, participation in sport is a rite of passage, an important aspect of socialisation. Yet, if Bradman developed close cricketing pals in his Bowral boyhood, they kept remarkably schtum afterwards. The rudimentary game with paling bat and kerosene tin wicket in some urban thoroughfare is one of Australian cricket's cosiest images: think of Ray Lindwall and his cobbers playing in Hurstville's Hudson Street, trying to catch the eye of Bill O'Reilly as that canny old soul walked by; or of the brothers Harvey playing their fraternal Tests behind the family's Argyle Street terrace in Fitzroy. Bradman's contribution to the lore of juvenile cricket, by contrast, is one of solitary auto-didacticism, his water-tank training ritual with golf ball and stump.

That carapace hardened as Bradman reached cricketing maturity, and set him still further apart. Where the archetypal Australian male is hearty and sanguine, priding himself on good fellowship, hospitality and ability to hold his alcohol, Bradman was private, reserved, fragile of physique and teetotal. Where the traditional Australian work ethic has been to do just enough to get by, Bradman was a virtuoso who set his own standards and allowed nothing to impede their attainment.

Australia in the late 1920s, moreover, was not a country that seemed likely to foster an abundance of remarkable men. It was a small subsidiary of Empire, with an ethnically and culturally homogenous population of six million. Even that big bridge was still to come. There were extremes of wealth and poverty, but social mobility was constrained both by economic hardship and the prevailing belief in an underlying social equality. Writing of Australia in 1928, the year of Bradman's Test debut, the American critic Hartley Grattan was amazed by the vehemence of this latter faith: 'Australia is perhaps the last stronghold of egalitarian democracy . . . The aggressive insistence on the worth and unique importance of the common man seems to me to be one of the fundamental Australian characteristics.' As D. H. Lawrence described it in his novel of 1920s Australia, *Kangaroo*: 'Each individual seems to feel himself pledged to put himself aside, to keep himself at least half out of count. The whole geniality is based on a sort of code of "You put yourself aside, and I'll put myself aside." This is done with a watchful will: a sort of duel.'

Bradman, however, was not a 'a common man', and he assuredly did not 'put himself aside'. In the words of Ben Bennison, who collaborated with the 21-year-old cricketer on *Don Bradman's Book*: 'He set out and meant to be king . . . To the last ounce he knew his value, not only as a cricketer but as a man.' R. C. Robertson-Glasgow recalled that, at his first meeting with Bradman at Folkestone in September 1930, the Australian was surrounded by piles of correspondence to which he was steadily reaming off replies. 'He had made his name at cricket,' wrote Crusoe. 'And now, quiet and calculating, he was, he told me, trying to capitalise on his success.'

The times may have been ripe for such individual aspiration. Certainly, Bradman's benefactors on that tour had no difficulty singling him out for gifts and gratuities, not least the Fleming & Whitelaw soap magnate Arthur Whitelaw, who bestowed a spontaneous £1000 (worth around £35,000 today) on Bradman after his Headingley 334. But nothing before or since has paralleled the Caesar-like triumph that Bradman's employers, the sports-goods store Mick Simmons Ltd, organised for him when the team returned to Australia, where he travelled independently of his team and was plied with public subscriptions and prizes in Perth, Adelaide, Melbourne, Goulburn and Sydney.

It was the beginning of a career in which Bradman showed conspicuous aptitude for parlaying his athletic talent into commercial reward. Leaving Mick Simmons in 1931, he signed a three-part contract worth more than £1000 a year with radio station 2UE, retailer FJ Palmer, and Associated Newspapers (proprietor Robert Clyde Packer, grandfather of Kerry). He endorsed bats (Wm Sykes), boots (McKeown) and books (three while he was playing, two afterwards), irked the Australian Board of Control by writing about cricket in apparent defiance of their dictates, deliberated over effectively quitting Test cricket to accept the Lancashire League shilling for the 1932 season, and swapped states in 1935 to further his career. At a time when Australian industry lurked behind perhaps the highest tariff barriers on earth, Bradman was the quintessential disciple of the free market.

No dispute that Bradman deserved every penny and more. No question of undue rapacity either. As that felicitous phrasemaker Ray Robinson once expressed it, The Don did not so much chase money as overhaul it. Equally, however, Bradman's approach betokens an elitism uncharacteristic of Australia at the time, and a quality that few today would willingly volunteer as a national hallmark.

It was this impregnable self-estimation—not arrogance, but a remarkable awareness of his entitlements—that distanced Bradman from his peers. Some criticisms of The Don by playing contemporaries were undoubtedly actuated by jealousy but, all the same, he seems to have been incapable of the sort of gesture that might have put comrades at their ease.

The philosophy of Bradman's playing career emerged again in his approach to administration and selection. Biographers have served Bradman poorly by glossing over his years in officialdom. His strength and scruples over more than three decades were exemplary; the foremost master of the game became its staunchest servant. But he largely missed the secular shift toward the professionalisation of sport in the late 1960s and early '70s. His attitude remained that, if a player was good enough, he could profit from the game through other avenues. Again, this does not seem a response of one who understood the struggles of others less blessed.

Discussing the rise of World Series Cricket, Bradman told Williams in January 1995 he 'accepted that cricket had to become professional'. Yet, as Dr Bob Stewart comments in his recent work on the commercial and cultural development of post-war Australian cricket, *I Heard It On the Radio, I Saw It On the Television*, cricket wages declined markedly in real terms during the period that Bradman was Australian cricket's *éminence grise*. When he quit cricket, the home Test fee was seven times the average weekly wage. A quarter of a century later it was twice the average weekly wage. Ian Chappell opined in his *The Cutting Edge* that the pervasiveness of Bradman's attitude to player pay within the Australian Cricket Board 'contributed to the success World Series Cricket officials had when a couple of years later they approached Australian players with a contract'.

Perhaps these paradoxes of the Bradman myth relate something about the complex Australian attitude to sport. As the Australian social commentator Donald Horne once put it: 'It is only in sport that many Australians express those approaches to life that are un-Australian if expressed any other way.' But, as Bradman enters his tenth decade fit for both commodification and canonisation, two questions seem worth asking, with apologies to C. L. R. James.

First: what do they know of Bradman who only cricket know? Surely it's possible in writing about someone who has lived for 90 years to do something more than prattle on endlessly about the 15 or so of them he spent in flannels—recirculating the same stories, the same banal and blinkered visions—and bring some new perspectives and insights.

Second: what do they know of cricket who only Bradman know? A generation has now grown up in Australia that regards cricket history as 6996 and all that. Where are the home-grown biographies of Charlie Macartney, Warwick Armstrong, Bill Woodfull, Bill Ponsford, Lindsay Hassett, Keith Miller, Neil Harvey, Alan Davidson, Richie Benaud, Bob Simpson, even Ian Chappell and Dennis Lillee, plus sundry others one could name? Such is the lava flow from the Bradman volcano, they are unlikely to see daylight.

So enough with the obeisances already. Yes, Bradman at 90 is a legend worth saluting. But as the American journalist Walter Lippman once said: 'When all think alike, none are thinking.'

An analysis of a marvel

By Charles Davis

Adapted from The Best Of The Best: A New Look At The Great Cricketers And Their Changing Times, *2000.*

After scores of books and thousands of articles, and more than 50 years, what can be said that is new about the career of Donald George Bradman? It does not take any great depth of analysis to identify his career as unique. Here is a batsman who scored double centuries more often than most of the other great batsmen scored centuries, part of an overall career so unlikely that it must be described, to paraphrase Douglas Adams, as not impossible, just very, very improbable. On deeper analysis, his career is no less extraordinary, but there is some suggestion of chinks in the armour that opponents might have been able to exploit, had not Bradman been able to maintain a near-impregnable psychological dominance for almost 20 years.

There are various ways of measuring batting prowess, but in nearly all of them where averages are involved Bradman is peerless, even when allowance is made for the high-scoring era in which he played. When suitable historical adjustments are made, allowing for the sometimes weak bowling he played against, Bradman's average (for comparison with the modern era) drops from its familiar 99.9 to about 85, but this is still more than one-third higher than anyone else. Although questions have been raised about his performance under pressure, it is worth noting that his four highest scores, (334, 304, 299*, 270) were all made in circumstances where, had he failed, Australia would have been in trouble. Bradman was better than anyone else in turning a high pressure situation into low pressure by the time he had finished.

One area where Bradman's reputation runs a little ahead of reality is in his scoring speed. When proper allowance is made for changing over rates, Bradman's speed, at 63 runs per 100 balls for his major innings, and 59 for his whole Test career, remains fast, but not as fast as some modern batsmen or a few of his predecessors such as Trumper. (Bradman's 309 in one day at Leeds in 1930, for example, would be worth about 220 per day at modern over rates.) A close look at the records shows that a few modern batsmen, for example Viv Richards and Sanath Jayasuriya, and all-rounders Ian Botham and Kapil Dev, scored faster than Bradman in all situations. Kapil Dev is the all-time leader, sustaining a rate of 79 runs per 100 balls for his whole career. Bradman is still near the top end of the scale, however, and the relentlessness of his scoring speed was one of his main weapons. Among Bradman's contemporaries, Stan McCabe was the only specialist batsman to score more quickly (62 runs per 100 balls, rising to 72 in his major innings).

If anything new can be teased out of the detailed record, it suggests that psychological dominance was a critical part of Bradman's achievements. Bradman's likelihood of getting out changed in an unusual way as his innings progressed, quite different than for any other batsman.

For scores below about 15, even though Bradman was very good at avoiding dismissal, his chances of dismissal were still within the range of other great batsmen. Hobbs, for example, was more reliable at reaching double figures. Once set, however, Bradman's chance of dismissal plummeted to only one-third of other leading batsmen, and above a score of 50 he is way ahead of anyone else in Test history. Specifically, Bradman's chance of dismissal before his next run stayed constant at about 0.5 per cent, whether his score was 50, 100 or 150. No other batsman in history has achieved a rate of better than 1.0 per cent, and for the typical all-time great batsman the rate is closer to 1.5 per cent. It was only at scores above 150 that Bradman's dismissal rate begins to rise and return to the mortal realm: most other top batsmen enjoy reduced dismissal chances above 150. The fact that Bradman's chance of dismissal is so low, and constant, specifically between 50 and 150, suggests a psychological factor. This is supported by some of the statements from opposing captains (such as G. O. B. Allen) to the effect that they expected the 'customary century' from Bradman, and once he looked like getting one they preferred to focus on the other batsmen while he went about it.

Further evidence comes from the only two series where Bradman did not enjoy psychological dominance, 1928–29 (before he established his reputation) and 1932–33 (the 'bodyline' series). Bradman exceeded a score of 40 in these two series just as often as he did in all his other Tests, but he did not reach 150 once. In short, his scoring between 50 and 150 now looks just like the typical superior batsman, and is nothing like Bradman's record at other times. His psychological dominance of bowlers appears to have applied only to good batting conditions and may also explain his almost complete failure to score well on poor pitches. Pick out the six worst pitches he had to bat on, pitches which are rare to non-existent today, and Bradman's total is just 27 runs. Without these innings, his average would have been 109!

Bradman could not have exploited his dominance over opposing bowlers if he did not possess great reserves of mental strength. This strength is manifested in aspects of his personality which have been often remarked on, his self-reliance, his semi-reclusive nature, and the social distance he maintained from colleagues. It was also shown in his critical first Test innings after World War II, when he demonstrated that nothing had changed, in spite of advancing years (38) and health problems, by scoring 187. There was some good fortune to come in that the bowling strengths of the teams Bradman had to face in this last phase were weak, but by convincingly outscoring a talented and successful new generation

of Australian batsmen in 15 Tests between 1946 and 1948 Bradman
demonstrated that he was more than a freak product of a single era.

No cricketer has ever performed like him and (this is stated as
unequivocally as probability could ever allow) no cricketer ever will.

NOT UNORTHODOX AFTER ALL

By Tony Shillinglaw

From an interview in England's Daily Post, *2000, in which
Shillinglaw, an English coach, explained how he began a campaign to
have Bradman's technique adopted as a model for young English
batsmen.*

I WAS SPEAKING TO a highly qualified coach and suggested the
Don Bradman technique, only to be dismissed and told his style was
unorthodox. I couldn't believe that the batting style of someone so
successful and so admired in the game could be dismissed that easily. If
I was in business and someone was 66 per cent more successful than
me, I would want to know exactly what he was doing.

ONE OF THE DIVINITIES

By Nelson Mandela

A remark by Mandela during a visit to Australia in 2000.

IN THE THIRTIES AND forties, at least in our country, we regarded
Sir Donald—we were tempted to regard him—as one of the divinities,
so great he was and such an impact he made.

HIGHER THAN EVEREST

By Simon Barnes

From an article in the London Times, *2001.*

THERE IS A GENUINE case for saying that Sir Donald Bradman was the greatest player of any sport that ever plied his trade. No one has ever dominated his sport as Bradman dominated cricket while he was playing it: no one has continued to dominate his sport after retirement.

Following his death this weekend, Bradman leaves behind not only imperishable deeds and impossible statistics, but also a curious conundrum about the anomalous nature of his own greatness.

Every sport has its great names, for much of sport is about heroes and their legends. These are names that resonate far beyond their own sports, and far beyond sport itself: Muhammad Ali, Pele, Babe Ruth, Michael Jordan, Martina Navratilova, Jack Nicklaus, Jesse Owens, Red Rum.

Each of these names represents an Everest. But the point about the Himalayan mountain range is that it is a family of giants. If Everest is the greatest of these, he stands in high and lofty company: first among the greats. The other peaks around it have, as it were, a right to be there. But the analogy simply doesn't work with Bradman. Bradman is not only Everest, he is also K2 piled on top. Bradman reaches skywards while the other giants of his game paw at the waistband of his trousers.

Where other cricketers peak, Bradman has merely found his stride. When others gasp through lack of oxygen at these rarefied heights, Bradman is in his natural element. Where others get vertigo, Bradman simply looks up, not down. And he carried on: without fuss, without rancour, without remorse.

It is a sporting cliché to say that all records will be broken. It is probably safe to say that Bradman's won't. He scored a century at the rate of just better than one in every three innings. His Test match average is 99.94. He made more than 300 runs on six occasions—very few players have done that once. He scored 37 double-hundreds. In the Test matches of his first tour of England, in 1930, he scored 254 at Lord's, 334 at Headingley and 232 at The Oval. That level of sustained brilliance simply isn't possible. A newspaper placard in England once read 'Bradman fails again'. He had narrowly missed a century.

Charles Davis, a scientist from Melbourne, has contrived a statistical system for measuring talents in different sports, published in his book *The Best of the Best*. He has drawn a bell curve for each sport, and found that it assumed the same shape in each sporting discipline. One thing spoils the neatness of this conclusion: Bradman.

'Statistically speaking, his career should never have existed,' Davis says. He has produced a 'Z-score' for the great: Michael Jordan 3.2, Jack Nicklaus 3.5, Pele 3.7, Björn Borg 3.15. 'A Z-score of two is exceptional,' Davis says, 'while three would put an athlete near the top of the all-time greats.' Bradman's Z-score is 4.4. To reach a comparable level in Davis's system, a footballer would have to score a goal per game over the course of 100 internationals, a golfer would have to win 25 major titles.

Bradman was, in short, talented beyond the confines of the medium for his talent. He was like Mozart writing pop songs, Shakespeare writing for *The Times*. His talent made his game virtually unplayable. Jack Hobbs, himself a great batsman and a legendary collector of centuries, wrote in this newspaper 49 years ago: 'I think the Don was too good: he spoiled the game. He got too many runs. The pot calling the kettle black? No: I was human; he got hundreds every time he went in . . . He was mechanical; he was the greatest run-getting machine of all time. I do not think we want to see another one quite like him. I do not think we ever shall.'

The notion that Bradman spoiled the game is interesting. I

remember playing schoolboy rugby with a boy called 'Jock' Mildenhall. Jock reached puberty at about the age of five, and by the time he was 12, stood over 6ft and weighed almost 14 stone. Every time he got the ball, he walked calmly from wherever he stood to the try-line and scored, with little boys festooned all about him like homunculi.

When Bradman played, the rest of the cricketing world was in a wrestling-with-your-dad situation. His presence in the side was frequently enough to end the match as a contest. The only way to stop him was physical force: the tactic of bodyline bowling was invented specifically for Bradman, and it caused a row between England and Australia that has never been forgotten or quite forgiven. And throughout the bodyline tour, Bradman still averaged 56: the nearest to failure he ever got. A Test average of 40 is reckoned to be the bench-mark of a seriously good cricketer.

It is almost unique for any person to be so much farther ahead of everybody else that ever lived in any field of life. My father will tell you that Mozart is the greatest composer that ever lived; I will tell you that Bach is better. And of course, we're both right. It is not even worth having an argument about.

True, most of sport is in some way quantifiable, and most of art is not. But the point is that Bach and Mozart represent lofty peaks of human attainment: and in terms of their achievement, you can't really separate them, save on the ground of personal preference. I spent last weekend in Amsterdam, and feel tempted to say that Vincent van Gogh is the greatest painter of all time . . . but a few hundred yards from the Van Gogh Museum lies a potent counter-argument with the Rijks-museum and Rembrandt.

Greatest writers of all time? I might suggest Homer, Dante and Joyce, but I'd be asking for an argument on several counts. Throughout history, great deeds have been emulated, great achievements have been equalled and surpassed, and then surpassed again. Sport provides a toyshop view of the real world, but it supplies us with an endless stream of vivid analogies. This, of course, is one of sport's eternal fascinations. Jack Nicklaus was always regarded as head and shoulders above any other golfer: but now we have Tiger Woods—who might just turn out to be golf's Bradman, and the only serious rival to Bradman as the greatest games player ever. But he hasn't done it yet: Bradman has.

The debate about the greatest footballer ever is a bar-room standard. It is the more pleasing and pointless because much of footballing excellence eludes statistics. Most people would say Pele, but Diego Maradona and George Best are part of the argument, and then you can throw in Johann Cruyff and Franz Beckenbauer, and it's last orders long before you're ready.

But you can't do the argument with cricket, because there isn't an argument to be had. In 1999, *Wisden Cricketers' Almanac* polled 100 of the great and good in cricket, asking each to name the five greatest cricketers of the departing century. Only one cricketer got 100 votes. At this stage, I suppose it is unnecessary to name him.

True, cricket is a small thing, played seriously in a handful of countries: it is hardly a universal pursuit. But the pattern is repeated time and again in all walks of human life that can be regarded as in any way competitive: that there is a cluster of greatness at the top, and then a reasonably sharp fall-away to the next level of achievement, and then a gradual broadening to an almost infinitely wide base of game triers.

Bradman breaks the pattern. Davis's bell curve doesn't work for cricket. 'It is Bradman who is anomalous, not the game of cricket,' Davis says.

Bradman was unique: the man who reached the peak of Everest and felt he had made a good start.

A UNIQUE SUPERIORITY

From an editorial in the Guardian, *2001.*

As SPORTSMAN, HIS SUPERIORITY is unique: if the golfer Tiger Woods can sustain his dominance for the next two decades, his achievement will merit comparison with Bradman's. Certainties in sport are dull, yet a Bradman double (or triple) hundred never was. He turned winning into an act of collective worship, drawing on the public's sense of wonderment that one performer could not merely dominate the stage but redefine the art.

CELEBRITY WITH A GLOBAL IMPACT

By Matthew Engel

From an article in the Sydney Morning Herald, *2001.*

WHEN A MAN DIES in extreme old age, full of honours as well as years, there is no tragedy: Sir Donald Bradman not only mastered his contemporaries, he outlived them too. But Bradman achieved such mastery that he not only dominated his field of endeavour, he came in a sense to embody it. Thus, now he has died, something of cricket has died too.

People will be sensing that today wherever the game is played. And that means just about every country on the planet. There will be sadness in the posh clubs of Buenos Aires, and among the expat business-men of the Baltic Republics. In Kabul and Kathmandu. In Vietnam, Vanuatu and Vancouver, which Bradman himself said had the most beau-tiful cricket ground in the world.

But there is an illusion here, of course. The world is not really in mourning. Cricket's administrators have placed a huge emphasis on development in the past few years. A mixture of idealism, fantasy and avarice has impelled them to try to push the game globally.

In reality, almost everywhere outside the 10 Test-playing countries, cricket is a minority sport played only by outsiders: sometimes just Western diplomats, most often these days the migrant workers and shopkeepers of the South Asian diaspora. The main newspapers will not be clearing the front page. Perhaps the *New York Times* or the more learned western European broadsheets will note Sir Donald's passing to give their readers a little insight into Australian quaintness (the knighthood itself providing an extra touch) just as this paper might record the death of a famous bullfighter.

However, Bradman's celebrity was so great within cricket itself that this is not just an important moment, it is one that has been long-anticipated, sometimes too much so. Several times before, there had been rumours of his death. One of the most widespread came on September 29, 2000: the final Friday of the Sydney Olympics.

This caused particular alarm in Australian newspaper offices which, until the good news came through that the Don was actually fine, had to consider how they might cope with the coincidence of these two huge stories. It also made the mind race, as to the response from the multitudes gathered in Sydney: grief from many; incomprehension from the rest.

First and foremost, the grief is Australia's. Many historians—hemmed in by the conventions of their calling—have been reluctant to admit that a mere sportsman could be a vital figure in a national maturing process. Yet Bradman was more vital to the growth of Australia's national unity and self-awareness than any mere politician. But it is cricket's grief too. In every continent, there are countries where the game really matters, and these are places where Bradman matters, too. These places embrace a quarter of the world's population, because India is included.

'Indians worship a multitude of gods', wrote the Bombay journalist Vasant Raiji in an article for the Don's 90th birthday in 1998. 'In Sir Donald Bradman they have their god of cricket. God is perfect. In the eyes of the Indians, Bradman is the perfect batsman. God is unseen. Indians have not seen Bradman play. God's ways are inscrutable. Indians cannot comprehend why, in spite of numerous pressing invitations, Bradman never came to India. Whatever happens is God's will. So if Bradman avoided India, it was Bradman's will. Disappointment, but no ill-feeling or rancour.'

The Indians should not feel especially slighted. Through the last two decades of his life, and to an extent even before that, Bradman spent much of his time composing polite and neatly-typed refusals of invitations. More and more, he withdrew from the world until he declined even to attend the Adelaide Test and his own 90th birthday party (which certainly did cause rancour). And the Indian response to his lifetime rejection of their adoration was not entirely passive either. In 1987 there was a plan to put a statue of the Don in Calcutta alongside those of Mahatma Gandhi and the poet Rabindranath Tagore. But when Bradman did not appear for the World Cup, the plan was dropped.

Vasant Raiji's article was entitled *The Unseen God*. By the end that's how the Don was regarded even in Adelaide. And it was truer still elsewhere. The only countries in which he played cricket aside from England and Australia were the US and Canada (on the tour of 1932) and Ceylon, when the ship to England docked there. Compare and contrast the working life of a modern cricketer.

It all added to the mystique, of course. In recent years, while his contemporaries racked up frequent flyer miles the way Bradman accumulated runs, he did not visit England either. He came in 1960, for the great international pow-wow on throwing, then appeared for a Lord's Taverners dinner in 1974. After that, no matter what the occasion, the entreaties were always refused.

But his reputation rests, more than anything, on the four visits he did make: 1930, 1934, 1938 and 1948. Australia had beaten England before Bradman, of course slaughtered them, indeed, in the special post-war circumstances of 1921. But before Bradman appeared, the English believed that their champion, Walter Hammond, was about to lead them to a new era of Ashes dominance. In fact, England did not win the Ashes again—except by foul means in 1932–33—until 1953, after Bradman's retirement. In that time, the whole balance of the relationship between the two countries had changed. Bradman destroyed England's cricketing authority; Bodyline destroyed England's moral authority.

No, the whole world is not joining us in mourning today. But much of the world is mourning. And it's possible to argue that Bradman's major legacy was to help alter the entire nature of Anglo-Australian relations. We are not mother and daughter any more but siblings: living far apart, inclined to argue at family gatherings, but deep-down affectionate still.

Bradman's role in that change perhaps surpasses anything else he achieved: even the 99.94.

TELL YOUR KIDS ABOUT BRADMAN

From an editorial in the London Sun, *2001.*

HE WAS ONLY FIVE foot seven tall—but he towered above the rest of his generation and subsequent generations like no other sportsman. Above all else, Bradman had a distaste for fame—in fact his celebrity seemed an embarrassment to him. His family came first. He was the original man with a hinterland. All that we can hope is that younger generations model themselves, as much as they are able, on Bradman—whether they are sportsmen and women or not. Tell your kids about Bradman. Buy them books. Tell them stories. The world would be a finer place with a few more like him.

BLISSFUL IGNORANCE

From an editorial in the London Daily Telegraph, *2001.*

THE DON IS DEAD; he had a good innings. What exactly made Bradman so much better than any other batsman? Averages tell their own story, but they do not tell us how he did it. Others may have imitated his grip, his footwork, his strokes. They cannot imitate his achievements. Even Edison's old adage about genius—'one per cent inspiration, 99 per cent perspiration'—does not apply: however hot the conditions, Bradman never seemed to sweat. We do not know why he was the best and, however expert we may be, we never shall. Bradman himself did not know either. Gray got it right: 'Where ignorance is bliss, 'tis folly to be wise.'

BEYOND ARGUMENT

By Martin Johnson

From an article in the London Daily Telegraph, *2001.*

THE BIGGEST SURPRISE ABOUT Sunday's sad news from Adelaide is that the great umpire in the sky chose to raise his finger before Don Bradman had the chance to rack up yet another century. For every other cricketing legend, living for eight years less than his batting average would represent being cut down in his prime, which is why the Don—given out on Sunday for 92—will never be remembered as anything other than the greatest batsman who ever played the game.

The arguments still go on as to whether Nicklaus was better than Woods, Pele better than Maradona, or Ali better than Louis, but if cricket is still around in 10,000 years no one will be claiming that anyone was better than Bradman.

ACKNOWLEDGEMENTS

THE EDITOR WOULD LIKE to thank the Bradman Foundation for its help and support in publishing this second edition of *Our Don Bradman*. The encouragement and co-operation provided by the foundation's chief executive, Richard Mulvaney, was especially valuable and, indeed, was indispensable to the development of the book into its expanded, illustrated form.

The editor is deeply grateful to the following people who have allowed their work to be reproduced for the first time in this edition. They are:

Neil Marks for an extract from his book *Tales From The Locker Room* (Ironbark Press, 1993) and for an extract from his book *Australian People, Australian Tales* (HarperCollins Publishers, 1999).

Charles Davis for an adaptation from his book *Test Team Of The Century* (Harper Sports, 2000).

Michael Parkinson for an extract from an article in the *Sun-Herald*, 1995.

Peter FitzSimons for an extract from an article in the *Sydney Morning Herald*.

Alan Jones for an extract from the foreword which he wrote for the first edition of this book.

Gideon Haigh for an extract from an article in *Wisden Cricket Monthly*.

Peter Roebuck for an extract from an article in the *Sydney Morning Herald*.

Don Watson for an extract from an article in the *Australian*.

Evan Whitton for an extract from an article in the *Sun-Herald*.

Rodney Cavalier for an extract from an article in *Sir Donald*

Bradman AC, co-ordinated by Mike Coward (Ironbark Legends, Pan Macmillan, 1998).

Frank Keating for an extract from an article in the *Guardian*, 2001.

Edward Docker for an extract from *Bradman And The Bodyline Series* (Angus & Robertson Publishers, 1978).

Peter O'Reilly for an extract from a taped speech that his father, Bill, made in Sydney in 1986.

Les Carlyon for an extract from an article in the *Age*.

Matthew Engel for an article in the *Sydney Morning Herald*.

Simon Barnes for an article in the London *Times*.

Martin Johnson for an extract from an article in the London *Daily Telegraph*.

The editor would also like to repeat his thanks to the following people who allowed their work to be used in the first edition of this book:

Dame Pattie Menzies for the extract from Sir Robert Menzies' book *The Measure of the Years* (Cassell Australia Ltd).

Arthur Mailey (junior) for several extracts from newspaper articles written by his father, Arthur Mailey.

Ken Mathers for an extract from a newspaper article written by his father, Jim Mathers.

Air Vice-Marshal Rodney Noble for an extract from *The Fight for the Ashes 1928–29* (George G. Harrap & Co Ltd) written by his father, M. A. Noble.

R. J. L. Altham for an essay by his father, H. S. Altham, reproduced in *The Heart of Cricket* (The Cricketer/Hutchinson).

Lord Tennyson for a passage from a newspaper article written by his father.

Jack Lindsay for an extract from the book *Don Bradman* (Phoenix House Ltd) written by his brother Philip Lindsay.

E. W. Swanton for the long passage from his book *Sort of a Cricket Person* (William Collins).

Retusa Pty Ltd for an extract from one of A. B. Paterson's radio talks, reproduced in *Song of the Pen: Collected Works 1901–41* (Landsdowne).

J. M. Kilburn for the extract from his book *In Search of Cricket* (Arthur Baker Ltd).

Bill O'Reilly for the passage from his book *'Tiger'—60 Years of Cricket* (William Collins) and for the passage from his book *Cricket Conquest—The Story of the 1948 Test Tour* (Werner Laurie).

Rowntree Hoadley Ltd for the Minties commercial jingle.

David Frith for his article in *Wisden Cricket Monthly*.

Charles Fry for excerpts from newspaper articles written by C. B. Fry.

Adrian McGregor for an excerpt from his book *Greg Chappell* (William Collins).

Virginia May for part of an article written in the *News Chronicle* by her father, Arthur Gilligan.

Mrs Frank Woolley for an extract from her late husband's book *The King of Games* (Stanley Paul & Co).

Laurence Le Quesne for a passage from his book *The Bodyline Controversy* (Seeker & Warburg).

Malcolm Gemmell, a trustee of Jack Fingleton's estate, for a newspaper article by Fingleton and for an extract from Fingleton's book *Cricket Crisis* (Cassell & Co Ltd).

John Boyd for his account of Bradman's visit to Blackheath.

O. Wendell Bill for his account of Bradman's innings at Blackheath.

Lynton Taylor for permission to reproduce a quote by him.

Allan Moyes for an extract from the book *Bradman* (Harrap) written by his father, A. G. Moyes.

Hamish Hamilton Ltd for a passage from Ben Travers's book *94 Declared* (Elm Tree Books/Hamish Hamilton Ltd).

Clifford Winning for a passage from his book *Cricket Balmania* (Balmain District Cricket Club).

Richard Cashman for an extract from an article he wrote for the *Cricketer*.

Bradman Weerakoon for an extract from a letter he wrote to Richard Cashman.

John Fairfax & Sons Ltd for an editorial, a letter and several articles which appeared in the *Sydney Morning Herald*.

John Arlott for a sketch which appeared in his book *Gone to the Test Match*.

Sir Leonard Hutton for a passage from his book *Fifty Years of Cricket* (Stanley Paul).

Margaret Hughes for extracts from four newspaper articles written by Neville Cardus.

Roy Fuller for a passage from his autobiography *Vamp till Ready* (London Magazine Editions).

Tom Downes for an extract from an article he wrote for the Sydney *Sun*.

Michael Parkinson for an excerpt from an article he wrote for the *National Times*.

The McCool family for an extract from Colin McCool's book *Cricket is a Game* (Stanley Paul).

Colin Cowdrey for a chapter from his book *The Autobiography of a Cricketer* (Hodder & Stoughton).

The Bodley Head Ltd for Hollis and Carter Ltd for a passage from G. F. McCleary's book *Cricket with the Kangaroo* (Hollis and Carter/Dymock's Book Arcade).

Alan Foley Pty Ltd for two items for which *Punch* holds the copyright—a passage from the book *The Punch Book of Cricket* (Granada) and for a verse which appeared in *Punch* magazine.

Alec Bedser for an extract from *Our Cricket Story* (Evans Bros Ltd) which he and his brother Eric wrote.

Dr Brian Robinson for extracts from two collections of writing by his father, Ray Robinson—*Between Wickets* (William Collins) and *After Stumps were Drawn: The Best of Ray Robinson's Cricket Writing* (William Collins).

Ralph Barker for a passage from his book *Ten Great Bowlers* (Chatto & Windus).

The Fender family for a passage from Percy Fender's book *The Turn of the Wheel* (Faber & Faber Ltd).

Keith Miller for R. S. Whitington's excerpt from the book which they wrote jointly, *Cricket Caravan* (Latimer House) and for an extract from his own writing in *Cricket Caravan*.

Adrian Deamer for an extract from a newspaper article by his father, Sydney Deamer.

Keith Dunstan for an excerpt from his book *The Paddock that Grew* (Cassell & Company Ltd).

Valerie Guareschi for excerpts from three books written by her father, Walter Hammond—*Cricket My World* (Stanley Paul), *Cricket's Secret History* (Stanley Paul) and *Cricketers' School* (Stanley Paul).

Bill Bowes for excerpts from his essay on Don Bradman in *Cricket: The Great Ones*.

The *Daily Express* for an excerpt from an article by Trevor Wignall.

Murray Hedgcock for a passage from an article he wrote for *Wisden Cricket Monthly* and for an excerpt from a letter he wrote.

Stanley Paul for a passage from A. A. Thomson's book *Cricket—The Golden Ages* (Stanley Paul).

Denis Compton for his essay on Don Bradman in *Compton on Cricketers Past and Present* (Cassell Ltd).

Trevor Bailey for a passage from his book *The Greatest of My Time* (Eyre & Spottiswoode).

Edward Docker for an extract from his book *Bradman and the Bodyline Series*.

In a few cases, the people able to give reproduction approval could not be contacted. The editor begs their forebearance and asks that they contact him as soon as possible care of the publisher.